SAMPLERS

By the same author
PATCHWORK

1 (*Overleaf*) *Mid- or second half of the seventeeth century. English. Linen, metal thread, and coloured silks on linen. Long armed cross, Montenegrin cross, double running, hem, satin, stem, detached needlepoint, chain and laid stitches and couched work.* $21\frac{1}{4} \times 10\frac{1}{2}$ *inches*

SAMPLERS

AVERIL COLBY

CHARLES T. BRANFORD COMPANY

NEWTON CENTRE 59, MASSACHUSETTS

First Published in the United States of America, 1965

LIBRARY OF CONGRESS CATALOG CARD NUMBER: 65-11616

© AVERIL COLBY, 1964

MADE AND PRINTED IN GREAT BRITAIN

Preface

Several books about samplers in Britain have appeared since the beginning of the century and it is inevitable therefore that there is a good deal of repetition in this book, but until the 1900s no serious attempt had been made to devote a book entirely to recording their history. As a result of an exhibition held in London by the Fine Arts Society in the Spring of 1900, Mr Marcus Huish wrote a book recording and illustrating samplers loaned for the exhibition by owners and collectors, which represented 250 years of their history; comparable specimens of embroidery during the same period also were shown. Earlier writers on the history of needlework had recorded various samplers from private collections, as illustrations for single chapters in which outlines of sampler making were given. In 1926, Sir Leigh Ashton followed Mr Huish with a book compiled from samplers in private and museum collections arranged in chronological order and accompanied by a short history of the work.

Magazine articles about small collections or single specimens have appeared from time to time and in books on embroidery, samplers have been included as illustrations, especially in technical books like Miss Etta Campbell's book on linen embroidery. A catalogue of samplers and embroidery in the National Museum of Wales compiled by Mr Ffransis Payne in 1939, contains an account of English and Welsh sampler work and a survey of its history from the early sixteenth century. A short volume on British samplers by Miss Eirwen Jones was published in 1948 and a privately printed catalogue, illustrating samplers in the collection of Lady Mary St. John Hope was published in 1949. In 1960, Mr Donald King, Deputy Keeper of the Department of Textiles at the Victoria and Albert Museum, wrote a comprehensive chapter on his researches into the history of samplers, which was illustrated by nearly 100 English, European, Asian and other specimens in the Museum collection.

There have been a number of private collectors in the past and among the best known were Dr Glaisher, Mrs Head, Mrs Longman, Lady Mary St. John Hope, Mr Andrew Tuer, Mr Marcus Huish and Mr John Jacoby; most of the important collections are now in Museums in this country as bequests from their former owners, or were sold and dispersed into various other collections.

Private collections have been made for a number of reasons other than just collecting mania; a few have been inherited, either of family work or a collection which had grown with time, a few have been bought or acquired because of the sentimental appeal of the patterns or inscriptions and for others, a collection has been built up because of interest in a special type or period of embroidery. More than a few samplers have been 'picked up in a junk shop' or at a village sale and a number have been rescued from use as cushion covers or 'chair backs'. Many framed specimens have been abandoned to moth, damp and dust, or eaten through by woodworm in the frame, testimony to the truth sewed by the 'virgins' who made them, that 'all must come to dust.'

A great deal has been done by museum authorities and individual students in tracing the ancestry of patterns before and after their arrival on samplers, especially those of the sixteenth and seventeenth centuries, and it has been my endeavour to bring a collection of these patterns and later ones, into a sharper focus than has been done before, except by Miss Louisa Pesel in her *Embroidery Notebooks*. Miss Pesel wrote of the old English sampler patterns that 'they contain certain elements which reflect our character not found so suitably for us in say, Italian or Russian work', and a number were shown in diagrams in her *Notebooks*.

I have not attempted any technical descriptions or diagrams of stitches in samplers, as Mrs Christie's *Samplers and Stitches* does this more adequately than I could hope to do. In samplers of all periods the patterns were worked by the counted thread of the material and with the exception of some small motifs from pattern books, all the drawings have been worked out on graph paper in the hope that their character will not be lost in the reproduction. As my skill as a draughtsman is very limited, I have had the untiring help of Norah Lee who has relieved me of all the drudgery of blacking in my pencilled sketches and I am most grateful for her ability and the many hours she has given to the work. The original motifs of nearly all the seventeenth-century pattern drawings are on samplers of the period in the collection of Dr Douglas Good-hart, who has given me the most generous help and encouragement. He has allowed me to make free use of his collection of *spot motif* samplers for study and drawings, as well as having photographs specially taken and allowing me the use of others, including that of the *band* sampler on the frontispiece and wrapper, and I have taken full advantage of his kindness and interest, for which I owe him my most grateful thanks.

I should like to acknowledge very gratefully all the help I have had from the several museum authorities with collections of samplers in their possession; from the Victoria and Albert Museum and especially Mr Donald King, who has given me permission to make use of what he has written on the subject of samplers, Miss Patricia Wardle, Research Assistant to the Department of Textiles for her help in going through the samplers, and Miss Helen Lowenthal for her suggestions and help with the symbolism of sampler patterns; from the Fitzwilliam Museum and particularly Mr Frederick Stonebridge, Keeper of the Department of Textiles who allowed me to work on samplers in the department and afterwards sent photographs and letters of help when needed, and also to Miss Dorothy Stevens, for so much detailed information about samplers from her experience of them; from St Fagan's Folk Museum of the National Museum of Wales and Mr Ffransis Payne who has permitted me to use information from the Museum guide which he compiled.

I have had much generous help also from Mr H. Schubart of the City Art Gallery, Bristol, Mr R. N. R. Peers, Curator of the Dorset County Museum, Dorchester, Miss Enid Dance, Curator of the Guildford Museum, the Hon Rachel Kay-Shuttleworth and the Gawthorpe Foundation, Gawthorpe Hall and Mrs Joanna Hutton, the Brontë Parsonage Museum, Haworth, to all of whom I owe much gratitude. I should like to acknowledge also, most valuable help in my work which I received from Miss M. D. Liggett, Chief Librarian to the Central Library, Guildford and to the staff of the Mobile Library of the Somerset County Library, which comes to my village. For the loan of books from their own needlework libraries, I have to thank Mrs Nathaniel Lloyd, Miss Etta Campbell and Mrs Anthony Otter; also to Mrs Hamilton-King of the Royal School of Needlework and Miss Sinclair Salmon of the Embroiderer's Guild, I owe my appreciation with thanks for their speedy help at all stages of this book.

My most especial gratitude goes to the owners of several hundred samplers who wrote to me but who, for lack of space, must remain anonymous to everyone but me. The drawings, verses, descriptions of samplers and even samplers themselves which they sent, were invaluable.

Finally I would like to thank my publishers, especially Mr Samuel Carr, for their friendly help, kindness and patience, especially for waiting without protest for a long overdue script.

Langford,   Averil Colby
Bristol.
Spring 1964

Contents

		Page
PREFACE		7
ACKNOWLEDGMENT		10
LIST OF ILLUSTRATIONS		11

Chapter		
One	*Origins and Pattern Books*	17
Two	*Flowers, Fruit and Trees*	31
Three	*Men, Birds, Beasts, Flyes and Fishes*	57
Four	*Buildings, Pyramids and Ships*	82
Five	*Friends and Relations*	90
Six	*Schools and Teaching*	110
Seven	*The Sixteenth Century*	143
Eight	*The Seventeenth Century*	153
Nine	*The Eighteenth Century*	169
Ten	*The Nineteenth Century*	197
Eleven	*The Twentieth Century*	223
Twelve	*Inscriptions and Verses*	234
BIBLIOGRAPHY		257
INDEX		259

Acknowledgment

The Author and Publishers wish to thank the following for allowing their samplers to be photographed:

Mrs Atkins, Bishop's Waltham, for fig. 212; The Curator, Brontë Parsonage Museum, for fig. 175; Mrs E. Carlton, Woolwich Arsenal, for fig. 215; Miss Dashper, Guildford, for fig. 178; The Curator, Dorset County Museum, Dorchester, for figs. 57 and 104; The Embroiderer's Guild, London, for figs. 221 and 222; Miss F. V. Gillet, Sevenoaks, for fig. 194; Mrs Gilson-Taylor, Stansfield, for fig. 124; Dr Douglas Goodhart, Carshalton Beeches, for figs. 1, 99 and 119; The Curator, Guildford Museum, for fig. 173; Mrs E. C. Greenhill, Darley, for figs. 200 and 201; Patrick Johnston Esq., Wrington, for figs. 62 and 121; Mrs Arthur Lee, Churchill, for fig. 64; Mrs. E. W. Leche, Salisbury, for fig. 127; Mrs Catherine Little, Compton, for fig. 213; Miss Valerie Lovell, Winchester, for fig. 218; Dr Nathaniel Lucas, East Grinstead, for figs. 101, 103, 123, 172 and 179; Mrs Moorey, Haslemere, for fig. 198; The Royal School of Needlework, London, for figs. 177, 204, 216 and 217; Miss Shepherd, Gillingham, Dorset, for fig. 199; Mrs. S. Sandeman-Allen, Stoke Fleming, for fig. 220; Lady Arthur Tansley, Grantchester, for fig. 214; Mrs Oscar Truscott, for fig. 219. They are also grateful to Mrs Truscott for permission to reproduce her designs which appear as figs. 10 and 211.

Thanks are due also to the following for permission to make drawings of patterns on samplers in their possession:

Mrs Beryl Anderson; Mrs A. B. Cotton; Dr Douglas Goodhart; Mrs Nathaniel Lloyd; Mrs Mooney; Mrs Oscar Truscott; the Directors of the Dorset County Museum, and of The Guildford Museum; The Syndics of The Fitzwilliam Museum; the Trustees of the Victoria and Albert Museum.

The Author and Publishers must thank also the following for permission to reproduce copyright photographs:

Samuel Carr Esq., London, for fig. 174; The Syndics of the Fitzwilliam Museum, Cambridge, for figs. 56 (T.1-1928), 60 (T.3-1938), 61 (T.11-1938), 96 (T.24-1928), 98 (T.57-1928), 105 (T.137-1928), 182 (T.68-1938) and 202 (T.9-1946); The Trustees of the Gawthorpe Foundation, Gawthorpe Hall, Burnley, for figs. 126, 181 and 193; Dr Douglas Goodhart, Carshalton Beeches, for fig. 100; The Director, The London Museum, for fig. 54; Quentin Lloyd Esq., for figs. 55 and 106; The Director of the National Museum of Antiquities of Scotland, Edinburgh, for fig. 102; The Director of the National Museum of Wales, Cardiff, for fig. 195; Mrs Swain, Edinburgh, for fig. 125; The Director, Temple Newsam House, Leeds for fig. 203; The Trustees of the Victoria and Albert Museum, London, for figs. 53 (X.1428), 58 (P.1730), 59 (V.570), 63 (P.1728), 65 (R.865), 95 (M.1501), 97 (R.864), 118 (70200), 120 (M.1499), 122 (77171) and 176 (67296).

The Illustrations

Figure		Page
1	English: mid- or second half of the seventeenth century. Linen, metal thread and coloured silks on linen	Frontispiece
2	Two patterns taken from Sibmacher's 'Schön Neues Modelbuch'	21
3	Fruit motifs taken from 'A schole-house, for the needle'	24
4	Flower motifs taken from ' A schole-house, for the needle'	25
5	Band pattern with reversed honeysuckle flowers	26
6	Formal honeysuckle motifs in a border pattern	26
7	Strawberry fruit and flower pattern	26
8	Carnation band pattern	27
9	Three eighteenth-century lily patterns	33
10	Twentieth-century lily pattern	34
11	Three seventeenth-century fleur de lys motifs in diaper patterns	34
12	Two eighteenth-century fleur de lys motifs	35
13	Two seventeenth-century honeysuckle motifs	35
14	Nineteenth-century Prince of Wales's Feathers motif	36
15	Daisy pattern	36
16	Arcaded daisy border	36
17	Seventeenth-century pansy border pattern	37
18	Seventeenth-century band pattern of pansy and strawberry motifs	38
19	Pansy motifs used in seventeenth-century diaper patterns	38
20	Eighteenth-century tulip motif	39
21	Types of all-over patterns with strawberries	39
22	A pear-shaped fruit	40
23	Diaper pattern with strawberry motif	40
24	Spot motif with three strawberry fruits	40
25	Pomegranate border pattern	41
26	Pomegranate motif in seventeenth-century diaper patterns	41
27	Pea flower with two buds and hanging pods	41
28	Pea flower and pods, with strawberry fruits and flowers and pansy patterns	42
29	Strawberry plant with three fruits	43
30	Squirrels from late eighteenth- and early nineteenth-century patterns	44
31	Seventeenth-century border pattern of rose-hips and leaves	44
32	Seventeenth-century robin with rose hips	45
33	Hazel nut spot motif	45
34	Diaper patterns with acorns and oak leaves	46
35	Acorn spot motif	46

THE ILLUSTRATIONS

Figure		Page
36	Grape and vine leaf band patterns	47
37	Vine pattern on a spot motif sampler	47
38	Rose flowerpot pattern	48
39	Stylised vine motif used in diaper patterns	48
40	Some vases used in flower pot motifs	48
41	Baskets, bowls and urns used in flower pot and fruit bowl patterns	49
42	Seventeenth-century lily-pot motif from a band pattern	49
43	Two flower pot and fruit basket motifs	50
44	Late eighteenth-century oak tree	51
45	Trees with characteristics of the sycamore	51
46	An elegant tree in cross stitch	52
47	Trees showing the eighteenth-century fashion for topiary	53
48	Conventional pyramid trees	53
49	Formal motifs resembling bushes	54
50	A weeping willow and urn pattern	54
51	Tree pattern hung with bell-shaped flowers	55
52	A popular rose-bush pattern	55
53	1598. Silk and metal threads on linen, with seed pearls and black beads	59
54	Last half of sixteenth century. Silk and metal threads on linen	60
55	Early seventeenth century. Linen thread on linen	60
56	1629. Silk thread on linen	61
57	1630. Silk and metal threads on linen	61
58	First half of seventeenth century. Silk, silver and silver-gilt threads on linen	62
59	First half of seventeenth century. Silk and metal threads on linen	62
60	Mid-seventeenth century. Linen thread on bleached linen	63
61	Seventeenth century. Linen and silk threads on linen	63
62	First half of seventeenth century. Silk thread on linen	64
63	1649. Linen thread on linen	65
64	Mid-seventeenth century. Silk, silver gilt and silver threads on linen	65
65	Mid-seventeenth century. Silk and metal threads on linen, with some sequins	66
66	Family figure patterns	68
67	Family figures, possibly the parents of the workers	69
68	Girl Guide figures on a gift sampler	71
69	'Trophies' typical of those carried by boxers	71
70	Nude boxer figure with floral motif	72
71	Pattern from 'Ornamente delle belle et virtuose donne'	74
72	Lion or leopard figures typical of all periods	75
73	A lobster, erect as in heraldry	75
74	Frog in double running stitch	76
75	Toad	76
76	A hare	76
77	Some of the innumerable dogs and cats	77
78	The occasional mouse	77
79	Peacocks 'in pride'	78

Figure		*Page*
80	*Ducks and geese in seventeenth- and eighteenth-century patterns*	78
81	*An attempt to put a bird into a tree*	79
82	*Two patterns of birds at a fountain*	79
83	*Fishes in seventeenth-century spot motif samplers*	80
84	*The peacock shown on the ridge tiles of a house*	84
85	*Small motifs indicating birds in the sky*	85
86	*Coffee and tea pot patterns*	86
87	*Jugs*	86
88	*Kettles*	86
89	*Bottles and wineglasses*	86
90	*A household object on Elizabeth Cromwell's sampler*	87
91	*Farm livestock*	87
92	*A grand piano*	87
93	*Door key patterns*	87
94	*Nineteenth-century bird motifs*	89
95	*Mid-seventeenth century. White linen thread on linen*	99
96	*1660. Linen thread on linen*	99
97	*1670. Silk and metal threads on linen*	100
98	*1675. Silk thread on linen*	100
99	*c. 1670–1680. Silk thread on linen*	101
100	*'August the 22nd 1710'. Silk thread on linen*	101
101	*Early eighteenth century. Silk thread on linen*	102
102	*1724–1725. Linen thread on linen*	103
103	*1729. Silk thread on linen*	104
104	*'June the 26 1734'. Silk thread on linen*	105
105	*1737. Linen thread on linen*	105
106	*'November the 25 1740'. Silk thread on worsted*	106
107	*Types of letters used in alphabets*	111
108	*Alphabet letters with flourishes in double running*	112
109	*Numerals worked in stitches which correspond to those used for alphabets*	113
110	*Crown and coronet patterns used for marking and decorative purposes*	114
111	*Reversed crowns in a border pattern*	116
112	*Linen mark in the household of Viscount Nelson, Duke of Bronte*	116
113	*A decorative crown*	116
114	*Striped stag in Philips and Goodday samplers*	121
115	*Swan on Elizabeth Clement's sampler*	122
116	*Christ's Hospital scholar*	123
117	*Cow and milkmaid from Sarah Fear's sampler*	124
118	*1752. Silk thread on wool*	127
119	*Late eighteenth century. Silk thread on Tiffany*	128
120	*1777. Silk and linen threads on linen*	128
121	*1778. Silk thread on satin, with some hair*	129
122	*1787. Silk thread on linen*	130
123	*1796. Silk thread on linen*	131

Figure		Page
124	*1799. Silk thread on linen scrim*	132
125	*Early nineteenth century. Cotton thread on fine muslin*	132
126	*Early nineteenth century. Cotton thread on net*	133
127	*1803. Silk thread on wool*	134
128	*Stylised carnation band patterns with double running*	146
129	*Narrow border patterns worked in double running with some satin stitch*	147
130	*Daisy pattern*	150
131	*Rose motif in Jane Bostocke's sampler*	150
132	*Carnation pattern*	151
133	*Grape and vine leaf pattern*	151
134	*Acorn and oak leaf band pattern*	151
135	*Grape and vine leaf all-over pattern*	152
136	*Seventeenth-century strawberry band pattern*	153
137	*Acorn and oak leaf band pattern*	153
138	*Arcaded honeysuckle band pattern*	154
139	*Rose spot motif*	154
140	*Three seventeenth-century pansy spot motifs*	157
141	*Diaper pattern with stylised rose motif and interlacing border worked in metal thread*	158
142	*Carnation border patterns showing painted lady and speckled varieties*	160
143	*Pansy motif used in band and spot motif samplers*	161
144	*Stylised carnation motif for a corner*	161
145	*Stiffly formal acorn band patterns*	162
146	*Acorns in a double border pattern*	162
147	*Carnation motif in a diaper pattern*	163
148	*'Lively worke upon a Sad and Solemne Ground'*	164
149	*Flower and fruit spot motif in outline only*	165
150	*Two rose border patterns typical of the transition period*	167
151	*Carnation motif used in band patterns*	169
152	*Eighteenth-century carnation motifs*	170
153	*Eighteenth-century honeysuckle motif*	170
154	*Honeysuckle border*	172
155	*Reversed carnation and honeysuckle border*	172
156	*Eighteenth-century heart patterns*	175
157	*Eighteenth-century tulip border pattern*	176
158	*Two variants of a late eighteenth-century tulip arcaded border pattern*	176
159	*Carnation flower pot pattern*	177
160	*Late eighteenth-century tulip flower pot*	177
161	*Heart pattern worked in hollie point*	178
162	*Crown worked in hollie point*	178
163	*Acorn motif with a heart border in hollie point*	178
164	*Acorn border in white work*	178
165	*Grape and vine leaf motif showing the use of darning stitches for veining*	179
166	*Some bird patterns found in matching pairs*	180
167	*Strawberry in a pot*	181

THE ILLUSTRATIONS

Figure		Page
168	An early nineteenth-century stag	182
169	Eighteenth-century stags	182
170	'Return of the Spies from Canaan'	183
171	Adam and Eve pattern	184
172	1818. Silk thread on wool	187
173	1823. Silk thread on linen	187
174	1825. Silk thread and chenille on linen	188
175	'March 1st 1829'. Silk thread on wool	189
176	183 . Silk thread on wool	190
177	c. 1834. Silk thread on linen with some hair	191
178	1837. Silk thread and beadwork on linen	192
179	1837. Silk thread on wool	192
180	1842. Silk thread on linen	193
181	Mid-nineteenth century. Silk thread on stocking web	194
182	1845. Silk thread on linen	194
183	Tulip motif	197
184	Mid-nineteenth-century tulip flower pot	197
185	Early nineteenth-century all-over tulip pattern	197
186	Strawberry border patterns	198
187	Cross stitch pattern for a gift pincushion	199
188	Flower motifs from border patterns in manuscript pattern book, 1840	201
189	Jasmine spray	202
190	Small motifs from 1840 pattern book	202
191	Canvas lace work pattern in Berlin wool work	205
192	'The Church', 1842	208
193	Mid-nineteenth century. Silk and wool threads on canvas	211
194	c. 1850. Silk on canvas, mounted on flannel	211
195	Mid-nineteenth century. Silk thread on canvas	212
196	c. 1870. Silk, taffeta, satin and ribbon	213
197	Late nineteenth century. Loom-made bead patterns on cotton thread	213
198	1875. Red silk on linen	214
199	'June 82' (1882). Hair, with some silk thread and crochet cotton on linen	215
200	c. 1900. Cotton and silk threads on flannel with some calico	216
201	c. 1900. Cotton and silk threads on cotton	216
202	1894. Silk and cotton threads on linen	217
203	1910. Linen thread on linen	217
204	c. 1910. Silk and gold thread on linen, with some cord	218
205	Peacocks with the tail 'close'	220
206	Rose flower pot	221
207	Rose motifs	221
208	Type of letters in an alphabet, 1909	224
209	A small figure pattern	225
210	Owl motif	225
211	Bishop's mitre used for kneelers in St. Leonard's Church, Watlington	229

15

Figure		Page
212	c. 1920. Linen and silk thread on linen scrim	235
213	1934. Wool thread on linen	236
214	1936. Linen thread on linen	237
215	1946. Cotton and silk on cambric	237
216	c. 1920. Silk and gold threads on figured silk damask, with jewels, laid work and couching in motifs for church embroidery	238
217	1952–1953. Silk and gold thread with spangles on purple velvet	238
218	1955. 1960. Silk thread on linen	239
219	1961. Wool thread on double canvas	240
220	1961. Silk thread on linen	241
221, 222	Two panels from a six-fold screen sampler	242

CHAPTER ONE

Origins and Pattern Books

The accepted form of needlework known as a sampler is a cloth on which a collection of miscellaneous stitches and patterns is worked in embroidery for use as a reference in future work. Embroidered samplers outnumber by thousands those which record other kinds of work, but examples showing patterns, stitches and techniques on textiles probably have existed for longer than is indicated in surviving types which have been found.

The derivation of the word *sampler* is from the Latin *exemplum*, meaning 'anything selected as a model for imitation—a pattern—an example'. The word 'exemplar', frequently given as the root, probably was an adjective derived from *exemplum* and which later became a noun when referring to 'a person who is an example to others'—usually for some virtue. In early English references to needlework samplers, the words *exemplar* or *exemple* are therefore, the nearest to the original word; other variants include *ensample*, *saumplerie*, *sawmpler*, *sam-cloth* and *sampleth*—the last two are said to have been the most common in the North of England. In *A Dictionary in Englyshe and Welshe* by Salesbury in 1547 the spelling is *siampler*, and in *Antiquae Linguae Britannicae*, John Davies gives 'Siampl, and Siampler, Examplar'[1] (1632). An earlier dictionary, *Lesclarissement de la Langue Francoyse*, published in 1530 and compiled by John Palsgrave, defines *sampler* as 'an exampler for a woman to work by', which indicates that by then it was no longer common for men to embroider as it had been in earlier centuries or if they did, women only had need of a sampler for their patterns. Some years later in Cotgrave's well known French–English dictionary of 1611, the translation of *exemplaire* is given as—'a patterne, sample or sampler . . . as example, president or precedent for other to follow or take heed by'.

There is no doubt that the original function of an embroidered sampler funda-

[1] F. G. Payne, *Guide to the Collection of Samplers and Embroideries*, p. 22.

mentally was educational and that it had a two-fold purpose; first that it should be an experimental exercise for learning and practice; and second, that it should serve as a reminder and a record of stitches and patterns. There is more than enough evidence of this in early existing samplers, and although there is reasonable proof that pattern samplers were made over a thousand years ago, it would not be illogical to believe that the equivalent of what is now called a sampler has been made wherever civilisation has advanced to the state of making cloth. The decoration of a plain surface is a natural development of hand work: 'the moment we make anything thoroughly, it is the law of nature that we shall be pleased with ourselves, and with the thing we have made; and we become desirous therefore to adorn or complete it . . . with a finer art expressive of our pleasure.'[1] It is also a necessary and instinctive action in almost every kind of pattern making—not the least in needlework—to experiment with an unfamiliar design or technique before beginning on the final work.

Textiles found in Egyptian burial grounds can be seen in Museum collections, which clearly are pattern samplers of an early age; they are in small fragments only, but the patterns remaining are quite distinguishable. One sampler of Coptic work is nine inches wide and less than six inches long and shows Christian emblems in *darning* stitch worked in red, blue, green and brown wools, in which the patterns are simple and scattered in arrangement; they are consistent with early types in English and other European samplers, although the date probably is between 400 and 500 A.D. A second example dating from the fourth century is composed of three fragments joined by *oversewing*; the patterns are geometrical in character and worked in *darning* stitch with linen thread on a linen ground but are more advanced in skill, resembling some of the motifs seen in English work more than 100 years later. Both these examples are kept at the Museum in Guildford and are illustrated in the Museum booklet.[2] A third Egyptian sampler in the Victoria and Albert Museum is more nearly contemporary with the early English examples and probably was made during the fifteenth or sixteenth centuries, with the patterns in *double running* and *darning* stitches worked with silk thread on linen.[3]

It is believed that the practice of sampler making travelled from the East across Europe, and Mr Donald King says in reference to Egyptian examples: '. . . it may be that samplers such as these served as prototypes for the European tradition. It is possible, indeed, that the initial development of amateur needlework in Europe owed more than has yet been recognised to the example of the Near East. The

[1] John Ruskin, *Lectures on Art Delivered before the University of Oxford in the Hilary Term*, 1870. Lecture iv, paragraph 97.
[2] R. Oddy, *Samplers in the Guildford Museum*, 1951.
[3] D. King, *Samplers*, plate 87.

patterns of the Egyptian samplers were used, as in Europe, on articles of personal and household linen, of which many have also been found in graves.'[1] The Egyptian patterns are geometrical and are similar to the diaper type used in early European and English examples, especially those of the 'S' and 'X' motifs which had a long life in English sampler patterns.

Before the use of pattern books was known, hand-to-hand exchange, or copying of existing patterns, were the only means of passing on designs to those who had not the skill to make their own, and it is not surprising to find so many similar and comparable features in early embroideries. From the early samplers individual patterns have been identified with the same kind of motifs on woodcuts, illustrated manuscripts, herbals, bestiaries, as well as the early printed pattern books from which the inspiration was taken before they were transferred by embroidery to the sampler, but the workers to whom these sources were available, were limited in number. In the Middle Ages the embroiderers were dependant on the Church for patronage and it followed that ecclesiastical work influenced the type of patterns and designs which were used. During this time when English embroidery was renowned for its perfection, it was worked both by men and women in the religious communities and upper class houses as well as in the Broderer's Guilds, but there is no evidence that samplers had any part in recording the patterns. It has been suggested that any which might have existed were swept away in the dissolution of the monasteries, but it seems unlikely, if they had been in general use, that all would have vanished without a trace and the most probable explanation of the absence of any samplers before the late fifteenth century, is that there were none. Written references give good evidence of their existence in the early years of the sixteenth century (Chapter Seven), but so many enthusiasms have come and gone in the history of England's needlework that it seems more likely that samplers 'had no apparent infancy'[2] and arose as a fashionable occupation for those with leisure to do embroidery as an occupation and not as a livelihood.

The earliest samplers recorded must have been made before pattern books existed and although ecclesiastic work was declining, domestic embroidery was not; it was in fact growing and by the middle of the sixteenth century was being used for important articles of clothing and household furnishing as a means of decoration. Fashion in dress and household textiles has been responsible for many changes for better and many for worse in the tradition of needlework, and richly embroidered clothing, as well as a lavish use of lace so popular in the second half of the 1500s, accounted for most of the enthusiasm for sampler making. Needlework occupied the greater part of the day—it was a way of life among

[1] *ibid.*, p. 4.
[2] M. B. Huish, *Samplers and Tapestry Embroideries*, p. 99.

women and girls in upper class households—and the sampler was indispensable as an alternative to memorising the multitude of patterns.

Books of printed patterns originated in Europe, numbers of those brought out during the 1520s having survived and are included in Museum library collections. Their popularity led to translation and publication in many countries, notably in Germany and France and in Italy where books of lace patterns were published in Venice. Among the earliest pattern books of which copies remain were those by Schonsperger in 1523–1524, Peter Quentel in 1527 and, of the Venetian books, *Esemplario di lavori* by Giovanni Andra Vavassorie in 1530 and in 1561 *La Vera perfettione del designo* by Giovanni Ostau, from which patterns can be found in surviving samplers.[1] Eventually pattern books came to be printed in England but not until later in the century. In 1586, *La Clef des Champs* by Jacques le Moyne was published at Blackfriars[2] and as may be inferred from the title, the patterns illustrated birds, animals and flowers, which had Latin, German, French and English titles. Referring to this book Mrs Morris identifies some of the animals with those in an earlier bestiary and the flowers as 'Le Moyne's own work and some of the original drawings for them are in the Victoria and Albert Museum'; that the illustrations were intended for embroidery patterns is made clear in the introduction, where they are described as being for every kind of needlework.

Many of the contemporary pattern books contained detailed introductions to the contents and frequently were dedicated to ladies noted for their skill in embroidery. After being published in France in 1587, an English translation of Frederic di Vinciolo's book *Les Singuliers et Nouveaux Pourtraits pour touttes sortes d'ouvrages di Lingerie* was published by John Wolfe with the title of *New and Singular Patternes and workes of Linnen* in 1591 and contained, we are told, patterns of 'seven Planets, and many other Figures serving for Patternes to make divers sortes of Lace'. Vinciolo followed this with another book in 1599, *Les Secondes Œuvres, et subtiles inventions de Lingerie*. The introduction to a book of patterns published by William Barley in 1596 entitled *A Booke of Curious and Strange Inventions, called the first part of Needleworkes* is more elaborate than most others. Having stated that first it was 'Imprinted in *Venice*, and now againe newly printed in more exquisite sort for the profit and delight of Gentlewomen of England', the patterns are described as '*Many singular and fine sortes of Cutworkes, Raised-workes, Stitches and open Cutworke, verie easie to be learned by the diligent practisers, that shall follow the direction herein contained*'. The dedication to Lady Isabel, Duchess of Rutland, and the verses which extol the value of the book for its

---

[1] Leigh Ashton, *Samplers*, Figures 20a and 20b.
[2] Barbara Morris, *The History of English Embroidery*, p. 6.

patterns, give a side glance at the social values attached to a high skill in embroidery
and some moral precepts, which may perhaps be quoted in full.

> The wit of man by several things is tride
> Some for the soule do bend their study still:
> Some on the seas do search the world so wide,
> In Alcomie some others tries their skill:
> Some other love the liberall Arts to learne
> The ground of knowledge thereby to discearne.
>
> But farre unfit for tender women kinde,
> Such toylesome studies altogether be:
> Although their wits most sharp and swift we finde
> Their milkwhyte hands the needle finer fits,
> With silke gold to prove their pregnant wits,

2   *Two patterns taken from the 1877 edition of Sibmacher's 'Schön Neues Modelbuch'*

> In needle works there doth great knowledge rest.
> A fine conceit thereby full soone is showne:
> A drowsie braine this skill cannot digest,
> Paine spent on such, in vaine awaie is throne:
> They must be careful, diligent and wise,
> In needleworkes that beare away the prise.
>
> This worke beseemeth Queenes of great renowne,
> And Noble Ladies of a high degree:
> Yet not exempt for maids of any Towne,

For all may learne that thereto willing be:
Come then sweet gyrles and hereby learne the way
With good report to live another day.

For many maidens but of base degree,
By their fine knowledge in this curious thing:
With Noble Ladies oft companions be,
Sometimes they teach the daughter of a king:
Thus by their knowledge, fame and good report,
They are esteemed among the noblest sort.

Then prettie maidens view this prettie booke,
Marke well the works that you therein doe finde:
Sitting at worke cast not aside your looke
They profit small that have a gazing minde:
Keep clean your Samplers, sleepe not as you sit
For sluggishness doth spoile the rarest wit.[1]

Of all the sixteenth-century printed patterns those of Johann Sibmacher's *Schön Neues Modelbuch* published in Nürnberg 1597, probably were the best known in English samplers. Certainly a number can be traced in surviving examples[2] and the patterns were reproduced not only in an English book of the seventeenth century, *The needle's Excellency*, but facsimile reproductions were published in Germany as late as 1866 and 1877. Two of the patterns reproduced in the 1877 edition are illustrated in full in Figure 2, although these two generally were worked in part only, as their full length over-ran the width of an average sampler. Sibmacher's patterns are accompanied by a direction at the head for the number of rows or threads required for the depth of each.

By the end of the sixteenth century the pattern books followed on each other's heels but specimens from the time which have survived, have done so in some cases, in a state of dilapidation. The practice of pricking off patterns directly from the printed page to the linen undoubtedly was the quickest and simplest method, but the life of the pages was shortened in proportion to the popularity of the patterns they contained and many of them in books which have survived whole or in part, show evidence of this treatment. Numbers of patterns can be identified in samplers made some years after they were published in book form and many of them most probably were copied from other samplers and not

[1] Quoted in 'Some Sixteenth-century Pattern-Books' by Margaret Dowling, *Embroidery*, June 1933, pp. 15–16.
[2] Leigh Ashton, *Samplers*, Figures 30a and 30b, 42a and 42b. D. King, *Samplers*, Plates 20, 24, 30. M. E. Jones, *British Samplers*, Figure 51.

always from the printed originals, which had been destroyed by harsh wear and tear. Destruction by pricking doubtless was the fate of early copies of *The needle's Excellency*, the book which has been mentioned as containing many patterns from *Schön Neues Modelbuch* and which is known to have run to 12 editions by 1640; surviving copies are rare and these are from the later editions only. Published by John Boler '*at the sign of the Marigold in Paule's Churchyard inlarged wth divers newe workes as needleworkes purles and others never before printed*', it was written and compiled by John Taylor, Thames waterman, traveller, publican and writer of verse and prose as the self-styled Water Poet. As was the custom, the patterns were introduced by a long preamble in verse for which John Taylor seems to have acquired much information about needlework listing names of stitches and foreign sources of 'rare patternes', with detail worthy of one who had made a life's study of the subject. He followed the fashionable line in praising distinguished needle-women and in his verses Catherine of Aragon and Queen Elizabeth I are among those chosen for commendation, the final couplet on Catherine of Aragon reading:

> Thus for her paines, here her reward is just.
> Her workes proclaime her prayse though she be dust.

The copy of the book in the library of the Victoria and Albert Museum has an unexpected addition to its antiquity in the written inscription on the fly leaf which runs:

> Olympia Dury Aprill the 22 1755
> Olympia Dury July 20 1751
> This book is one hundred and
> five teen years old.   115
>
>   1751
>   1636
>   ——
>   115
>   ——

and a little way beneath this calculation, a later owner has added:

> 1839
> 1636
> ——
> 203   Oct. 19 1839
> ——

Another pattern book at about the same time was the well-known *A scholehouse, for the needle* by Richard Shorleyker; first published in 1624 it contained

3   *Fruit motifs taken from 'A schole-house, for the needle'*

patterns which have been identified in embroidery [1] and in samplers, and in one of these made soon after this date several birds, fishes and flowers are represented. [2] Lace patterns were included, as well as those for other embroidery, as the preamble states:

> Here followeth certaine Patternes of Cut-workes: newly invented and never published before. Also sundry sortes of spots as Flowers, Birdes, and fishes, etc. and will fitly serve to be wrought some with gould, some with silke, some with crewel in coullers: or otherwise at your pleasure. London. Printed in Shoe Lane at the signe of the Falcon. Richard Shorleyker.

Many of the small motifs in this book have survived to be adapted and used in present-day twentieth-century embroidery, especially the flower, fruit and leaf sprays, and those which are smaller still have been used as all-over and filling patterns [3, 4]. In addition to the patterns, instructions for enlarging or reducing the size of a motif are given at the end of the book, with a specimen page ruled into squares to illustrate the accompanying explanation: 'I would have you know that the use of these squares doth showe, how you may contrive any work, Bird, Beast or Flower: into bigger or lesser proportions according as you shall see the cause: as this if you enlarge your pattern divide it into squares; then rule a paper

[1] 'An Embroidered Shirt of the Seventeenth Century' by E. Rolleston, *The Embroideress*, Volume I, pp. 79–80.

[2] Leigh Ashton, *Samplers*, p. 8, Figures 4a, b and 5. D. King, p. 7, *Samplers*, Plate 4.

4   *Flower motifs taken from 'A schole-house, for the needle'*

as large as ye list, into what squares you will: Then looke how many holes your pattern doth containe, upon so many of your holes of your ruled paper draw your pattern.' Not so many years ago this method was being taught as a so-called new way of enlarging a design.

The fashion for including small creatures, caterpillars, butterflies, snails, flies, beetles and so on, in Elizabethan and Stuart embroidery, filled the pattern books with them in great variety. In 1650 William Simpson published *The second book of flowers, fruits, beasts, birds and flies exactly drawn*,[1] and a little later, about 1660, appeared *A Catalogue of Plates and pictures that are printed and sould by Peter Stent dwelling at the Signe of the White Horse in Guilt Spur Street betwixt Newgate and Py Corner*, and among the books offered for sale were *Books for Drafts of Men, Birds, Beasts, Flowers, Fruits, Flyes and Fishes* with *One Book of Birds sitting on sprigs* (p. 40) *One book of Beasts, One book of Branches, One Book of Flowers* and *Nine plates of Emblems* which summarise the types of patterns commonly in use in the seventeenth century. Numerous *figure* patterns of Royal personages from *King Henry the 8* to *James 2nd son of the late K.*, of biblical notabilities from *Adam and Eve* to *Moses lifting up the Serpent in the Wilderness* were offered, as well as *the 4 seasons of the Year* and *the 5 Senses*[2] among the other patterns which were in demand for embroidered panels and caskets.

Another source of patterns in the seventeenth century was that of the illustrated

[1] A. L. Kendrick, *A Book of Old Embroidery*, p. 118.
[2] M. Jourdain, *English Secular Embroidery*, pp. 68–69.

herbals from which the black and white drawings were easy to reproduce as embroidery patterns, and it was not unusual for some English and European books to contain illustrations of flowers for students of botany or gardening which were intended to serve the double purpose of providing patterns for embroidery also. Decorative patterns of flowers and fruit for samplers and embroidery,

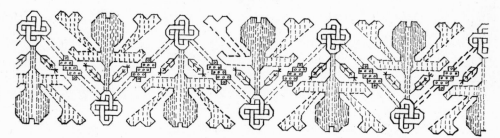

5 Band *pattern with reversed honeysuckle flowers worked in* double running *and* satin stitches. *Seventeenth century*

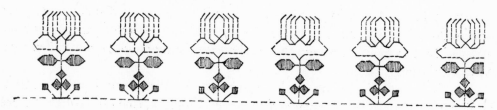

6 *Formal* honeysuckle *motifs in a border pattern. Seventeenth century*

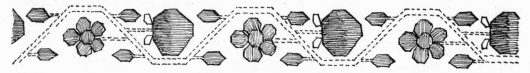

7 Strawberry *fruit and flower pattern. Seventeenth century*

whether formal or naturalistic, outnumbered the geometrical designs in what has been described as 'an age when a whole nation went mad about flowers'.[1] The demand for them continued into the eighteenth century to the extent of illustrations from a seed catalogue of 1730 being reproduced in *The Flower Garden Displayed* brought out by a London nurseryman, Robert Furber in 1732, which he recommended as being 'very Useful, not only for the Curious in gardening but the

[1] Wilfred Blunt, *The Art of Botanical Illustration*, p. 131.

26

8   Carnation band *pattern. Seventeenth century*

Prints likewise for *Painters*, *Carvers*, Japaners, etc., also for the Ladies, as patterns for working . . .'[1]

Patterns on eighteenth-century samplers showed decreasing reliance on the old printed books for their source and the popularity grew for the more naturalistic type of floral designs resembling those on the printed textiles of the time, especially the Indian painted calicoes. The formal and geometrical patterns did not die out altogether but a change, as with most transitions, took place gradually, although samplers up to the middle of the century showed examples of the old patterns. Of those which have been recorded, two Sibmacher patterns are known to have been worked on eighteenth century samplers—one dated 1699–1700[2] and the other 1729[3]—and others can be traced, but in the main pattern books were out in favour of the school mistress, whose repertoire was limited by her taste. The professionally drawn sampler had been a means of increasing the range of the costly and rare pattern books which were beyond the means of many in the early seventeenth century, and linen pieces with pattern outlines drawn ready for working, were sold especially for samplers. Evidence of this is shown on two specimens illustrated; both were made during the first half of the century; the dated example [57] shows patterns partly worked and of those on the other [59], half of the motifs are completed with embroidery and the rest are shown in drawn outline only. The same professional, or by this time more commercial touch, is found again, notably in the *map* samplers, from the third quarter of the eighteenth century, many of which were printed directly on to the material and some had

[1] *ibid.*, p. 135.
[2] Leigh Ashton, *Samplers*, Figure 30.
[3] *ibid.*, Figure 42.   D. King, *Samplers*, Plate 30.

also the name of the printer or publisher, as well as other information added (pp. 125–136). There appear to have been no printed paper patterns or any other kind of commercial guidance for making *map* samplers except for those maps drawn ready for working on the fabric, which accounts, no doubt, for the fact that some *maps* possess more individuality than conventional samplers.

Prepared canvas or linen, printed with patterns to be worked generally in *cross* or *tent* stitch, became popular in the nineteenth century, but the increase in the numbers of printed pattern books, with detailed instructions and suggestions for working, did away with the last need for samplers as go-betweens, except for some in Berlin wool work. With the advent of this fashion in needlework about 1805, charts on squared paper and printed in colour, originated in Berlin and travelled with little delay to this country, together with the brightly coloured wools for working the patterns. Such was the demand for them that by 1840, 14,000 designs are known to have been published especially for this work.[1] In spite of this flood of printed patterns, or possibly because of them, quite a number of samplers were made in Berlin wool work, generally recording patterns of the floral and geometrical types for borders, corners and ground work and show an interesting return to the early *spot motif* method of recording ([*193*] and p. 205). Other patterns taken from the printed charts influenced the choice of subjects, especially those of a pictorial nature, found in samplers throughout the century, although not all by any means, are worked in Berlin wool; rustic scenes, buildings (whole or in ruins), figures in all manner of dress from that associated with Biblical characters to the current fashion and animals of many kinds both wild and domestic, especially pet cats and dogs [*77*], reflect the obsession for the work.

Small pattern books, miniature in size and no doubt printed for children, were popular from the middle of the century. A typical example is entitled *The Embroidery and Alphabet Sampler Book*; measuring $2\frac{1}{4}$ by $2\frac{3}{4}$ inches, a stiff green cardboard cover encloses a concertina strip of paper—one and a half yards long—folded into 15 sections, each containing a number of small patterns. Animals, ships, houses, household objects [*86–93*] six different alphabets, six sets of numerals, floral and geometrical patterns, initials and seven Christian names for girls, Charlotte, Rose, Elizabeth, Emily, Sarah, Ellen and Maria in elaborate flower-decorated letters. Published by 'Groombridge and Sons. 5. Paternoster Row. London' it was sold at 'PRICE SIXPENCE'. Inside the cover of one copy written in neat copper plate, is '6d or 1d pattern' so that a nice little profit was in prospect if each section had been sold separately. This book probably was one from which patterns were taken for some of the Bristol Orphanage samplers; the alphabets, numerals and 28 of the figure patterns in it are identical with those shown on a

[1] Barbara Morris, *Victorian Embroidery*, pp. 19 and 20.

sampler of 1874 illustrated by Sir Leigh Ashton, from one of the Muller Homes.[1] A similar book printed in 1851, contained patterns identical with some of those already mentioned, as well as a double page pattern of 'The Crystal Palace. Exhibition. 1851'.

The size and shape of early samplers were largely determined by the material available and in many of them the length of the sampler was that of the woven width of the linen, the selvedges being at the ends of the work and the sides hemmed. This was an economy in material and may account for the approximate uniformity in the length of the seventeenth-century samplers. There is no evidence that there was a conventional length or width and although there is no doubt that her samplers were indispensable to the embroiderer, it is unlikely that valuable linen would have been cut especially for this purpose. The long narrow shape is the most typical of early samplers, although some exist which are very nearly square, but there was sufficient width in a narrow strip to record or practise enough of the *spot* motifs, consisting of single motifs in colour of all types including the small devices used in groundwork, and the *band* or border patterns, which were worked either with lace stitches in white thread, or other patterns in coloured silks. In the finished examples of both types the greatest economy is seen when the worker had the planning in her own hands [100] but wider spacing is seen in most of those which had been professionally drawn [54], otherwise it seems that the individual made her sampler to suit her needs and the narrow widths were the more easily rolled to go into the work box. Wooden or ivory rollers were used sometimes on which to keep the work, but these have not survived as well as have the samplers and are rare and difficult to find. Later samplers were put away folded as evidenced by the fold marks, until the eighteenth century when samplers ceased to be of practical use and became a fashionable form of decorative embroidery designed to be hung in a frame.

It was not until the nineteenth century, when sampler-making had become a school exercise, that printed directions appeared for a regulation size for samplers. In Caulfeild and Saward's *Dictionary of Needlework* of 1882, the following paragraphs were headed '*To Make a Sampler*'.

Take some Mosaic Canvas, of the finest make, and woven so that each thread is at an equal distance apart. Cut this 18 inches wide and 20 inches long, and measure off a border all round of 4 inches. For the border, half an inch from the edge, draw out threads in a pattern to the depth of half an inch, and work over these with coloured silk; then work a conventional scroll pattern, in shades of several colours, and in TENT STITCH, to fill up the remaining 3 inches of the border. Divide the centre of the Sampler into three sections. In the top section work a figure design. (In the

[1] Leigh Ashton, *Samplers*, Figure 63.

old Samplers this was generally a sacred subject, such as Adam and Eve before the Tree of Knowledge.) In the centre section work an Alphabet in capital letters, and in the bottom an appropriate verse, the name of the worker, and the date.

(2) An oblong square of canvas, more or less coarse, upon which marking with a needle in Cross Stitch or otherwise is learned, Common canvas usually measures from 18 inches to 20 inches in width. In this case, cut off a piece of about 4 inches deep from one selvedge to the other. Then cut the remainder along the selvedge into three equal parts, so that each strip will be about 6 inches in width. These strips must each be cut into four parts, and this will make a dozen samplers, 8 inches long and 6 inches wide respectively. This size will contain all the letters, large and small, besides numerals.

Then follows directions in detail as to hemming the raw edges and a reference to an earlier paragraph on *Marking*, from which an extract is given in Chapter Six (p. 115).

By the end of the nineteenth century embroidery pattern books were easily available and plentiful, but so many different kinds of work were done by hand that the time and interest which had been given to embroidery alone, was taken up with the Fancy Work so beloved of the Victorian age. Such things as Crochet, Macramé and Tatting had no need of samplers; pattern books such as Weldon's *Practical Publications*, Higgin's *Handbook of Embroidery*, Caulfeild and Saward's *Dictionary of Needlework* and many others anticipated every problem with instructions and illustrations and samplers had outlived their need.

CHAPTER TWO

Flowers, Fruit and Trees

The presentation and detail of individual patterns may vary from one sampler to another according to the choice and taste of the worker, but throughout all of them there is a noticeable basic tradition in the selected subjects and their arrangements. This is most apparent in the flower patterns but occurs also in some of the formal and other decorative motifs, as well as in animal and human figures, and yet it appears unlikely that tradition and the demands of fashion could influence the persistent choice of some subjects in samplers over several centuries, irrespective of changes and variety of stitches. The immediate origins of many patterns have been traced, but it seems that one could look even further than a traditional use of some patterns which occur from the sixteenth century onwards and a possible explanation may lie in a deeply rooted but unconscious attachment to symbolic forms, to which embroiderers had become accustomed in ecclesiastic and heraldic work. Religious conviction and superstition have kept alive symbolic representations and with the virtual extinction of church embroidery by the middle of the sixteenth century, the embroiderer's allegiance then was transferred to domestic needlework, at a time when professional broderers were employed in the big houses and with other members of the households, carried out the work on large hangings and furnishings, on which many of the designs were emblematic. Combined with the Tudor love of emblems was a growing fashion for elaborate embroidery on clothing and doubtless these also were responsible for the continuance of patterns which had recognised meaning as well as decorative value. An added stimulus to this industrious age was the fervent belief that idleness was sinful, a sin for which needlework was held to be the means of salvation in the eyes of John Taylor writing in verses *In Prayse of the Needle* early in the seventeenth century:

So what deserves more honour in these days
Than this? which daily doth itselfe expresse
A mortal enemy to idleness

and offered the most exalted of examples in Queen Mary Tudor:

Her greatness held it no disreputation
To hold a needle in her royal hand
Which was a good example to our Nation
And banish idleness throughout the land.

Various opinions have been given as to whether there was or was not any foundation for believing that embroidery motifs had emblematic meaning and among them Miss Jourdain thought it extremely improbable that there was any intended significance at first, but allowed that *caterpillar* and *butterfly* patterns 'later acquired Stuart symbolism'[1]; another writer at the end of the nineteenth century, Lady Marian Alford, produced many examples supporting symbolic meaning in patterns which had survived from earlier civilisations.[2]

Mediaeval sources, from which the first sampler makers took their patterns, had developed from earlier drawings and paintings, which in their turn had derived from even earlier, primitive kinds of decoration. Primitive art was full of superstition and religious significance and made no great distinction between human and animal figures—bird- or animal-headed male and female figures represented godlike beings and many other patterns illustrating myths and religious beliefs had animal, bird or plant shapes. Gods could be recognised by the symbolical shapes associated with them and it was believed that the drawing of the symbol became animated with the spirit of the deity, until eventually only the symbol remained but without losing its original significance. A familiar example which has survived is the Owl—associated with Minerva, Goddess of Wisdom— and still used to represent Wisdom and Learning.

Many symbols were absorbed into later religions when their original associations had faded, and were adapted to fit into decorative patterns on vestments and furnishings and on paintings of a religious nature. In Christian religious art symbolic patterns showing interpretations of Good and Evil are legion; they are also at the root of nearly all embroidery design, whether ecclesiastic or domestic, but while traditional symbolism in church embroidery is intentional, that in domestic needlework is carried on unintentionally. Nowhere is this more apparent than in samplers, and especially in the patterns with their origins in plant life. In every century flower, fruit and leaf patterns outnumber all others; animal and

[1] M. Jourdain, *English Secular Embroidery*, p. 33.
[2] Lady Marian Alford, *Needlework as Art*, 1886, p. 85 *et seq.*

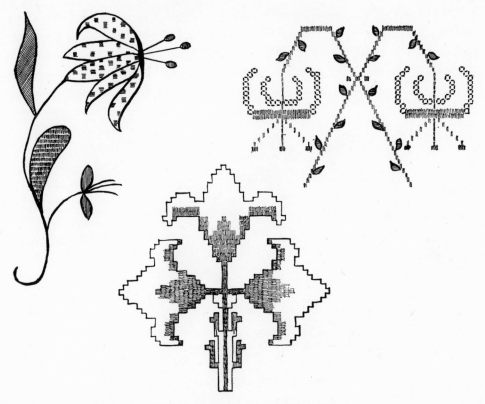

9   *Three eighteenth-century* lily *patterns*

bird patterns are included in many, as also the smaller creatures such as butter-flies, snails, 'flies and wormes' [65, 98], much loved and much used in patterns especially throughout the seventeenth century, but plant forms whether fruiting or in flower, in naturalistic or conventional shapes, are found abundantly in embroidery and in almost every sampler. Poets and writers of the seventeenth century were very much alive to the needlework of their time and Milton's observations in 1637 on patterns used in embroidery might equally well be of those on a sampler which he had seen:

> Bring the rathe primrose that forsaken dies,
> The tufted crow-toe, the pale jessamine,
> The white pink, the pansy freakt with jet,
> The glowing violet,
> The musk-rose, and the well attir'd woodbine,
> With cowslips wan that hang the pensive head,
> And every flower that sad embroidery wears.[1]

[1] John Milton, *Lycidas*, lines 142 to 149.

33

The plant patterns seem, nearly always, to be those associated traditionally with the Christian virtues, especially the ones which symbolise the attributes of the Virgin Mary and the Holy Child seen in paintings in which either or both are the central figures. The sixteenth century samplers illustrated [53, 54] contain flowers which persist in patterns throughout the history of sampler making and can be recognised as the *rose, carnation, lily, iris, marigold, cowslip, honeysuckle* and the *strawberry* plant, bearing fruit as well as the blossom. The Rose—an early pagan symbol signifying Earthly Love in association with Venus, or Pride and Victory in Roman symbolism — became the Flower of Heavenly Bliss and of Divine Love when seen with the Virgin Mary. The Carnation, Pink, Dianthus (literally 'Divine Flower') or the Gilly Flower of heraldry, has much the same symbolic meaning as the Rose, but its pagan origin was as the Flower of Zeus. The immaculate Lily, as the Flower of Heaven was the symbol of Purity or Chastity and the Lilium candidum or Madonna Lily, is seen with the Holy Virgin in relig-

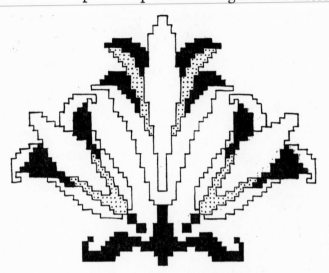

10 *Twentieth-century* lily *pattern*

11 *Three seventeenth-century* fleur de lys *motifs in diaper patterns*

34

ious paintings, especially in those of the Annunciation. The Lily is represented also, in a stylised shape as the Fleur de Lys, in one known sixteenth-, and a number of seventeenth-century samplers in lace and in embroidery patterns [11, 12, 54, 59]. The pattern continued until the nine-teenth century but then it seems only to be recognisable as the 'Prince of Wales's Feathers' sometimes found in the Bristol Orphanage work or other kinds of school samplers [14]. Its origin is variously given; as an adaptation of the Oriental *lotus*, symbol of Fecundity—as a representation of the *iris* or *royal lily* in the heraldic

12   *Two eighteenth-century* fleur de lys *motifs*

Fleur de Luce—and 'as the Lily of France...it was once a conventional frog'.[1] The Honeysuckle is the symbolic flower of Enduring Faith and one suggestion of its origin as a pattern, is that of a derivation from the Tree of Life 'refashioned and combined with the graceful ingenuity of Greek art and covering a mixture of sacred and traditional emblems'[2] [13]. It was a favourite flower of the Tudors and also of Shakespeare as the Eglantine and the Woodbine; as a country flower

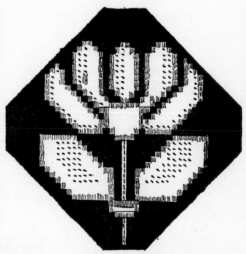

13   *Two seventeenth-century* honey-suckle *motifs*

[1] Lady Marian Alford, *Needlework as Art*, p. 95.
[2] *ibid.*, p. 101.

it has an old traditional power of averting the evil eye, a comforting choice of pattern for the worker whose work at times appears to be bewitched.

A number of smaller flowers which are seen strewn in the grass of gardens or meadows in which the Holy Mother and Child are painted, do not seem to be looked upon as sacred flowers with a separate symbolism for each but they occur

14 *Nineteenth-century* Prince of Wales's Feathers *motif*

15 Daisy *pattern. Eighteenth century*

nevertheless with those which have, in pictures and embroidery. The Marigold, belonging to the Flowers of the Sun (the gold florets symbolise the rays of light), the Cowslip, also called Herb Peter and supposed to represent the Keys of St Peter with its hanging florets, the Violet and the Daisy—flowers of Humility—and the Pansy, commend themselves for colour and shape and for the simple virtues [*15–19, 130, 140, 143*].

While the types of sixteenth-century patterns continued unchanged into the seventeenth, flowers in samplers became more numerous and varied and among the most popular were the *columbine, thistle, cornflower, pansy, tulip* and the fruiting and flowering *vetch* or *pea*. The Columbine is a complex flower in religious symbolism; its name is taken from the five birdlike florets, resembling the columb or dove and because of this, usually it signifies the Holy Spirit of which the Dove is the recognised symbol. The grouping of the flowers sometimes is composed of three blooms—the number of the Holy Trinity—and sometimes of seven, the symbolic number of True Perfection, signifying the seven gifts of the Holy Spirit. The number of flowers in embroidery varies, especially in the *spot*

16 *Arcaded daisy border. Seventeenth century*

motif samplers in which a branch or spray is shown with one full flower and a bud, symbolic of the Mother and Child [57, 58, 65]. A border pattern in *cut* work with four flower heads is shown[1] [63], the number of the four Evangelists; in another example a single flower was composed of seven florets, possibly in an attempt at Perfection but this number is given also to the flower in heraldry. As a sampler pattern, the *columbine* does not appear after the last part of the seventeenth century and generally speaking this is true also of the *daffodil* which is seen in a number of early *spot* motifs but not apparently as a border pattern, although it appears in isolated examples from time to time, all of which are worked in colour.[2] As a symbolic flower it does not represent one of the Virtues, which may account for its lack of popularity although it acquired a remotely Christian connection later on, as the name Lent Lily implies. In its wild state it is a meadow flower, the ancient *Lilium affodilus* and as *Asphodelus* is supposed to have been the flower of Persephone, Queen of the Underworld where it bloomed in the Meadows of the Damned and as such a highly unsuitable subject to perpetuate in samplers. As a national emblem it belongs to the Principality of Wales where it is synonymous with the *leek*. The Thistle does not seem to have been used until after the accession of James I to the English throne and although in symbolism it represents the Major Sins[3] presumably its presence in sampler patterns was in order to represent the National emblem of Scotland as an expression of patriotism, as it appears often with the Rose of England after the union of the two countries in 1603. It is shown also as a single spray with one full flower and one bud [139] but it seems more often to be among patterns of the heraldic kind [131, 141]. A beautiful sampler of 1660 shows the *thistle* with a *rose* and with a *shamrock* of Ireland in cutwork with needlepoint lace stitches, and each scale of the *thistle* calyx is *detached* [96].

The *pansy*, Shakespeare's *Love-in-Idleness*, is seen in nearly every coloured sampler known to have been made from the beginning of the seventeenth century

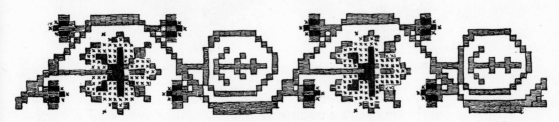

17   *Seventeenth-century* pansy *border pattern*

[1] M. B. Huish, *Samplers and Tapestry Embroideries*, Figure 41. D. King, *Samplers*, Plate 18.
[2] D. King, *Samplers*, Plate 37.
[3] E. Haig, *Floral Symbolism of the Great Masters*, p. 33.

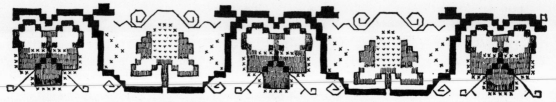

18 *Seventeenth-century* band *pattern of* pansy *and* strawberry *motifs*

but so far none has been found in white work patterns. It was popular as a pattern in all embroidery and the purple and yellow flower is said to have been a favourite of Queen Elizabeth I, who used it as a pattern for some of her own needlework. This could have accounted for its first popularity and it stayed in samplers until the end of the eighteenth century, with a few isolated examples occurring in the first thirty years of the 1800s, but *pansy* patterns were outlived by those of the *rose, carnation* and others found in the early samplers. One of the botanical names of the *pansy* is the *Herba Trinitatis*, which gives an indication of religious significance and a name for the wild pansy of the Northern counties—the *Trinity Violet*—is still used because of its appearance of having 'three faces under one hood' [19]. Trilobed and trefoil shapes are age old symbols of the Holy Trinity and are used in scores of flower and leaf patterns, as well as other triple arrangements, such as three flowers on one stem, three sprays in one vase and so on.

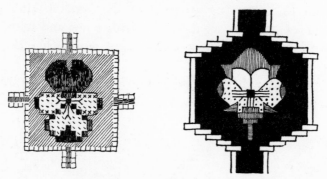

19 Pansy *motifs used in seventeenth–century diaper patterns*

The *tulip* and the *tulip* pattern originated in the East; the flower itself was not known in Western Europe until the middle of the sixteenth century and very little of it was known even then in England. Its cup-shaped flower has since become the emblem of the Chalice, a strange and obscure journey from its association with necromancy in the Middle Ages. As a sampler pattern it was not as popular as other flower patterns in the seventeenth century and it does not appear to have been used as a motif for a continuous border until the eighteenth century [157, 158]. It is seen in lace patterns as a single flower on a stalk, as in the *Garden of Eden* [60], behind the *Angel* in the *Visitation of Sara and Abraham* [60] and another worked in needlepoint by Sarah Fletcher in 1668.[1] A sturdy bloom in *tent* stitch[2] and others of more elegant form in coloured silks, arrived in samplers after the middle of the seventeenth century[3] and from the beginning of the eighteenth century it became almost an equal favourite with *carnation* and *rose* patterns [20].

20   *Eighteenth-century tulip motif*

Fruit patterns follow the same kind of tradition as that of the flowers; all-over and diaper patterns and numbers of seventeenth-century *spot* motifs are seen as naturalistic branches bearing flowers, leaves and fruit; *band* samplers on the other hand, have arrangements of a more formal kind, often of fruit and leaves in a repeating pattern in order to make a decorative border [31, 36, 145, 146, 164, 186]. The *pear* is considered by some as being more likely to be the Forbidden Fruit than the apple and generally it appears in the *spot* type of motif but rarely as a border pattern [57, 62]; a pear-

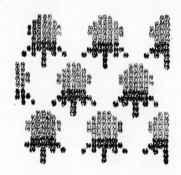

21 *Types of all-over patterns with* strawberries. *Seventeenth century*

[1] Leigh Ashton, *Samplers*, Figure 21.
[2] D. King, *Samplers*, Plate 1.
[3] Leigh Ashton, *Samplers*, Figures 24a and 24b.

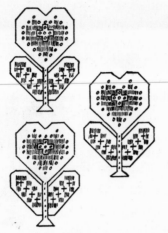

22   *A pear-shaped fruit thought to be the fig. Seventeenth century*

23   *Diaper pattern with* strawberry *motif. Seventeenth century*

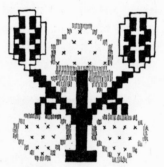

24   Spot *motif with three* strawberry *fruits. Seventeenth century*

shaped fruit seen in some patterns is thought to be the *fig* [*22*] which is another claimant for consideration as the Forbidden Fruit, on the grounds that its leaves clearly were the most conveniently to hand at the time of the Fall. In 1735 Elizabeth Spear worked two *cherry trees* and an *olive tree* between them on her sampler [*104*]; the *olive*, significant of Peace and Goodwill is a rare subject for a pattern but the *cherry*, one of the Fruits of Heaven, appears in several patterns as a fruiting branch, either held by a bird or with a bird perching upon it [*65, 97, 100*].[1]

The *pomegranate* occurs in a number of white and coloured samplers from the sixteenth century. The fruit had great religious meaning symbolising the Hope of Eternal Life and as an emblem of the Christian Church, it was shown open on one side to disclose its countless seeds. As an heraldic emblem it belonged to the

[1] Leigh Ashton, *Samplers*, Figure 15; also D. King, *Samplers*, Plate 1.

Royal family in the sixteenth century, being one of the badges of Queen Catherine of Aragon and of her daughter Queen Mary I, which no doubt encouraged its use in embroidery. A sampler of 1643, now in the Fitzwilliam Museum collection, shows a pomegranate tree bearing four fruits and four leaves in *cut* and

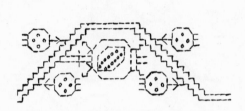

25   Pomegranate *border pattern*. 1598

26   Pomegranate *motif in seventeenth-century diaper patterns*

27   Pea *flower with two buds and hanging pods. Seventeenth century*

drawn work with *needlepoint* stitches,[1] but in coloured samplers a single pomegranate fruit is used as a *spot* motif among the diaper patterns more than as a pattern on its own [26]. Exceptions to this are found in an occasional border pattern [25] and as a fruit-bearing branch, with one large and one small fruit in the Mother and Child type of pattern, on a coloured sampler of the mid seventeenth century.[2]

Several plant patterns bearing fruit as well as flowers appear in early samplers and one which seems to have been popular is that of the white flowered Pea.

[1] Leigh Ashton, *Samplers*, Figure 9.
[2] D. King, *Samplers*, Plate 1.

28   Pea *flower and pods,* with strawberry *fruits and flowers and* pansy *patterns. Seventeenth century*

The pattern has few variations and may possibly have had an heraldic origin without the flowers, in the *Broom Pod* of the Plantagenets, but the sampler motif
consists usually of a flower on an upright stem, bearing also two buds and two
hanging pods open to show the seeds [*27*]. The *pea* flower and pods are shown with
good effect in a small seventeenth-century sampler in the collection of Dr Goodhart, a drawing from which is illustrated [*28*], but it was clearly preferred as a
spot motif in most samplers in the 1700s. Stylised patterns of *pea pods*, with or
without flowers are included in Shorleyker's pattern book, but the subject does
not appear in samplers until about the middle of the century and then in its more
naturalistic form, when it would seem that the garden pea, introduced into
England during the time of Queen Elizabeth I, had become well known as a
vegetable. In some motifs the flower resembles more that of the bean in colour,
being white with a dark keel, but the fruiting pod undoubtedly is intended to be
that of the pea.

The *strawberry* in early patterns appears usually as a plant bearing fruit as well as flowers as it does in paintings of the Virgin and Child, where it is seen with the small low growing plants of the flowering meadows and gardens surrounding the central figures, as well as among the decorative patterns on draperies and background hangings of many paintings with the same association [3, 21, 24, 29]. It

29   Strawberry *plant with three fruits. Seventeenth century*

has been described as a 'very perfect fruit with neither thorns nor stone, but sweet, soft and delicious all through and through. Its flowers are of the whiteness of innocence and its leaves almost of the sacred trefoil form and since it grows upon the ground, there is no possibility of its being the dread Fruit of the Tree of Knowledge. Its meaning always appears to be that of perfect righteousness'.[1] The combination of the fruit and flowers in coloured work was a familiar and decorative subject and combined with its religious associations, it was obviously much loved as a sampler pattern, although probably no other flower or fruit, except perhaps the *carnation*, began so well as a decorative pattern or continued so long, but having lost its freshness on the way, by the nineteenth century it had become one of the most copied and hackneyed of sampler border patterns [186].

[1] Elizabeth Haig, *Floral Symbolism of the Great Masters*, p. 269.

The dread Fruit of the Tree of Knowledge aroused no fears in makers of samplers. The whole well laden tree appears from early in the seventeenth century and with rare exceptions, in a faithfully maintained tradition; *Adam's* position was on the left of the pattern, *Eve's* on the right and the *Serpent* wound

30   Squirrels *from late eighteenth- and early nineteenth-century patterns*

in an anti-clockwise direction facing *Eve*, who succumbed to temptation with the Forbidden Fruit in or touching her hand, in *cut* work, *drawn* work, *satin* stitch, *double-running* or *cross* stitches for nearly 400 years [*55, 60, 171, 172, 176*]. There are, of course, the exceptions. In 183 , Sophia Stephens chose to show the Garden of Eden before the Fall, with *Adam* and *Eve* standing away from the *Tree*, whereon are many *apples* but no *Serpent*; instead, *Birds of Paradise* perch on the branches

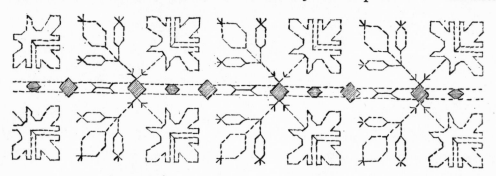

31   *Seventeenth-century border pattern of* rose-hips *and* leaves

and doubt as to the truth of it is forestalled by words embroidered below the pattern, 'Birds of Paradise' [*176*].[1] A nameless artist of the seventeenth century, however, preferred the scene after the Fall. In *cut* work and needlepoint stitches the *Angel with the Flaming Sword* advances upon the guilty pair, both of whom hold in place their fig leaves; his work done the *Serpent* droops in the *tree* and a

[1] D. King, *Samplers*, Plate 51.

32 *Seventeenth-century* robin *with* rose hips

squirrel eating a nut, bears witness on the ground before a bearded *Adam*, who usually is shown clean shaven—a somewhat unlikely condition [*60*]. In early Northern symbolism the *squirrel* represents Mischief and although it is found in many samplers, it is especially appropriate when associated with the Fall [*30*].

The number of *apples* shown upon the Tree varies from a perfunctory five to as many as 30 or more but the average number is about 15; the number usually is an odd one to allow for a balanced Tree and a single fruit at the top, but although imagination has led workers to include a number of details in the pattern, none has left a space on the Tree to show where the Apple of Temptation once grew. In some American samplers the Tree carries seven *apples* representing the Seven Deadly Sins, but the number in British samplers seems to be governed by the height of the Tree.

A rare but distinctive fruit pattern is that of the *rose hip* without the *rose* flower; both the

33 Hazel nut spot *motif. Seventeenth century*

45

34 *Diaper patterns with* acorns *and* oak *leaves. Seventeenth century*

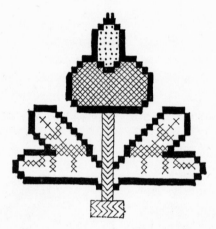

35 Acorn spot *motif. Seventeenth century*

examples illustrated come from seventeenth-century samplers [*31, 32*] and a small pattern is shown also in the Elizabeth Cromwell sampler [*62*].

Nuts are not overlooked among the patterns; both *acorn* and *filbert* or *hazel nuts* are seen in early samplers but the latter seem to disappear after the end of the seventeenth century, although the *acorn* has not yet fallen from favour and it seems probable that it will never do so in embroidery. It appears with or without the *oak leaf*, as a *spot* motif on its own [*35*] or enclosed within one of the many diaper or arcaded border patterns [*34, 134, 137, 145, 146, 164*], and was a popular pattern until the first part of the eighteenth century. The *oak leaf* is used in heraldry and as one of the National emblems, the fruit and leaf of the Oak appears among decorative patterns, especially in times of patriotic enthusiasm and many

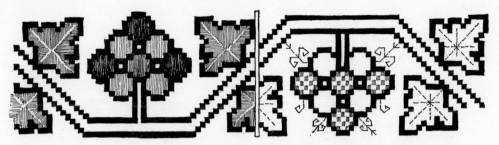

36 Grape and vine leaf *band patterns. Seventeenth century*

samplers bear witness to their popularity. A number of patterns are based on the 'prim acorn', but in spite of this there is a greater variety in its presentation than in any other fruit or flower pattern [*3, 34, 35, 69, 134, 137, 145, 146, 149, 163, 164*]. A pattern which is rather similar to some of the *acorns* but which cannot be compared with it in popularity, is the *filbert* or *hazel nut*. Various little nut-like

37 Vine *pattern on a spot motif sampler. Seventeenth century*

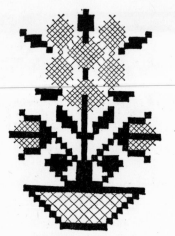

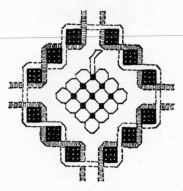

38 Rose *flower pot pattern.*
Eighteenth century

39 *Stylised* vine *motif used in diaper patterns. Seventeenth century*

patterns can be found in seventeenth-century samplers, but few as delightful as the *spot* motif taken from one of Dr Goodhart's samplers [*33*].

A fruiting *vine* pattern occurs in a number of early samplers from the sixteenth century, but as a subject the Vine did not provide inspiration for sampler workers for more than about a hundred years, although isolated examples can be found later. It is one of the subjects deeply associated with church embroidery in a tradition supported by biblical references and the symbolical significance of a tree with spreading, fruit bearing branches. The pattern in Alice Lee's sampler shows the essential character of the Vine in its arrangement as a continuous all-

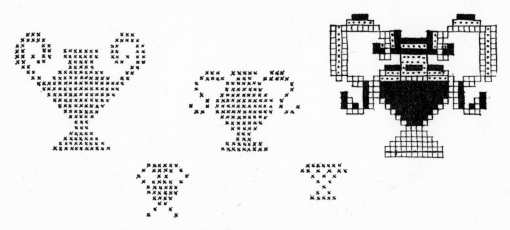

40 *Some vases used in flower pot motifs. Eighteenth century*

48

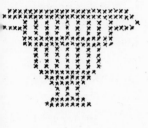
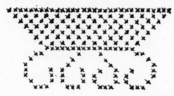

41 *Baskets, bowls and urns used in flower pot and fruit bowl patterns. Eighteenth and nineteenth centuries.*

over design [*133, 135*]. Other versions of it in the seventeenth century can be divided into two types, the naturalistic *spot* pattern—usually seen with a curving stem carrying one large and one small bunch of *grapes*, one or more *leaves* and a *tendril* [*37*]—or the stylised forms found in the diaper patterns, and in those of the borders in *band* samplers [*36, 39*].

A pattern representing flowers or fruit contained in a vase, bowl or basket has come to be looked upon as belonging exclusively to the sampler, probably because of its persistence in examples of the eighteenth and nineteenth centuries [*43, 167*]. It is a type of pattern with a distinctive character; the *flowers* form a balanced, pictorial motif often of enough impor-tance to be used as the chief pattern of a sampler. With some exceptions the patterns are symmet-rical, whether they contain one or several *flowers* and the container in which the *flowers* are shown, although varied, has become part of the pattern's tradition. The *flowers* are similar in design to those in the border or *spot* patterns, with the *carnation, rose* and *tulip* as the most popular, especially in the *cross* stitch samplers of the early nineteenth cen-tury [*38, 159, 169, 184, 206*]. The repetition of the pattern has tended to emphasise its likeness to the symbolical *flower pot* or *lily pot* in paintings

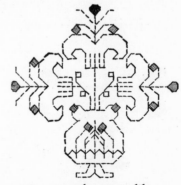

42 *Seventeenth-century* lily-pot *motif from a* band *pattern by* Hannah Dawe

of the Annunciation or the Adoration, a pattern familiar to religious symbolism, which probably had its pagan origin in the Gardens of Adonis, the God of Vegetation. The *flower pot* in religious art is shown either of glass—symbolising the purity of the Holy Virgin—or of earthenware, symbolical of her lowly birth, and some of the embroidered patterns seem to attempt this difference in their presentation of a solid or transparent container [40, 41]. With reference to a pattern of a *carnation* in a pot illustrated in *The History of Lace*, Mrs Bury Palliser described it by saying 'the Flowerpot of the Annunciation was worked in "hollie point" on the crown of the infant's cap or "biggin".'[1] and this symbolic interpretation of the type of pattern has been accepted more or less, during the last 50 years, as being its origin. Although it was not universal in sampler patterns until the eighteenth century, occasionally early examples are to be found, notably one of a *rose* and two *columbines* in Elizabeth Cromwell's sampler [62] and another of a *lily pot* with three *lilies* which occurs in an arcaded *border* pattern made by Hannah Dawe, also in the seventeenth century [42].[2] It is unusual to find this pattern in borders.

Fruit is represented in *bowl* or *basket* patterns, arranged with leaves and heaped into a pyramid to make what must be the most familiar of sampler patterns [43]. Its probable and most immediate origin was in the reproductions of fruit in paintings, especially in those of the Mother and Child; a good example is that of

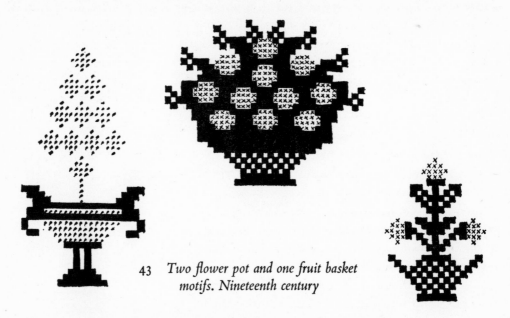

43 *Two flower pot and one fruit basket motifs. Nineteenth century*

[1] Mrs Bury Palliser, *The History of Lace*, p. 272, Figure III, 1875 (3rd edition).
[2] M. B. Huish, *Samplers and Tapestry Embroideries*, Plate xiii.

the bowl of fruit in Botticelli's '*Virgin and Child*', which might well have been the inspiration for the first of the numerous patterns in samplers, even to the design on the bowl. Patterns of *cornucopias* with *flowers* and *fruit* are found sometimes in eighteenth-century samplers, but they are not as frequent as the *flower pot* or *fruit basket* patterns.

Formal decorative patterns recognisable as trees can be found in a few early seventeenth-century samplers, but they are distinct in type from the naturalistic *tree* patterns which occur in numbers of early samplers of lace or coloured silk embroidery. The fruiting trees in Alice Lee's samplers of 1598 [53] are the earliest dated examples but with the exception of the *Tree of Knowledge* and others of a similar kind, *tree* patterns did not become popular

44   *Late eighteenth century* oak *tree*

until about 1740. Earlier than this, the fruit-bearing tree, similar in type to the Tree of Knowledge pattern, is found with male and female figures in dress of the period in which the work was done, standing on each side of the tree, taking the

45   Trees *with characteristics of the* sycamore. *Eighteenth century*

46 *An elegant* tree *in* cross *stitch by Susanna Gellett. 1800*

places of the Original Sinners in patterns of the Temptation. Other motifs, less easily recognisable as trees, appear to have developed from earlier *tree* patterns. In very early Eastern art a *core* or *pyramid* typifying the core was associated with the Tree of Life—the Holy Tree of Paradise—and from various translations of this symbol throughout the history of embroidery, it appears to have arrived on samplers in some of the cone-shaped patterns recorded on them [*98, 100, 120*]. Of these the *pineapple* and the *pomegranate* show the most direct descent and it has been suggested that the *honeysuckle* pattern could be an elaboration of the *Tree of Life* (p. 35). Another motif which is common in seventeenth- and eighteenth-century patterns shows an even stronger resemblance to an Oriental version of the

47　*Trees showing the eighteenth-century fashion for topiary*

48　*Conventional pyramid trees*

49 *Formal motifs resembling bushes*

Tree, in which two *beasts* are chained to opposite sides of the main stem, often in attitudes of praise or homage.[1] This pattern which is illustrated on Figure 120 (in the third border pattern from the top of the sampler) shows *tree* motifs with an intervening linking pattern, which appear clearly to be the remains of the original animal forms.[2]

During the seventeenth century, fruit-bearing trees were used in *band* patterns, but a gradual change in the conception of a sampler in the eighteenth century, from a work record to a pictorial exercise in embroidery, brought with it a

50 *A weeping wil-low and urn pattern of the 1820s*

desire for naturalistic design and all manner of *tree* patterns were evolved in consequence. The more naturalistic they were the better, if one can judge from their number and variety and *oak*, *ash*, *willow* and *sycamore* especially, can be distinguished from the forestry of the century's patterns which continued into the middle of the 1900s [*44*, *45*]. The *weeping willow* was used in many samplers after the death of the Princess Charlotte in 1817 [*50*, *178*]; other varieties, botanically unknown, owed their peculiarities to the imagination of the workers, but they were in keeping with the general character of the samplers. In Ann Day's work [*123*] the trees obviously were consistent with her frivolous outlook on the responsibilities of shepherding

[1] Lady Marian Alford, *Needlework as Art*, Plates 21 and 23.
[2] M. B. Huish, *Samplers and Tapestry Embroideries*, Plate vii, D. King, *Samplers*, Plate 12. M. Jourdain, *English Secular Embroidery*, Plate facing p. 182.

and one of the patterns in a sampler made by Susanna Gellett in 1800, shows an elegance not usually achieved with *cross* stitch [46].[1]

The conventional pyramid *trees*, although following the symbolic cone pattern, were greatly encouraged no doubt by the eighteenth-century fashion for

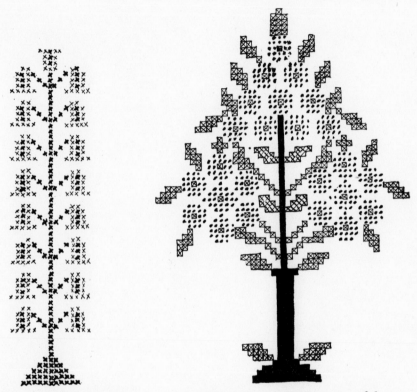

51 Tree *pattern hung with bell-shaped flowers. Eighteenth century*

52 *A popular* rose-bush *pattern of the eighteenth and nineteenth centuries*

topiary, while keeping to the traditional shapes [47, 48]. Their first appearance on samplers was a little half hearted by comparision with the enthusiasm with which they were treated as the eighteenth century progressed, but at whatever period the conifer type of *tree* was used, *cross* stitch was the method of embroidering it. All manner of stitches can be found in other types of *tree*; *satin* stitch, *French knots*, *stem* and *chain* stitches were used freely and *couched* chenille was especially popular for the *trees* in the pastoral scenes of the eighteenth century and in the early years of the nineteenth. A variety of *leaf* patterns, many of them of

[1] Leigh Ashton, *Samplers*, Figure 55.

doubtful pedigree, were used to make formal little motifs resembling bushes more than trees during these periods [49]; numbers of them had flower-like patterns also. A popular pattern resembled a standard rose bush more than a tree [52] and other *tree* patterns were hung with bell shaped and various flower patterns [51].

CHAPTER THREE

Men, Birds, Beasts, Flyes
and Fishes

Patterns representing human figures have been attempted in embroidery for many centuries, but during the last 400 years some familiar types have come to be looked upon as belonging only to samplers. Human figures in ecclesiastical and domestic embroidery patterns had had a long and ancient history by the end of the sixteenth century, but they appear only occasionally in samplers before the middle of the seventeenth century and can be grouped roughly into four types. The most numerous are the *biblical* figures, associated with well-known stories from the Bible; then those which may be described as *family* figures, on the grounds that often they appear to represent members of the worker's family and are shown in dress of the period; a third type is known as the *boxer*, a controversial, mis-shapen little figure which appears in samplers approximately within the span of the seventeenth century, although a few examples stray into those of the first half of the 1700s; and lastly there are the *mermaids*, which should perhaps be classed with the bestiary patterns.

According to the present evidence, *Adam* and *Eve* were the earliest of the biblical figure patterns and possibly the first of any human figure patterns, to be worked on a sampler. Early examples are seen in the white lace samplers and seem always to be on linen, generally embroidered with linen in *cut, drawn* and *needle-point* stitches, the fine work giving a lightness of touch to their presentation which exonerates any lack of anatomical elegance; this is especially so in Mrs Lloyd's sampler [55]. In work of later years, most of the angular small figures were worked solely in *cross* stitch and are just amusing, with little merit as examples of needlework. Other biblical subjects of the seventeenth century are treated in the same way as the *Adam and Eve* patterns, as can be seen in the *Visitation of Abraham* and Sarai [60] which in this instance was worked on the same sampler as *Adam and Eve* and is unusual, as biblical subjects generally are seen singly.[1] A rare pattern of another group of figures recalls the story of *Judith and Holofernes*, in which colour has been added to the white lace by the use of gold silk thread in *bullion* stitch for the *curls* of *hair* on the head of Holofernes; Judith and her maid have gold silk *hair* also, including *eyebrows* worked in *buttonhole* stitch [61]. A curious fashion grew up in the first half of the seventeenth century for the inclusion of religious figures in all kinds of embroidery and so great was the enthusiasm that the playwright Jasper Mayne recorded its effects in some detail in 1639:

> Sir she's a Puritan at her needle too . . .
> . . . She works religious petticoats, for flowers
> She'll make church histories. Her needle doth
> So sanctify my cushionets, besides
> My smock sleeves have such holy embroideries,
> And are so learned, that I fear in time
> All my apparel will be quoted by
> Some pure instructor.[2]

This fashion persisted throughout the seventeenth century, flagging a little towards the end perhaps, but the pattern merchants did all they could to encourage their use; Peter Stent sold in 1662 *Abraham offering Isak, Adam and Eve, Susanna and the Elders, Moses offering up the Serpent in the Wilderness.*[3] The subject of *Solomon and the Queen of Sheba* was popular also and a sampler with this pattern was worked by An Smeeth in 1654, showing the *Queen of Sheba* wearing a necklace of seed pearls.[4] Bible subjects of the eighteenth century were worked in coloured silks and contained much detail but few changes of subject, scenes of the *Sacrifice of Isaac* and others from the life of Abraham seemed especially popular. The *Return of the Spies from Canaan*, which appears in some late eighteenth-century patterns, is illustrated [170], but by this time *cross* stitch was being used for most of the *figure* patterns and they had lost much of their character. There are of course, the exceptions and one made by Mary Young during the years of 1811 and 1812, possesses a sense of pattern and liveliness which are all too rare at this period. The subject of the main pattern is entitled *Jacob's Vision*, in which Jacob lies on his stony pillow beneath the wide rungs of a ladder going up into the clouds, with two lines of 'the angels of God ascending and descending on it' —those ascending were worked with the backs of their heads showing and those

---

[1] Also in Leigh Ashton, *Samplers*, Figure 12.
[2] *The City Match*, Act II, Scene 2.
[3] M. Jourdain, *English Secular Embroidery*, p. 69.
[4] In the Collection of the Fitzwilliam Museum. Reference no. 28, 81.

53   *1598. Silk and metal threads on linen, with seed pearls and black beads. Back, cross, Algerian eye, arrowhead, satin, chain, ladder and buttonhole stitches. Also detached buttonhole fillings, couching, speckling, two-sided Italian cross stitch, bullion and French knots. Signed, Iane Bostocke. 14 × 16¾ inches*

54 *Last half of sixteenth century. Silk and metal threads on linen. Cut and drawn work with needle-point fillings. 36½ × 6 inches*

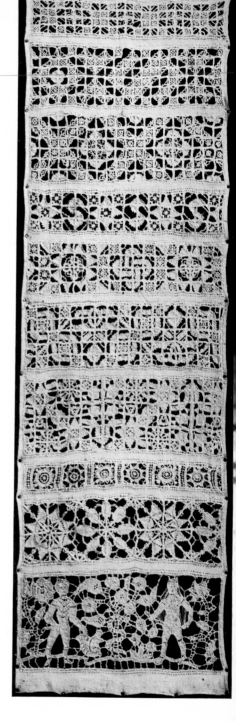

55 *Early seventeenth century. Linen thread on linen. Cutwork with needlepoint fillings. 19½ × 6 inches*

56   1629. *Silk thread on linen. Cross and Holbein stitches with lace fillings. Signed, Elizabeth.* 26½ × 6⅜ *inches*

57   1630. *Silk and metal threads on linen. Tent, plaited braid, rococo, back and detached filling stitches.* 21 × 8½ *inches*

58 *First half of seventeenth century. Silk, silver and silver-gilt threads on linen. Tent, plaited braid, detached filling, back, plaited Gobelin, chain, rococo, interlacing and two-sided Italian cross stitches with detached fillings. Signed, M.R. 21 × 16¾ inches*

59 *First half of seventeenth century. Silk and metal threads on linen. Tent, rococo, double running and encroaching Gobelin stitches. Some original drawings shown unworked. 16 × 9½ inches*

60 *Mid seventeenth century. Linen thread on bleached linen. Cutwork and needlepoint stitches. Figures showing Abraham and Sarai greeting the Angels, and Adam and Eve and the Angel with the Flaming Sword.*
$7\frac{1}{8} \times 5\frac{3}{4}$ *inches*

61 *Seventeenth century (detail). Linen and silk threads on linen. Satin and Roumanian stitches with needle-point lace fillings and some buttonhole stitch. Figures showing Judith and her maid with the head of Holofernes.*
Whole sampler $27\frac{3}{4} \times 5\frac{3}{4}$ *inches*

62   *First half of seventeenth century. Silk thread on linen. Holbein, darning, stem, buttonhole, Roumanian, cross, outline, detached buttonhole, four-sided and chain stitches with some French knots. Signed, Elizabeth Cromwell.* $24\frac{3}{4} \times 7\frac{3}{4}$ *inches*

63   1649. Linen thread on linen. Cut work.
Signed S.I.D., A.I. 18¼ × 6½ inches

64   Mid seventeenth century. Silk, silver gilt and
silver threads on linen. Tent, rococo, Hungarian,
Florentine, cross, interlacing, Algerian eye, chain,
and plaited braid stitches, with bullion knots and
couched work. 22½ × 8½ inches

65   *Mid seventeenth century. Silk and metal threads on linen, with some sequins. Tent, rococo, plaited braid, double plaited braid, cross and double running stitches with eyelet holes, oriental punched work and interlacing. Signed M.P. Initials drawn but unworked. 21 × 16¾ inches*

descending were given faces. A smaller pattern on the same sampler represents the figure of *Hagar* beside a large *bottle* lying on its side and the abandoned *baby* lies beneath a bush; the relevant verse from the Bible is given below the pattern:

And the water was spent
in the bottle and she cast
the child under one of the
shrubs. * Gen. 21 ver. 15 *[1]

Angel patterns away from a biblical context occur seldom in the seventeenth century. A winged, angel-like figure in a voluminous white garment appears in some mid-century samplers, but figures seen in eighteenth- and nineteenth-century examples resemble *cherubim* rather than the *angel* figures in earlier work. The *angels of Jacob's Vision* are exceptional, being clothed in bottle green and rather bottle shaped in outline, but the more commonplace patterns show a winged figure clothed in flying draperies—sometimes only a ribbon—and carrying a *sword* when connected with *Adam and Eve* patterns, or more often they are blowing *trumpets* when included among the collections of miscellaneous patterns of the nineteenth century. The *Lord's Prayer* [118] and the *Ten Commandments* [103], verses taken from the Bible and from books of *Moral Songs*, often are accompanied by flying *angels* in conventional robes or by winged heads of cherubim appearing above or below silken or woollen *clouds*; others wear long tunics and coats, and hold palm leaves and trumpets.[2]

Patterns representing the Crucifixion are rare in British samplers and occur only about the middle of the nineteenth century. An example of 1842 contains the *Crucifix*, the *crosses* of the *two thieves* and two female figures[3] and a Welsh sampler dated 1823 is illustrated in the booklet issued by the National Museum of Wales, showing the *Crucifix* only.[4] Similar patterns exist in other samplers but the subject was more common in European examples made half a century before; in them, patterns which represented the *Instruments of the Passion* sometimes were included.[5] The subject of the Crucifixion is used in some of the nineteenth century *puzzle* samplers (p. 186) in which three *Crosses* are worked in outline and biblical quotations worked across and within the outlines.

Discounting the traditional fig leaves of the *Adam and Eve* pattern and the nude *boxer* figures, *figure* patterns in general were dressed in the fashion of the time in which the sampler was made [66–8]. Clothing given to the biblical characters

[1] Leigh Ashton, *Samplers*, Figure 12.
[2] Leigh Ashton, *Samplers*, Figure 39.
[3] Collection of the Fitzwilliam Museum. Reference no. 38. 65.
[4] F. G. Payne, *Guide to the Collection of Samplers and Embroideries*, Plate xiii.
[5] Leigh Ashton, *Samplers*, Figure 65b. D. King, *Samplers*, Plates 59 and 66.

is of the same period as those of the contemporary *family* type, which follows the practice in mediaeval art, so that *Abraham and Sarai* in Stuart costume is no more incongruous than Bible characters of religious paintings being represented in mediaeval clothes; in fact, it is partly because of the clothing on *figure* patterns that an approximate period can be assessed for some undated samplers, which had been taken (directly or by copying) from early printed pattern books.

Human figures of the *family* type were not popular until the eighteenth

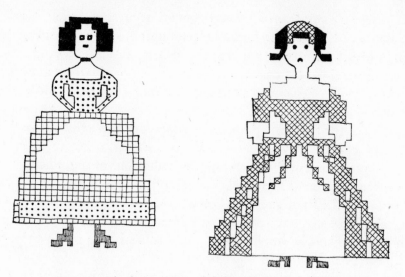

66   *Family figure patterns. Mid-eighteenth century*

century, but nevertheless they are found from time to time in the different kinds of samplers before then. An early example of the seventeenth century of silk and metal threads embroidered on linen, contains two *human figure* patterns and although it is undated, the initials 'I.R.', the type of embroidery and the costume of the figure, indicate its period as that of James I, 1603 until 1625.[1] The larger of the two standing figures is of a woman in a full skirted dress, wearing a ruff and holding a fan, the smaller—a male figure—wears doublet and hose with ruff and a high hat, and is much the same as that seen under the name of Elizabeth Cromwell in her sampler [62]. The first dated sampler to include figure patterns is an early Stuart example in the collection of the Dorset County Museum at Dorchester [57]. The date is 1630 and again the initials, 'C.R.', are those of the reigning monarch; the figures are of a man and woman in Stuart dress and the fact that they are holding hands suggests that they represent man and wife and possibly the parents of the worker. Stuart dress is shown in white *cut* and *drawn*

[1] D. King, *Samplers*, Plate 2.

work samplers throughout the century except where the figures have been taken from early pattern books.[1] *Family* figures occur more often after the middle of the 1600s; embroidered in colour and worked in a variety of stitches which range generally speaking, from *tent* and *satin* stitches in the seventeenth century, *satin* and

67   *Family figures, possibly the parents of the workers. Eighteenth century*

split stitches until the middle of the eighteenth, to *cross* stitch by the middle of the nineteenth century and onwards. The earliest figure patterns consist either of one figure, man or woman, or a man and woman standing side by side and sometimes holding hands [67] or of a man and a woman standing each side of a fruiting tree in the manner of the *Adam and Eve* pattern[2]; the last type is found in *band* samplers and not among *spot* motifs, which had almost died out by the end of the seventeenth century. That there are the inevitable exceptions to this classification can be seen by the figure patterns in the Joyce Leedes sampler of 1675 [98] some of which are on horseback; and in another pattern of the *spot* motif type in 1776, figures are shown beside a fruiting tree.

During the same period a distinctive kind of pattern with a *family* figure motif is found among the *band* samplers and usually given a place of importance at the bottom of the work. The figures, alone or in pairs, are shown either standing or sitting surrounded by a pattern of flowers or fruit in the form of an arbour. There are a number of versions of the pattern but all are so strongly reminiscent of the mediaeval *Hortus Conclusus* or Enclosed Garden of the Holy Virgin of religious art, that once more an old symbolical pattern seems to have come to life again in the sampler. The Enclosed Gardens of the paintings are surrounded on three sides by a wall or hedge, on or in front of which are growing

[1] Leigh Ashton, *Samplers*, Figures 21 and 30.
[2] *ibid.*, Figures 8b and 25.

flowers or fruiting trees verging on to a flowered meadow in which the Virgin is seated; among others are those which show the Virgin in a rose bower, or within a trellised arbour over which grows a fruiting vine. A sampler 'wrought' by Rachel Loader in 1666 shows two standing figures within an arbour of fruiting *Vine*, flanked by other fruit-bearing trees[1]; Mr Marcus Huish illustrated a sampler of 1668 in which a woman feeding a squirrel is seated in an arbour of flowers and a small canopy is embroidered over her head within the arbour,[2] but by the beginning of the eighteenth century the top of the *arbour* pattern had shrunk a little, revealing in some samplers, the figure of *Queen Anne* holding the Orb and Sceptre, with *flowers* on each side, and only a canopy over her head [*101*]. The pattern in a similar sampler in the collection of the Victoria and Albert Museum, contains *Queen Anne* but the canopy is omitted altogether, and a *fruiting tree* has taken the place of the *flowers* in the previous pattern.[3]

A number of patterns of the *family* type include among them figures representing members of the household who were not necessarily members of the family, especially small negro boys as servants or pages—a reflection of upper-class fashion in the eighteenth century—who are shown in attendance on other family figures. A well-known sampler of 1761 of the Philips family, contains figures of mother, father, five daughters, a son with his clerical tutor, a child's nurse with the youngest daughter, a white servant, a negro servant and a small negro page[4]; this sampler is an unusual and good example of its kind but many others exist although not all are as successful in workmanship and design. It is possible that none can have more of the family feeling than a small sampler with an indifferently worked miscellany of patterns round a single figure in a tricorne hat and an inscription which reads 'This is my Dear Father'.[5] Other small figures seen in patterns of sailing *ships* in the last part of the eighteenth century, may well be intended to show that the occupation of the father or other member of the family was connected with the sea. The Philips sampler has just such a pattern with wild birds and animals foreign to this country surrounding a sailing ship, with a commanding figure amidships who could be none other than Mr Philips when far from home. Occasionally the inclusion of a figure on board has defeated the worker and although the ship may be drawn to its last halyard, the figure is seen with no more than head and shoulders showing above deck.

A number of samplers in the later part of the eighteenth century have patterns of figures in imaginary shepherd and shepherdess costume; all are coloured and

---

[1] In the Collection of the Fitzwilliam Museum. Reference T. 39–1928.
[2] M. B. Huish, *Samplers and Tapestry Embroideries*, Plate IX.
[3] D. King, *Samplers*, Plate 28.
[4] M. B. Huish, *Samplers and Tapestry Embroideries*, Plate xxii. Leigh Ashton, *Samplers*, Figure 48.
[5] D. King, *Samplers*, Plate 42.

two in a sampler of 1779, now in the Fitzwilliam Museum, are described by Mr Huish as 'two figures posing as mock shepherd and shepherdess and decked out in all the vanities of the time'.[1] Another figure of 1796 is that of a *shepherdess* (with a bewildered *lamb*) who has had a

few more vanities added to her costume with a *fan*, a bouquet of *flowers* on her *crook* and three black ostrich feathers on her hat[123]. A variety of other types of figures appear in *landscapes* and *rural scenes* on nineteenth-century samplers; young men in rustic costume, women in classical draperies, some-times playing a musical instrument and seated under a *weeping willow* are typical of the contemporary idea of design for embroidery. The

68   Girl Guide *figures on a* gift *sampler. 1923*

figure motif however, virtually disappears by the end of the nineteenth century, except, for odd little patterns on school or gift samplers during the first few years of the twentieth century [209] and occasional family records worked in cross stitch.

   The period in which the *boxer* pattern appeared in samplers was in the first half of the seventeenth century—the earliest example in this book is dated 1629 [56]—but although it was found commonly throughout the century, within a hundred years or so its popularity was on the wane and occasional examples only, occurred in samplers up to about 1750. The pattern is of the repetitive type found usually in *band* samplers and consists of figures worked in facing pairs on each side of a floral motif, although a number of patterns show only one *boxer* to each floral unit [56, 70]; from the early part of the seventeenth century until the beginning of the eighteenth, isolated *boxers* are inserted in some samplers,

69   'Trophies' *typical of those carried by* boxers. *Seventeenth century*

[1] M. B. Huish, *Samplers and Tapestry Embroideries*, Plate xxvii.

apparently at random and without the accompanying motif [*62, 98*].[1] About 60 years ago it was thought that the *boxer* figure was so called 'presumably because of their attitude and costume',[2] but the name has no historical or traditional foundation and is relatively modern, being used only since about the end of the last century. The earliest figures had no costume and although one hand is raised in what might be called a pugnacious gesture, the figure invariably is shown in the position of squaring-up in one direction and facing in another, which is not a conventional attitude for boxing [*70*]. The upraised hand holds an object which has been described as a *trophy*, the form of which changes almost from one sampler to another although commonly it resembles a *flower* or *fruit* motif. Usually it is small and in proportion to the size of the figure and although at times it is difficult to identify, some shapes clearly include *acorns, honeysuckle, daisy, pear* with two *leaves*, a *branching stem* or possibly a *fern*; a *heart* or heart-shaped *cup* is carried in patterns of the mid-seventeenth century [*69*]. Larger trophies resemble a bush on a thick stem and to one of these in a sampler of 1742, a perching bird was added.[3] In earlier samplers the figures are in outline, worked with *double running* or *back*

70 *Nude* boxer *figure with floral motif worked in double running and satin stitches. Mid-seventeenth century*

[1] Leigh Ashton, *Samplers*, Figure 42. D. King, *Samplers*, Plate 30.
[2] M. B. Huish, *Samplers and Tapestry Embroideries*, p. 32.
[3] M. B. Huish, *Samplers and Tapestry Embroideries*, Plate xix.

stitches but gradually clothing of various kinds was added to nearly every example and by the middle of the century, those in outline became less common—whether due to increasing modesty or a fashion for figures in costume, is now too late to tell. Once clothing was added to the pattern, few are identical; doublet and hose were popular; frequently the hose is there and no doublet and on others short trunks—sometimes striped—are worn by the figure. Despite their small size, the figures were given dress with recognisable details in fashion at the time of working; wide brimmed and feathered hats, long curls, white collars covering the shoulders and high boots; some are padded so that the figure stands in relief. Occasionally one *boxer* of a pair has long strands of black silk hanging from the back of the head, too long for the male Stuart fashion and obviously intended for a female *boxer*. A sampler by Jean Porter in 1710 shows the familiar *Adam and Eve* pattern with *boxers* instead of the traditional figures; all the usual items of the Fall are included except the fig leaves.[1]

There has been speculation from time to time as to the origin of the *boxer* pattern. In 1900 Mr Huish noted that it had 'puzzled almost all the collectors who possess specimens containing it' and with reference to the object or *trophy* held by each figure he wrote that 'it negatived the idea of their being combatant figures and it almost with certainty places them in the character of the Greek Erotes, the Amores of the Romans or the cupids of the Renaissance' and 'the little figures themselves preserve a singular uniformity of costume which again points to them being the nude Erotes, clothed to suit the times in a tight-fitting jerkin and drawers'.[2] Commenting on the pattern in 1910, Miss Jourdain said—'Small short-skirted figures holding objects in their hands are met with in lacis or darned netting and it is possible that these and the 'Boxers' (in) samplers are rude renderings of the processional figures'.[3] Miss Dorothy Stevens wrote in 1946 that 'they are merely the putti of Renaissance design and carry in their hands not "dice boxes", "fool's baubles", etc., but acorns, fruit, flowers etc. appropriate to the design in which they appear'.[4] The most recent research into the origin of the figures has been done by Mr Donald King and in an article on the results of his work he compares the attitude of the boxer and its position in relation to the floral motif, with that of a pattern, common in early European pattern books, in which a pair of lovers exchanging gifts is represented.[5] One of the comparable patterns is taken from a Venetian publication of 1570, *Ornamente delle belle et virtuose donne* where the girl is being given the choice of the Flower of Youth from the young

[1] *ibid.*, Figure 7.
[2] M. B. Huish, *Samplers and Tapestry Embroideries*, pp. 32 to 34.
[3] M. Jourdain, *English Secular Embroidery*, p. 182.
[4] 'Samplers' by D. Stevens, *Embroidery*, December 1946, p. 4.
[5] 'Boxers' by D. King, *Embroidery*, Winter 1961–1962, pp. 114–115, Fig. 129.

71   *Pattern from* 'Ornamente delle belle et virtuose donne', *1570*

lover, or of the elderly suitor, symbolised by the Tree of Maturity in the background [71]. From other illustrations, Mr King shows the probable transfor-
mation from Continental origins and suggests that its introduction into this
country was by copying directly from European embroidery. Noticeable
similarities in the *human* figures of the original pattern and those of the metamor-
phosed *lovers*, are in the attitude of the male *figure* with his gift held in an out-
stretched hand towards the herbaceous remains of human characteristics of head,
arms and feet of the girl. In this explanation Mr King adds one more to the sampler
patterns to which a symbolic origin can be attached and what he has to say about
it can be applied equally to others—'The generations of schoolgirls who copied
this border in their samplers can have had not the slightest inkling of its origin and
meaning. This is a curious example of the way in which a traditional pattern will

74

survive for centuries, though almost every detail is changed and its original significance long since forgotten.'[1]

The need for skill in embroidering heraldic emblems, accounted for the inclusion of numbers of patterns in samplers. On rare occasions the arms of a family concerned with the making of the sampler can be identified among the patterns; one known example is signed 'M.C.' and contains the coat of arms of the family of Chichester of Arlington, Devon[2] although several other samplers in museums and private collections contain examples of royal coats of arms, probably put on record for patriotic reasons [54].[3] Nevertheless, it is a reasonable supposition that heraldry was the motive behind the presence of many *spot* patterns which seem at first only to be decorative, such as *mermaids*, *birds*, *animals* and some *flowers* and *trees*, and are seldom seen in *band* samplers. The badge of the *mermaid* in heraldry has a history of several hundred years before its known recording on a sampler in

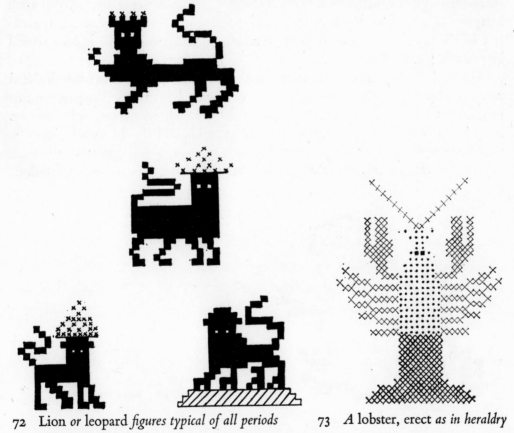

72   Lion *or* leopard *figures typical of all periods*   73   *A* lobster, erect *as in heraldry*

[1] 'Boxers' by D. King, *Embroidery*, Winter 1961–1962, p. 115.
[2] Leigh Ashton, *Samplers*, Figure 22.
[3] *ibid.*, Figures 2 and 5.

the seventeenth century and although the *figure* usually is shown with *comb and mirror*, instances occur in which one or both are omitted [*58, 63, 65, 98*][1]; a *mermaid* in 1668 is shown playing a flute to some unappreciative dogs.[2] The pattern in embroidery can be compared with that in the well-known fourteenth-century tapestry of *The Apocalypse*, of '*The Harlot seated upon the Waters*', combing her hair and looking at her reflection in the mirror in her hand; the folds of her long gown falling on the water, resemble the tail of a mermaid. Mermaids appear first on samplers which are undated but ascribed to the early part of the seventeenth century; they are fairly common among the *spot* motifs, generally worked in fine detail, especially in the scale patterns on the *tail* and in some examples found in lace patterns, the *hair* is shown in loose strands of linen thread hanging from the *head*.[3] The reflection in the *mirror* is treated also with imagination and most details of the hair and face are faithfully copied, regardless of the position of some mirrors, in which no reflection of the holder would be possible [*61, 63, 65*].

74 Frog *in double running stitch. Seventeenth century*

It is established that printed pattern books accounted for numbers of individual motifs and some of these were heraldic in character, but many other patterns not so accounted for, correspond with types of heraldic charges commonly used on furnishings and clothing of upper class households and the livery of their retainers, as well as on small personal belongings such as bags, purses and book covers. The charges included almost every kind of bird and beast, real or fabulous

75 Toad. *Seventeenth century*

76 *A hare*

[1] *ibid.*, Figure 14.
[2] M. B. Huish, *Samplers and Tapestry Embroideries*, Plate ix.
[3] Leigh Ashton, *Samplers*, Figure 22.

77 *Some of the innumerable* dogs *and* cats

and many fishes, reptiles and insects. Animal patterns are among those on the earliest samplers and have the characteristics of heraldic beasts such as the *lion* or *leopard* [72], the *unicorn*, *dragon* and *stag* [168, 169]; many of the smaller creatures also, are identical in their presentation on samplers and in heraldry. It has been assumed that the placing of some was solely for the purpose of filling in spaces between larger patterns but it seems that quite a number of *fishes*, *reptiles*, *insects* and *snails* were embroidered with heraldic presentation in mind. The *lobster* is borne erect in heraldry as it is in samplers [73]; *reptiles*—the *frogs*, *toads* [74, 75], *lizards* and *serpents*—are shown with the back of the head in heraldry and frequently

78 *The occasional* mouse

so in samplers. The heraldic serpent is borne *curling* and *erected on its tail* in many charges and also *knotted* or *nowd*, and both aspects are used in samplers[1]; the serpent of the *Adam and Eve* pattern has its counterpart in heraldry on a pillar and in church embroidery it symbolises the virtues of *healing* and *wisdom*. *Animal* patterns in samplers which correspond with those of heraldic charges are nearly always identical in presentation; the *elephant* and the *camel* occur in both, occasionally as *spot* motifs, and other animals which are common in samplers are characteristically heraldic also and include the *horse*, the *ass*, the *sheep*, *lamb* and *goat*; the *boar*, *porcupine*, *hare* [76], *rabbit*, *hedgehog*, *squirrel* [30] and innumerable *hounds*, *dogs* and *cats* [77] and the occasional *mouse* [78], but by the eighteenth century these patterns were not as common and heraldic intention had reached vanishing point. Patterns which represent cattle occur only rarely; an early

[1] D. King, *Samplers*, Plates 1 and 4.

79   Peacocks *'in pride'. Eighteenth and nineteenth centuries*

example is seen in Elizabeth Cromwell's sampler, but they are not common until
the eighteenth century and after then they appear in numbers of the rural pictorial
patterns. A Somerset sampler of 1790 contains a *milkmaid* in conjunction with a
cow pattern and is typical of the change in character of all animal patterns [*117*].

80   Ducks *and* geese *in seventeenth- and
eighteenth-century patterns*

Bird patterns in early samplers also showed characteristics common to heraldry and ecclesiastic work; the *pelican in her piety* [53] is identical in each; the *owl* perched or standing, is borne full face always in heraldry and in sampler patterns [53, 58, 210]; the *peacock* is the same also, *in pride* or with the tail *close* [62, 79, 84, 205]; the *swan* appears in a number of patterns resembling that in Sibmacher's pattern book as well as in heraldic charges [115]. Numbers of small bird patterns contain recognisable species in seventeenth-century examples—the *parrot* or *popinjay* [57], also the *falcon* [58] the *duck* and the *goose* [80]; many smaller birds stand or perch on fruiting branches or are holding fruit in the beak. Among separate items advertised by Peter Stent (1662) is 'One Book of birds sitting on Sprigs' from which a number in samplers were probably taken. Many familiar kinds of birds are recognisable, *finches, magpies, blackbirds* and *robins* but none remotely resembling Phyllyp Sparowe; *Birds of Paradise* appear in some eighteenth-century patterns, generally among the flower patterns and once, in 183 , in the *Garden of Eden* [176]. The heraldic character of *bird* patterns persisted longer than that of the *animals*; the wing positions in particular—spread while standing or *displayed*, raised as if about to take off—*rising* or *rousant*—and spread actually in flight or *volant*, remained very much the same even under the onslaught of *cross* stitch [94, 166]. Formal bird patterns were particularly popular in nineteenth-century

81 *An attempt to put a bird into a* tree

samplers and outnumber the animal motifs; they were placed frequently in facing pairs each side of *flowerpot* or *tree* patterns or sometimes the pairs were arranged

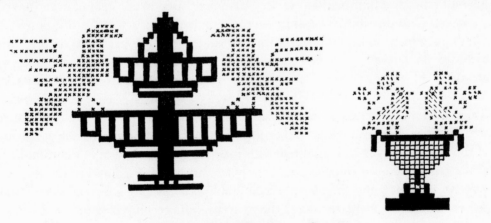

82 *Two patterns of* birds at a fountain

on or above the *trees* and occasionally an attempt was made to put the *bird* into the *tree* [81] until it seemed that with these and other innumerable contrivings, each worker was trying to outdo the other. A number of patterns with the subject of *birds at a fountain* are found in samplers from the middle of the eighteenth century until about the end of the nineteenth [82]; sometimes the birds are omitted but in either case the pattern resembles that in church embroidery of *doves drinking at a fountain* which symbolises Eternal Life.

Fish patterns have never been as popular as bird and animal motifs, although seventeenth-century samplers contain a few examples in the heraldic manner; as a

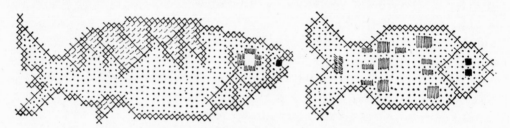

83   Fishes *in seventeenth-century* spot *motif samplers*

Christian symbol the *fish* has been used in decorative church work for nearly 2,000 years but only odd little representations appear from time to time in samplers. A panel in Elizabeth Cromwell's sampler shows a pattern of a *fish* swimming in *water* with a *swan* sailing overhead [62], and two illustrations show patterns taken from other contemporary samplers [83], but the *fish* as a pattern was not common in secular embroidery until about the middle of the 1950s. Since then *fish* motifs in great numbers and variety have been used in all types of embroidery.

Insects were distributed lavishly over seventeenth-century *spot* motif samplers, a fashion which had continued from embroidery of the previous century and included *flies, moths, butterflies* and *beetles*, as well as caterpillars and creeping creatures. All were advertised in publishers' lists of printed pattern sheets for sale; '*Books for Drafts of . . . Fruit, Flyes and Fishes*', '*The second book of flowers, fruicts, beasts, birds and flies exactly drawn*', also '*flies and wormes*' gave a wide choice to embroiderers, but amusement rather than unqualified admiration is felt for many of the motifs, drawn and coloured with little regard for the laws of entomology in the representations of *butterflies, dragonflies,* large and small and *beetles* in great variety, in which the *ladybird* is recognisable. *Caterpillars* and *centipedes, grasshoppers* and *garden snails*, thronged the patterns, but creeping creatures and beetles died out with the seventeenth century; butterflies kept their popularity throughout the eighteenth and nineteenth centuries and some are found in school samplers early in the twentieth. The *bee* is not a frequent motif in samplers, although a few can be found among seventeenth-century patterns [*62*]; about the middle of the eighteenth century a pattern of a *skep* surrounded with small *cross* stitch marks, usually in black and intended to represent flying *bees*, was popular for a time.

CHAPTER FOUR

Buildings, Pyramids and Ships

Houses and other buildings became popular in patterns from about the middle of the eighteenth century, but before this architectural subjects were rarely found. The earliest motif which could be considered as a kind of habitation was that of a small *tent* or *pavilion* which appeared in some of the white lace samplers of the seventeenth century; none is recorded on coloured samplers, although many can be seen in embroidered panels, mirror frames and caskets of the period, especially in *stump* work. The *pavilion* pattern had few variations, each consisting of a domed *canopy* from which tent-like *hangings* fell to the ground and appeared to be looped, tied or folded back in one place to make an opening[1] [60]. In some patterns the front of the hangings was worked in *detached* stitches, so that the two sides of the opening actually could be folded back and tied with a bow; the edges of the *canopy* and *hangings* often are ornamented with fine lace. A sampler in the collection of the Victoria and Albert Museum contains a *pavilion* with these features and two *figures* in Stuart costume are shown standing within the pavilion; two smaller *tents* can be seen in the background.[2] Background positions are the most usual for *pavilions*, where they give an effect of distance and perspective behind the more important foreground figures and it is most probable that the origin of the pattern is heraldic—certainly it bears a strong resemblance to the *tent* in heraldry. Another feature of this Stuart sampler is that of a small *house* or *cottage* which is also part of the background pattern and probably is the earliest pattern of this type in samplers, although in later periods, *house* patterns were common to many. Worked in *drawn* and *needlepoint* stitches, this seventeenth-century *cottage* has one *window* and two *chimneys* and a *door* in *detached* stitches which is open to a pathway leading to the house.

[1] M. B. Huish, *Samplers and Tapestry Embroideries*, Plate VI. Leigh Ashton, *Samplers*, Figures 12 and 21. D. King, *Samplers*, Plate 18.
[2] Leigh Ashton, *Samplers*, Figure 17. D. King, *Samplers*, Plate 22.

Another pattern which was popular in seventeenth-century embroidery was that of King Henry VIII's Palace of Nonesuch, with its towers, pinnacles and battlements and at least one smoking chimney, but few of them were included in sampler patterns and it seems that only one has been illustrated in an example of the first half of the seventeenth century.[1] A palace of a later date was recorded on a sampler of about 1813 and is an unpalatial brick mansion on which, in words along the roof as on some hotels, 'Queen's Palace' is embroidered and another pattern which appears in a miniature *Sampler Pattern Book* is one of the 'Crystal Palace' (p. 29).

Solomon's Temple was the subject for some remarkable examples of architecture in the 1800s; it was popular in England and Wales until the middle of the century and even more so in America, and in many examples the *building* is accompanied with inscriptions giving the biblical proportions and nearly always the name of the Temple. Elizabeth Spear, who must have had a meticulous mind, named several patterns on her sampler, among them a massive gateway which she named 'THIS IS KING SOLOMON PORCH' [104]. From this pattern it is clear that other *porches* similar in character which occur quite frequently in samplers, sometimes with pennants instead of birds on the turrets,[2] were intended to be 'the porch before the temple of the house', although patterns of the whole *temple* do not appear always to include the *porch*. Some of the *Temple of Solomon* patterns take up the centre of the work, or at least a good proportion of it; all are large buildings, some surrounded by railings and it must be admitted that handsome as no doubt they were, the designers' ideas on the architecture seem to have been somewhat overshadowed by thoughts of Brighton Pavilion or Victorian main-line railway stations; fortunately they are named and some are accompanied by relevant quotations from the *Book of Kings*. A sampler of 1808 at one time in the Collection of Lady Mary St John Hope shows the *temple* with the words below:

So he built the house and
furnished it and covered the
house with beams and boards
of cedar. I Kings. Chap. vi. Ver ix.[3]

Of two examples in the National Museum of Wales one is called simply 'Solomon's Temple' and the other of 1830 has an inscription across the front of the building itself:

And Solomon built the House of the Lord in 7 Yr's I Kin VI".[4]

[1] Leigh Ashton, *Samplers*, Figure 15.
[2] *ibid.*, Figure 47. Mary E. Jones, *Samplers*, Figure 29.
[3] *Some Pictures and Samplers from the Collection of Lady St. John Hope.* No. 30.
[4] *Guide to the Collection of Samplers and Embroideries.* Plates XIII and XVI.

Another Welsh sampler contains a pattern of St David's Cathedral[1] and an English school sampler from the 'Cock Road Daily School' bears a cathedral-like edifice marked 'The Church' [180, 192].

Castles and battlemented archways and ruins were popular also, during the nineteenth century, and generally were set in a country scene with *trees* and a *landscape*. A realistic pattern of 'PENRHYN CASTLE NORTH WALES' dominates a mid-century Welsh sampler [195] of which Mr Ffransis Payne writes: 'The view on this sampler is apparently a copy of a lithograph by W. Crane of Chester published about 1840 by Potter and Co., of Caernarvon. The same view occurs on a wool picture no. 206' (in the National Museum of Wales).[2] In a slowly descending scale of grandeur, mansions of almost palatial proportions are numerous in the nineteenth century and similar features seen in many suggest that they too were taken from pictures or from printed patterns. Some probably represented the home of the worker; 'Horse Hill House near London' suggests this in the sampler illustrated [176] while another containing a *house* with garden, *trees*, *flowers* and *figures* might have been the home and family of Mary Pether who did the work in 1839.[3]

Houses of less pretentious style and dimensions than the *mansions* were the most common of the nineteenth-century patterns; it was usual for a *house* and a

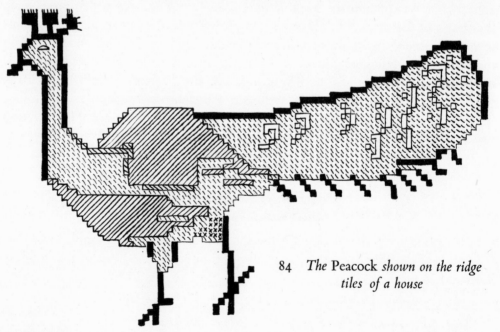

84   The Peacock *shown on the ridge tiles of a house*

[1] *ibid.*, p. 32.
[2] *ibid.*, p. 63.
[3] D. King, *Samplers*, Plate 52.

cottage to be worked on one sampler, especially those which included a rural scene, and probably they represented the big house and an estate cottage or as happened frequently, the house was a farmhouse in a field with a cottage nearby. In order to include as many patterns as possible in the space of the sampler, *birds* or *squirrels* perched or sat on the roofs and chimneys as well as on the trees; in one case a *peacock* was shown on the ridge tiles of a house[1] [*84*], and in others *dovecotes* are attached to the roof top or included in the surroundings of the house, especially in the garden [*118*]. Many *houses* are Georgian in character, brick built with the glazing bars, fanlights and other features of the period, and although most appear to be country houses, some have a trim urban aspect, with a flight of steps to the front door and occasionally a small front garden with neat, formal flower beds. The presence and degree of importance of *chimneys* appear to depend on the worker's sense of pattern rather than anything else; occasionally there is none at all, but two are accepted generally as the most fitting number for a balanced pattern. In one case of an excess of zeal in the achievement of symmetry, *smoke* was added emerging from the two *chimneys* but was shown blowing away in opposite directions.[2]

Cottages usually were given one *chimney*—almost a sign of social distinction— and sometimes they have only one storey; a thatched *roof* also, often indicates a cottage and this is shown by the use of loose *split* or *satin* stitches and sometimes applied brown *chenille* work. Most cottages had trees nearby or overhanging, and when they were situated in a *field*, the practical addition of a *pathway* was put from the *door* to the *field gate*; small motifs indicating *birds* in the sky are seen above nearly all cottage

85   *Small motifs indicating* birds *in the sky*

patterns [*85*]. *Schools* and religious meeting *houses* often were indicated by higher *windows* or in the case of religious buildings, a *cross* sometimes was added. *Windmills* were common in pictorial patterns of farm houses and country scenes and these, usually accompanied with patterns of farm livestock and pet animals [*77, 91, 118*] doubtless were incentives and of interest to the children who were a little bored with their alphabets and numerals and put together small patterns of their own choosing to make up a picture of home surroundings [*86–9, 93*].

Household objects connected with daily life probably began with the *door key*

[1] Leigh Ashton, *Samplers*, Figure 36.
[2] M. B. Huish, *Samplers and Tapestry Embroideries*, p. 56, Figure 21.

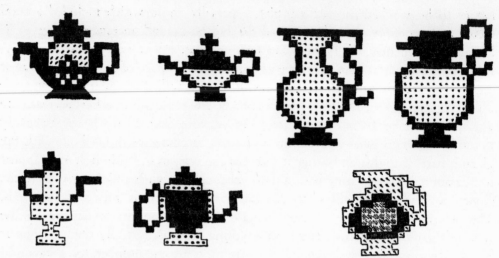

86 Coffee *and* tea pot *patterns. Eighteenth*
    and nineteenth centuries

87 Jugs. *Nineteenth century*

patterns of the seventeenth century, of which that on Elizabeth Cromwell's sampler is one of the earliest [*90*, *93*]; even in these small motifs there is variety of pattern, the most interest being in those of early date. The same can be said of the *coffee* and *tea pots*, which occur in numbers of samplers from the middle of the eighteenth century [*86*] and later on they were joined by *jugs* [*87*], *kettles* [*88*], *bottles* and *wineglasses* [*89*]. Furniture hardly ever is attempted, although *chairs* are found occasionally in European patterns; but we had to wait until 1933 for a *grand piano* [*92*].

Other small patterns of an architectural character are included in early samplers, especially those dating from the reign of James I; these are variously described as *pyramids* or *obelisks*. The basic shape is that of a narrow high pyramid, with an ornamented pediment which varies in detail with almost every example;

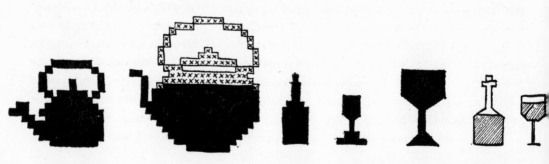

88 Kettles. *Nineteenth century*

89 Bottles *and* wineglasses. *Nineteenth century*

90 *A household object on Elizabeth Cromwell's sampler*

91 *Farm livestock*

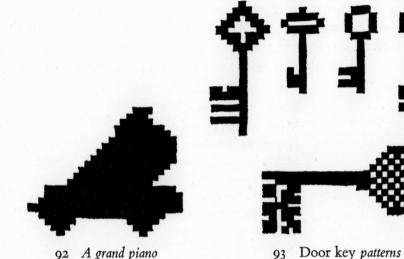

92 *A grand piano*   93 Door key *patterns*

on a sampler in the Victoria and Albert Museum collection it is a 'V'-shaped motif[1] and on two samplers illustrated [*59, 100*] one ends in a point and the other with a rounded knob which is repeated as feet under the pedestal on which the pyramid rests. Not all the patterns include the *pedestal*, which sometimes is without pattern, but those illustrated are ornamented with small chequered squares. The *pyramid* is found in embroidery made during the first 50 years of the seventeenth century and Miss Jourdain refers to the occurence of the motif in much of the wood carving and silver work of the early part of this period. The embroidered pattern usually is worked in silver or silver gilt thread and, used as a *spot* motif on a dark ground, often alternating with other motifs such as small *flowers*, *hearts* and so on in all-over patterns and especially on small pieces of work, such as bags and purses. Reference is made also by Miss Jourdain to examples of these embroideries in the

[1] Leigh Ashton, *Samplers*, Figures 11 and 13. D. King, *Samplers*, Plate 5.

possession of the Victoria and Albert Museum and a quotation is given from an inventory made in 1614 on the death of Henry Howard, Earl of Northampton— 'An orenge tawney nighte bagge embroidered with silver piramides and flowers.'[1] In samplers the *pyramid* is shown as it would be used, generally in a small panel of four or five motifs in silver thread, embroidered on a ground of dark silk *tent* stitch.

From about the beginning of the eighteenth century ornamental *columns* occur, generally appearing in pairs but with no other architectural feature; most are decorated with chevron [100], diagonal or horizontal stripes and bands and sometimes a *flower* pattern is arranged as if climbing the column and continuing at the top, forming something like a triumphal arch, to enclose an inscription or a decorative motif. *Birds*, *squirrels* or *flower pot* patterns are some of those which form pediments to the *columns*; *flower pots* with *carnations* in an especially elaborate pattern surmount those in Harriot Taylor's sampler and the pattern, with the title 'THE TEMPLE OF FANCY', encloses her name and age (which was seven) and a verse:

> Not Land but Learning
> Makes a Man complete
> Not Birth but Breeding
> Makes him truly Great
> Not Wealth but Wisdom
> Does adorn his State
> Virtue not Honour
> Makes him Fortunate
> Learning Breeding Wisdom
> Get these three
> Then Wealth and Honour
> Will attend on thee.[2]

Patterns which surround the words of the *Lord's Prayer* or the *Ten Commandments* sometimes are shown as small arches supported on slender pillars, between which are the inscriptions [103]. The resemblance between these patterns and the painted wooden panels bearing the same words which were hung in churches during the eighteenth and nineteenth centuries, makes it reasonably certain that they inspired the sampler patterns. The *pillars* and *arches* often are embroidered in brown silks and made to resemble carved wood in the patterns.

Sailing ships appear from time to time among sampler patterns. The earliest of them have one *mast* amidships and *pennants* flying fore and aft. In outline and

[1] M. Jourdain, *English Secular Embroidery*, p. 61.
[2] D. King, *Samplers*, Plate 48.

94   *Nineteenth-century* bird *motifs*

character they are almost identical with the heraldic *lymphad* with the exception of the oars and it seems that this is the most probable origin for the pattern. In later examples, extra *masts* and the addition of *sails* only elaborated but did not alter the basic shape of the hull, until *steamboats* made their appearance towards the end of the nineteenth century. *Ships* are used commonly as *spot* patterns among the nineteenth century *bird, flower* and *pet dog* motifs [94] but they seem to be more at ease sailing the high seas in the *map* samplers where as many as 19 have been recorded on one *map*.[1] 'M. F' launched two in her sampler which she worked in hair—dark brown for the *hull* and a silvery grey for the sails, perhaps her own and her mother's hair [121].

[1] A. Tuer, *The History of the Horn-Book*, Cut 197.

CHAPTER FIVE

Friends and Relations

Many samplers were intended to be objects of permanent interest, not only to the maker and her immediate family but to all the friends and relatives. Records on samplers of family events such as marriages, births and deaths were common from the beginning of the eighteenth century and gave much the same kind of information as usually is written into the Family Bible; others consisted almost entirely of inscriptions indicating that they were intended as gifts, and occasionally these took the form of a letter. The *epistle* sampler dated from the end of the seventeenth century and those which have survived generally are small and consist of a narrow border surrounding the 'letter' which was worked usually in *cross* stitch with silk thread, so that the letters were distinct. The earliest recorded *epistle* measured six by nine inches and is dated 1693; it was worked entirely in capitals in silk *cross* stitch on linen but the 'letter' covers only a little more than half of the sampler, there is no border pattern and the edge is unfinished. The letter runs:

> DEAR MOTHER MY DUTY I REMEMBER
> UNTO THE AND MY DEAR LOVE UNTO MY
> SISTER WHEN I SAW MY FATHER LAST
> HIS LOVE WAS TO THE BUT I THOUGHT
> IT LONG BEFORE I SAW THE BUT I DID MY
> ENDEAVOUR TO RITE UNTO THE NO MORE
> BUT THY DUTYFULL DAFTER S F
> FROM WANSTEAD 1693
> THE 25 OF THE 5 MONTH[1]

There are no punctuation marks and no intervals between the words on the sampler. So far no other *epistle* samplers of the seventeenth century have been found but a number of eighteenth century examples are known, with inscriptions

[1] Leigh Ashton, *Samplers*, Figure 28.

and patterns in keeping with the period. Mr Tuer illustrates an *epistle* from Deborah Iane Berkin in 1778, in which the *cross* stitch letter, two insects and a flower motif are contained within a flowing floral border; both writer and recipient were called Deborah:

Dear Debby
I love you sincerely
My heart retains a grateful sense
of your past kindness
When will the hours of our
Separation be at an end
Preserve in your bosom a Remembrance
of your Affectionate
Deborah Iane. Berkin
Bristol
May 1st   1778.[1]

A few years earlier than Debby's letter a rhyming *epistle* sampler was sent to her friend by a nine-year-old girl, Frances Incledon-Webber, who was to die at the early age of 21:

An Epistle from a young lady to her
Beloved Friend
Were paper wanting or pen to send
My best and kindest wishes to my Friend
Should ever chance all usual means deny
My needle thus should that loss supply
For sure Lucinda they have little art
That want the means who dictate from the heart.
Frances Incledon—Webber
In the ninth year of my
Age
August 30th   1769

The value of some samplers in the minds of the workers at least, is left in no doubt by the numbers which were made especially as gifts for members or friends of her—or his—family. Sixteenth- and seventeenth-century samplers were of greater value than those made in later periods, (of which the worth was almost entirely sentimental) and were considered as suitable items to be included not only in household inventories (p. 156) but also as a bequest in a will, as that of Margaret Thomson, whose sampler was left to her niece Alys as early as 1546. In more recent years when samplers had acquired antiquarian value, bequests of collections

---

[1] A. W. Tuer, *The History of the Horn-book*, p. 429, Cut 202.

have been made to the several Museums in England, Scotland and Wales. It seems probable that the sampler made by Iane Bostocke in 1598 [53] was intended for the child Alice Lee—whose birth two years earlier was recorded in the inscription—as a working sampler to be ready when she began her needle-work in three or four years time. There seems no better reason for the inscription otherwise and however high the hopes for her as a child prodigy, she could hardly have needed a sampler at the age of two. The sampler makers of the eighteenth century were not as generous with their work as those of the nineteenth when quite a number of *gift* samplers were made but they are smaller in size than the other more conventional kind of sampler. A small *gift* measuring seven and a half inches long by five and a half wide, was given on 'June 25 1790' by

> Mary Sharp to Mary Limmer
> This Gift my friend
> To the I send
> In hope to be approved
> I have done my best
> I do protest
> for one so well beloved.[1]

A heart-shaped sampler made in 1796 bears the name of three girls, Mary Ives Iane Mumer and Hannah Hopkins and the inscription 'Be unto me kind and true as i be unto you', which may have been a gift sampler; it seems too small to have been the work of three children, as the overall measurements are $5\frac{3}{4}$ by $4\frac{3}{4}$ inches only. A sampler which is smaller, $2\frac{7}{8}$ inches wide and $3\frac{1}{8}$ inches long was worked in silk on tammy cloth early in the nineteenth century, bearing an inscription only:

> Absent or dead
> Still let a sister be dear
> A Sigh the absent claims
> The dead a tear
> D H to A H

and another, smaller still measuring roughly two inches in diameter was worked by a nurse to a family of children—a Mrs Scott and known as 'Cotty'—who gave the sampler to their mother in about 1850 [194].

Nineteenth-century *gift* samplers usually were more ornamental than earlier samplers of the type, sometimes with a verse appropriate to an occasion, and flower and other patterns—one of which is often a heart—as well as a simple decorative border [199]. A sampler made in 1849 contains two rows of small

---

[1] In the Collection of the Fitzwilliam Museum, 28 / 165.

patterns in the centre—a small house, a boy and girl, two dogs and some trees, which give the impression of representing the family and their background. The accompanying verse seems an odd choice for a sampler but the circumstances of its making are not known.

> FAREwell my dear brethren
> my Lord bids me come
> Farewell my dear children im
> now Going home bright angels
> Are WhisPring so sweat in my ea[r]
> AWay to thy saviour thy sPirit W[e]
> Bear.
>
> William harrss the gift to his
> mother mary ann Jones work[d]
> bY mbrown aPri 9th 1849.

Possibly William harrss (Harris?) were the christian names only and his surname being the same as his mother's, 'mbrown' thought it unneccessary to mention it. A happier atmosphere, with the same destination in mind, is lent to a sampler worked in fine blue silk *cross* stitch on perforated cardboard—a kind of work popular in the late nineteenth century for samplers, illuminated texts, mottoes, book markers and so on, as well as for *marking* exercises for children, card being cheaper than canvas. The sampler in question has a geometrical *cross* stitch border pattern and was made by Thomas Sharp when aged about 12 years old, as a birthday gift for a small girl whom in due course he married:

> A Birthday Wish,
> Many happy returns of the day of thy birth
> Many seasons of sunshine be given
> May God in his mercy prepare you on earth
> For a birthday of Glory in Heaven
> September 8th 1877.

In 1879 'B.L.' embroidered a hymn and a text with patterns of horizontal borders, plants, crowns and hearts in a sampler:

> Alberta Hubbard
> a gift from her cousin B.L.
> May 31st 1879.[1]

But one of the longest inscriptions of religious verse was embroidered on a curious piece of work in the form of a sampler made by a woman prisoner in Bedford Gaol, as a gift for the Governor's daughter [*199*]. Her name was Annie Parker and after her signature is embroidered 'Done by her with her own hair

---

[1] F. G. Payne, *Collection of Samplers and Embroideries*, p. 81, no. 146.

June 82.' and below 'Presented by her to Miss D. A. Roberts.' The work is very finely done on close linen and the hair has shades of golden brown throughout; the panels of linen are hemmed and outlined with *feather* and *double feather* stitches in cotton thread and the joining seams and surrounding pattern of the sampler are of crochet. There is a smaller but similar piece of work in the Black Museum at Scotland Yard, made in 1879 by a woman prisoner named Ellen Parker, whose record was that of a confirmed dipsomaniac, who had been gaoled 50 times for drunkenness. During the course of one term of imprisonment, she had a cell companion—in prison for the same reason—who had with her a small baby. Ellen Parker helped to nurse the child during an illness and made such an impression on the mother, that she asked for a souvenir to remind her of the help and kindness she had received; in due course the sampler was made with the materials Ellen Parker had to hand, those of her own hair for thread and a piece of her head scarf to work on. It seems certain that these two samplers were made by the same woman, as Ellen Parker was known also as Annie and the methods of working, patterns, inscriptions and making up have many similarities. She died in 1884.

Other samplers which pay tribute to public figures and benefactors outside the family are found from time to time and two which reflect the social conditions of their time have survived from the 1830s. At that time a normal working day for children doing factory work was 12 hours—compared with 10 hours for a 'convicted felon' in prison—for which the weekly payment for a child was one shilling. These conditions were the cause of great concern to men who were in daily contact with the results on the health and education of the children, and among those working for a reduction in hours was the Reverend George Stringer Bull. This work resulted in the passing in 1847 of the 'Ten Hours Bill'', 15 years after it was presented in 1832, in which a child's working day was reduced to ten hours and which earned for the Reverend Stringer Bull the name of the 'Ten Hours Parson'.[1] Two samplers commemorate his work in the parish of Bierley, close to the factories of Wakefield and Bradford, and contain inscriptions which clearly are the work of children. One with the date added in ink—1831—has religious verses and beatitudes appropriate to the poor and the persecuted, and is inscribed:

A token of respect from Martha Crook
to the Rev. G. S. Bull. Incumbent of Bierley
the Factory Child's Friend and protector.
May the Lord bless you and make you prosperous
in the factory child's cause.

[1] J. C. Gill, *The Ten Hours Parson*, Christian Social Action in the Eighteen-Thirties.

The second sampler has an inscription contained within a simple *cross* stitch border:

A small token of Grati
tude and respect, from
the Bowling Lane Ev
ening Scholars to their
kind Friend and Bene
factor, the Rev, G. S.
Bull. incumbent at
BYERLEY
18   32

Memorial samplers appear first about the middle of the eighteenth century. The example believed to have been made soon after the death of Queen Elizabeth I, at the beginning of the seventeenth century, is one on its own (p. 155), as no other sampler of that time has survived or is recorded which contains any inscription other than initials, a name, or a date and even these are rare. During the second half of the eighteenth century when *puzzle* samplers became a fashionable affectation (p. 186), a memorial in the form of an acrostic was worked by 'T.B.' entitled:

An Acrostic
On My Late Dear Sister
Jane Emery Day
died Sepr 14 1792.

Jealous of Self. deeply possess'd
And rested twas within her breast
No allowed sin in her was seen
Early forsook bane paths of sin.

Earnestly She enquired th' way to God
Marked well She did. each step She trod
Eager pursued it through CHRIST's Blood
Righteousness divind She gloried in
Yea Confessed herself nought in sin.

Dearly high favoured Youth thou
Ascended art to JESUS now
Yields Him the Crown eternal through.[1]

An inscription on an undated and unsigned Welsh sampler is devoted entirely to the deaths of a father and his four children, possibly worked by the mother as her name is not on the sampler, so presumably she was still alive.

[1] F. G. Payne, *Guide to the Collection of Samplers and Embroideries*, no. 103 (p. 69).

To
the memory of
John Perry,
who departed this life
January, 14th 1845;
Aged 66 years.
Also
his four children.
Thomas Perry
who departed this life
June 12th 1818,
Aged 17 months.
Thomas Perry
who departed this life
August 25th 1838;
Aged 25 years.
Richard Perry,
who departed this life
January 5th 1841;
Aged 25 years.
Jane Perry,
who departed this life
January 1st 1845;
Aged 23 years.

Man dieth, and wasteth away; yea, man giveth up the
ghost, and then where is he?   Job 14th, 10th.[1]

This melancholy record is not typical of samplers which note a bereavement;
it is more usual for a single member of a family to be commemorated in this way,
the sampler being made in the form of an *In Memoriam* card. Sometimes a wife is
added to the husband's name in later years and John Twaites's father was included
almost as a postscript, although he died some years before his son.

In memory of my beloved Father
John Twaites who died April 11 1829
Life how short—Eternity how long.
Also of
John Twaites
My grandfather who died Dec. 31, 1814.[2]

[1] F. G. Payne, *Guide to the Collection of Samplers and Embroideries*, no. 72 (p. 63).
[2] M. B. Huish, *Samplers and Tapestry Embroideries*, p. 57.

Others contain a few more details of age and the name of the place where the family lived, as one to the memory of the great-grandfather of the present owner, made, signed and dated by his married daughter Hannah Jackson: 'H.J. 1884.'

> In Affectionate Remembrance of
> Thomas Sanderson
> who died at Soulby, near Kirkby
> Stephen. Feb 23rd 1875 in his
> 80th year.
> A few more years shall roll
> A few more seasons come
> And we shall be with those that rest
> Asleep within the tomb.

The deaths of children are often included in samplers devoted to one generation of a family, but they seem to be treated in a matter-of-fact way and are noted in the chronological order of the family record. In nearly every instance of a long family, the death of an infant born in the early years of the marriage, is followed by the birth of another given the same name, as with the two boys named Thomas in the Perry family. The record of the Slater family shows greater persistence in this tradition, although the deaths are inferred and not actually mentioned. Thomas Slater was born in 1666, Abigail in 1673, Elizabeth in 1700, Susan was 'Borne August 16 1701' and Mary 'on Feb ye 8 1702'; another Elizabeth arrived in February 1704, another Abigail on 'Nov 1 1706' and another Thomas in June 1708. Having achieved a long awaited son, Mr and Mrs Slater apparently had no more children; their names are not given but the inscription includes the verse beginning: 'Deare Parents I Address Myself To You.' (p. 108) and the fact that:

> SUSAN SLATER MADE THIS SAMPLER AND
> FINISHED IT NOVEMBER THE 24 DAY 1709[1]

Hannah Fieldhouse adopted a different and shorter way of recording the living and the dead of her family:

sen^r	sen^r		isnot	isnot		jun^r	jun^r	
W F	H F	N F	S F	E F	J F	S F	W F	H F I F

Although family records usually constitute the main part of the work, Mary Young's brothers and sisters are subordinate in importance to *Hagar* and *Jacob's Vision* (p. 58).

Most family records contained births only and of these the earliest by at least a hundred years is that of Alice Lee in 1596 who:

---

[1] F. G. Payne, *Guide to the Collection of Samplers and Embroideries*, no. 13 (p. 47).

WAS:BORNE:THE:23:OF:NOVEMBER:BE
ING:TWEESDAY:IN:THE:AFTER:NOONE:1596 [58]

The parents, and sometimes grandparents, headed the samplers with the names of their children in two columns below, as in that of the Markham family, with 'Their Children in Rotation of Birth', and the names of two who died, within *tablets* at the foot of each column[1]; and also in that of 'the births of s & s drakes family' but in this work a touching addition is a circular plait of fine baby hair within a thin blue line of *tent* stitch, beneath the name of each child [177]. It was made by a member of the Drake family, 'mary ann drake' who signed the sampler and possibly she was an aunt. Mary, the only daughter of a farmer in Axmouth, Devon named Benjamin Gage and of Elizabeth his wife, recorded 'The Names and Time of Nativity of the Children'—six of them—at the age of '5 years and 10 months' and added 'The above were baptized in Axmouth Church'. As a rule there is no indication as to where the makers of the samplers lived except in the case of some school samplers. Sarah Taylor recorded her own birth and missed out no relevant detail on her timing:

> Pray excuse my mean endeavour. Ill strive to
> mend and be obedient ever saith the daughter
> of Iohn Taylor by ann his wife was born on su
> nday the 26 day of November at 5'oclock in th
> morning 1769 Anno
> Dom Sarah Taylor Aged 10 1779[2]

American genealogical samplers contained more detailed records than English, Scottish or Welsh examples. Parents and grandparents were included and under appropriate circumstances, the second and even third marriages of parents; in one family record, spaces were left for the deaths to be filled in as they occurred.[3] Samplers of other nationalities do not include inscriptions and recorded events, other than the name of the worker, sometimes a place name, and a date.

Some samplers are believed to have been made by more than one member of a family by the fact that they carry several names in a position which indicates that they may be signatures. Edward Bacheler and Ruth Bacheler embroidered their names together, with the date 1717, on a sampler to which it is believed they both contributed.[4] A Scottish sampler dated 1762 contains the names of Robert, Jean and Christan Henderson and was illustrated by Mr Huish,[5] who believed that it

[1] D. King, *Samplers*, Plate 56.
[2] F. G. Payne, *Guide to Collection of Samplers and Embroideries*, p. 38.
[3] 'The Genealogical Sampler' by Estelle Harris, published in *Daughters of the American Revolution Magazine*, Volume LX, no. 12, December 1926.
[4] Leigh Ashton, *Samplers*, Figure 36.
[5] M. B. Huish, *Samplers and Tapestry Embroideries*, Plate XXIII.

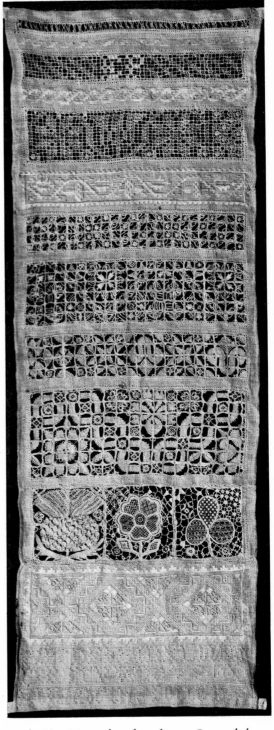

95   Mid seventeenth century. White linen thread
on linen. Drawn work, satin, double running and
hem stitches, with eyelet holes and bead work. The
beads are royal blue. 18 × 5 inches

96   1660. Linen thread on linen. Cut and drawn
work, needlepoint fillings, satin and eyelet stitches.
Signed, Elizabeth Potter. 21 × 7½ inches

97 *1670. Silk and metal threads on linen. Tent, cross, brick. Gobelin, plaited braid, double plaited braid, darning, double running, pile darning, satin, split and interlacing stitches. Signed, Elizabeth Branch. 21¼ × 8 inches*

98 *1675. Silk thread on linen. Double runnin... back, satin, cross, long-armed cross, buttonhole, ste... chain, eyelet and needlepoint stitches. Signed Joyce Leedes*

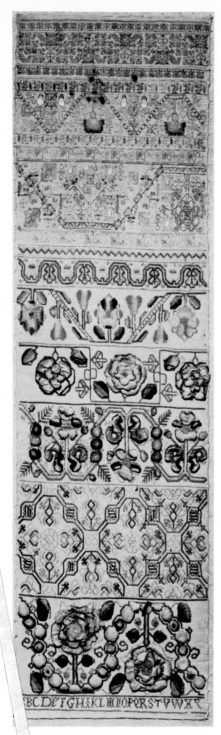

99 *c. 1670–1680. Silk thread on linen. Double running, satin, cross and detached buttonhole stitches, with some French knots. 26½ × 7½ inches*

100 *'August the 22nd 1710.' Silk thread on linen. Satin, split, cross, back, stem, chain, detached filling, rococo and eyelet stitches. Signed, Elizabeth Goodday 30 × 6½ inches*

101 *Early eighteenth century. Silk thread on linen. Cross, satin, eyelet, split stem, chain and back stitches. Signed, Sarah Bishop.* 15 × 8½ *inches*

102   *1724–1725. Linen thread on linen. Hollie point and geometrical satin stitches with cut work.*
Signed, Jenny Grant. $9\frac{1}{4} \times 8\frac{1}{2}$ inches

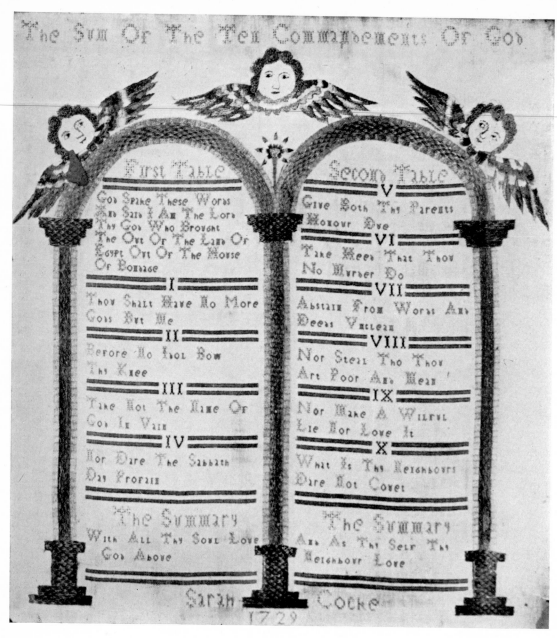

103   *1729. Silk thread on linen. Cross, satin, back and stem stitches with some French knots.*
Signed, Sarah Cocke. 13 × 12 inches

104 'June the 26 1734.' 1735. Silk thread on linen. Satin, tent, cross, stem, eyelet, split and chain stitches. Signed, Elizabeth Spear. $42\frac{1}{2} \times 10$ inches

105   1737. Linen thread on linen. Cut work, hollie point and geometrical satin stitches. Signed S.B. $9\frac{1}{2} \times 8\frac{1}{4}$ inches

106 'November the 25 1740.' Silk thread on worsted. Satin, eyelet, foursided cross, split, chain, stem, cross, and back stitches. Signed, Mary Whitehead. 11 × 13 inches

was made by Robert, as his name was worked in a darker colour and appeared more prominently, but it seems more likely that all three children did the work. Numbers of samplers in the seventeenth century were worked from both ends of the material (p. 148), so that some patterns always are seen reversed and a reasonable explanation for this is that, as an economy, two workers in a family could have used the same piece of linen and still kept separate records.

Collections of samplers made by different members of a family, and often from different generations, are fairly common and some are of historical interest. A member of the Field family—which is descended from Oliver Cromwell—has a small collection beginning with the seventeenth-century sampler signed by Elizabeth Cromwell [62] (p. 164) followed by others dated, and signed or initialled by later generations of the Fields [121]. The Brontë sisters made their sad samplers at Haworth Parsonage (now the Brontë Parsonage Museum) with others of the Branwell and Brontë families (p. 219).[1] A nineteenth-century Welsh family— father, mother, three sons, and a daughter each made a sampler which hung round the walls of their cottage, and there are innumerable examples of one child having made a series of samplers during her schooldays (p. 138).

The duty owed to their parents has been an all important background in the lives of many generations of young sampler makers, and inscriptions, rhymes and verses in their work have emphasised it from all possible angles. Acknowledgements to them as a source of learning are the most usual (p. 108), although sometimes the parents come after the teacher in a position of importance, but in one way or another the significance of family unity and affection is a common theme. In a rather prosy homily in 1809, Mary Harrison, a sister of Elizabeth Harrison, who made the sampler on figure 178, worked on her sampler:

ADVICE

Listen to the affectionate counsels
of your parents; treasure up their precepts
respect their riper judgment; and enjoy, with
gratitude and delight, the advantage resulting
from their society. bind to your bosom by the
most endearing ties, your brother and sisters,
cherish them as your best companions, through
the variegated journey of life; and suffer no
jealousies and contentions to interrupt the
harmony which should ever reign with
you.

[1] M. B. Huish, *Samplers and Tapestry Embroideries*, Plates XXXV, XXXVI, XXXVII.

The words on the inscription make it clear that the choice of this and many others like it were selected and dictated by their elders and not chosen by the children themselves, although from time to time self-assertion on the part of the worker is fairly clear. In 1810, 'A. Lingard', condensed much the same sentiments as those of Mary Harrison, into four lines:

> How happy it must be
> How pleasing Lord the sight
> When mutual love and love to thee
> A family unite.

Some inscriptions were addressed specifically to one or both parents, in some cases lines in prose or verse can be found which were composed especially for needle-work, and in many other, after the middle of the eighteenth century, verses from Dr Isaac Watts' *Divine and Moral Songs* were used. A favourite composition entitled 'To My Much Honoured Parent' is contained in samplers throughout the nineteenth century, the first and last couplets of which were the most popular:

> On this Fair Canvas does my needle write
> With Love and Duty both this I indite
> And in these lines dear Parent I impart
> The tender feelings of a Grateful Heart.

Another in much the same strain was repeated on many hundreds of samplers:

> Next unto God, dear Parents, I address
> Myself to you in humble Thankfulness
> For all your care on me bestowed
> The means of Learning unto me allow'd
> Go on, I pray, and let me still persue
> Those Golden Arts the Vulgar never knew.

Several variations of this occur from time to time, some from mistakes in copying but one at least from a change in the usual circumstances of Martha Britton, a love-child who was brought up by her aunt, and in 1857 the inscription had a feeling of sincerity in the words 'Next unto to God, dear Aunt, I do address' of the first line and the verse ended with 'Those Golden Arts the Friendless never knew'. Other verses were chosen which expressed the filial hopes of a six-year-old, Eleanor Sarah Hooper at that age in 1846, in words which were more suitable to her years:

Behold the labour of my tender age
And view this work which did my hours engage
With anxious care I did these colours place
A smile to gain from my dear Parents face
Whose care of me I ever will regard,
And pray that God will give a kind reward.

CHAPTER SIX

Schools and Teaching

The earliest of school lessons consists in learning the alphabet, and letters in alphabetical order, as distinct from those used for signatures and inscriptions, appeared among *band* sampler patterns sometimes during the first 30 years of the seventeenth century. These are supposed usually, but not always, to be the work of children and their arrival coincided with the period in which a sampler ceased to be a worker's pattern reference and became a means of teaching a child to do embroidery. Although no alphabet seems to have been recorded on a sampler before the 1620s, one was included in Giovanni Ostau's pattern book in 1561 (p. 20) and a version of it, from A to V, was reproduced on a late seventeenth-century sampler[1] and early in the eighteenth century John Brightland's *Grammar of the English Tonge*, published in 1711, also contained an alphabet of capital letters intended for embroidery, headed 'Sampler Letters', but by this time alphabets were common in all samplers whether made at home or in school.

A full alphabet occupied at least one row across the width of a sampler as a rule, but the amount of space used depended not only on the measurement of the sampler but on the size of the letters, whether minuscules or capitals or both, and the type of stitchery used. Miscalculations in the spacing of the letters often accounted for some being omitted altogether, while other workers, not to be defeated, overflowed them into the decorative border or put the misfitting consonants into a space above or below the original row; occasional alphabets ran in reverse order. A solution to the problem in some eighteenth-century samplers was to group the letters:

B		E		H		L		O		R		V		Y
A	C	D	F	G	I	K	M	N	P	Q	S	T	W	X	Z

[1] Leigh Ashton, *Samplers*, Figures 20a and 20b. D. King, *Samplers*, Plate 25.

107   *Types of letters used in alphabets, worked in* satin, eyelet, four-sided *and* cross *stitches. Seventeenth, eighteenth and nineteenth centuries*

Other samplers, notably those made in the Bristol Orphanges, contained several alphabets up to as many as 20, each of a different type and size; beginning with capital letters, the succeeding alphabets diminished in height until the letters in the last, generally of *cross* stitch minuscules, measured only a fraction of an inch [*198*]. Most samplers contain from one to six and in many the letters were doubled or trebled as they proceeded: AA BB CC, AAA BBB CCC, or Aa Bb Cc and so on, showing different methods of working, especially in each of the capitals, although the kinds of stitches used in alphabets have been limited to those which produce the clearest outline [*107*]. The most common were *satin* stitch, *eyelet, four-sided* and *cross* stitches, with ornamentation and flourishes added in *double running* during the eighteenth century [*108*]. Alphabets in *cut* work, such as that in Ostau's pattern book are rare, although initials, names and dates are sometimes worked in this way in seventeenth-century samplers [*63*].[1]

[1] Leigh Ashton, *Samplers*, Figure 8b. D. King, *Samplers*, Plate 18.

The letters J and U were included rarely before the end of the eighteenth century; letter Z, as often as not, was left out altogether as it was unlikely to be needed and the letter Q was worked sometimes as a reversed P – ꝗ, although both ꝗ and Q are seen together in some alphabets, of which the early ones usually consisted of capitals only, and with few exceptions, were worked in *cross* or *satin* stitches. A seventeenth-century exception is shown on a sampler made and signed by 'ANNE GOWER' in which the capitals were worked alternately in *satin* and *eyelet* stitches and took up three rows across the work. This sampler is undated but

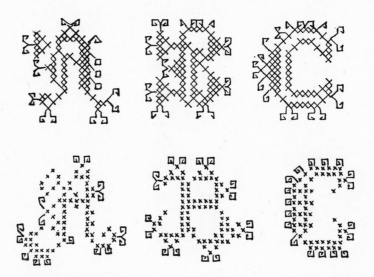

108 *Alphabet letters with flourishes in* double running. *Eighteenth century*

probably it was made early in the reign of King Charles I; Anne Gower married an American, Governor Endicott and left England for America in 1628, taking her sampler with her.[1]

There is now no means of knowing whether this sampler was made during or after her schoolroom days, but it is known that samplers were used for teaching the alphabet as well as stitchery by 1627, from lines in *Apollo Shroving* written by William Hawkins in that year:

> Take out thy fescue and spell here in this one-leau'd booke
> Tell the stitches in this sampler of black and white.

[1] Leigh Ashton, *Samplers*, p. 6 and Figure 6.   This sampler is now in the Essex Institute, Salem, United States of America.

The fescue was a pointer made from a number of different materials—wood, bone, straw, wire or quill and used in school especially in teaching letters of the alphabet from a horn-book. In the *History of the Horn-book*, Mr Andrew Tuer quoted from Halliwell's Folio Shakespeare: '. . . the fescue was an important instrument in the process of instructing from the horn-book.'[1] In the first place a horn-book consisted of letters of the alphabet written or printed on paper which was mounted behind a thin transparent layer of horn, on a small wooden tablet with a handle. *The Lord's Prayer* as well as the alphabet was learned from a horn-book and both are common characteristics of so many samplers which were to appear later. The connection between the two is remarked upon by Mr Tuer in writing of samplers: 'The sampler . . . served in fact, the purpose of a horn-book to so many generations of little girls.'[2] Numerals were not included in early horn-books, neither were they among sampler patterns other than in dates, until about the middle of the 1600s; one of the earliest is that on Elizabeth Calthorpe's sampler of 1656, where she embroidered a short row of digits from 1 to 9: she must have miscalculated her spacing so that by the time she had got to number seven there was room only for a half-size figure 8 to be put in before 9 finished the row.[3] Digits from 0 to 9 were usual in the seventeenth century and seem to have been added to complete a row across a sampler after the end of an alphabet; further numbers were put in where space allowed. By the eighteenth century full rows of numerals were common and often more than one set from 1 to 12—or sometimes

1 to 24 or more—were worked, in stitches corresponding to those used for alphabets on the same sampler [109]. Rows of three-figure numbers seen in the Orphanage samplers were identification numbers given to the children and used instead of their names [198] which was a practice in many nineteenth-century schools and not only in orphanages.

In addition to the advantages of learning spelling and embroidery at one and the same time, embroidered letters and numbers were needed for marking and listing increasing stores of household linen which had resulted from the more prosperous

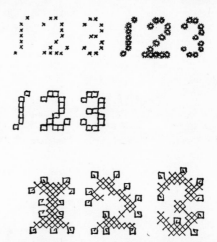

109 *Numerals worked in stitches which correspond to those used for alphabets*

[1] A. W. Tuer, *The History of the Horn-book*, p. 24. Single Volume edition, 1827.
[2] *ibid.*, p. 415.
[3] Leigh Ashton, *Samplers*, Plate I.   This sampler is now in the collection of the Fitzwilliam Museum.

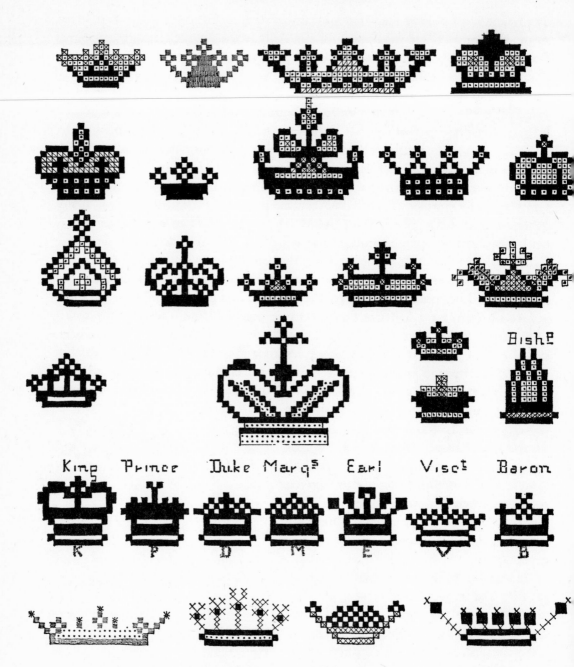

110 Crown *and* coronet *patterns used for marking and decorative purposes.*
Eighteenth and nineteenth centuries

way of life of the seventeenth century, and it may well be that this task was laid on children who had proved their ability on their samplers. Certainly children of the early nineteenth century were expected to do so; among subjects taught to schoolgirls, different kinds of needlework were listed separately among school classes and the children's attainments in '... Writing, Grammar, Geography, Sewing, Darning, *Marking*, Arithmetic, ...' and so on were noted individually. Many school samplers of the same period consisted largely, and sometimes entirely, of alphabets and numerals, some of them on fine linen and worked in single strand fine black silk which at first sight appear to have been done with pen and ink. The instructions for teaching in schools are typified by those given in *A Manual of the System of Teaching Needlework in the Elementary Schools of the British and Foreign Schools Society* in 1821, where the 10th Lesson was devoted to *Marking*. The canvas, which was of the same quality as that for *Darning* (p. 137), was hemmed and a 'straight row marked round as directed by the Monitor, four threads from the hem. . . . When the row is finished they (the children) *mark* the capital and small letters of the alphabet and the figures from 1 up to 10: having a pattern before them to show the regular distances'. The first sampler was marked with red cotton but the second was composed of finer materials.[1] By 1828 *marking* seems to have become the main function of a sampler, as in John Walter's *English and Welsh Dictionary*, it is defined as 'a marking alphabet wrought by girls at school',[2] although in earlier samplers the same description was used when a child 'marked' her sampler by adding her name, as in that of Ann Walters (p. 119).

In households of the nobility, coronets suited to their rank were added above the initials marked on the linen and although numbers of *crown* and *coronet* patterns in samplers were used as decorative motifs only, the first purpose of this type of pattern was for marking [110, 111, 113]. Linen at one time belonging to Lord Nelson— Viscount Nelson, Duke of Bronte—and now on loan to the Maritime Museum, Greenwich, is marked 'N B', with the coronet of a Viscount over the letter 'N' and that of a Duke above the 'B' [112]. *Crown* patterns over initials are common in samplers and although some may indicate noble rank, it is unlikely that all examples do this and a suspicion of affectation in some cases is perhaps, not unjustified.

Instructions for *marking* were given, not only in school; by 1882 they had moved into print in Caulfeild and Saward's *Dictionary of Needlework*, in which a paragraph is devoted to the subject. 'At the present date Marking in England is almost exclusively confined to pockethandkerchiefs, bed linen and woollen materials. . . . The marking of linen may be effected in a variety of stitches: in

[1] Extracts taken from a copy at the Fitzwilliam Museum.
[2] F. G. Payne, *Guide to the Collection of Samplers and Embroideries*, p. 34.

Cross Stitch, Embroidery Stitches and Chain-Stitch; but the orthodox style is after the first-named method.' This was accompanied by an illustration showing *cross* stitch letters worked in squares with instructions to 'Procure ingrain red cotton, and work upon Linen of coarse texture. . . . Form the letters with CROSS

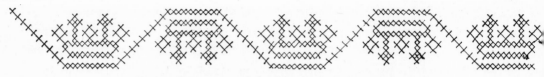

III   *Reversed* crowns *in a border pattern. Nineteenth century*

112   *Linen mark in the household of Viscount Nelson, Duke of Bronte. Early nineteenth century*

113   *A decorative* crown. *Early nineteenth century*

STITCH, . . . counting the linen threads as squares'—instructions which appear to have been followed very faithfully in samplers at the end of the nineteenth century. With further instructions and diagrams for working letters and numerals in other kinds of stitches with 'ingrain coloured sewing cotton, to be had in Turkey-red and blue, and sold in small balls and reels; the numbers running from 40 to 120 in tens', the last word seems to have been said on *marking*.

Although the making of a sampler was no mean task for a child of about seven or eight to accomplish, in the seventeenth century it was the beginning only, of her education in needlework which took her through the making of a coloured sampler, a *lace* and *white* work sampler and an embroidered casket—at that time called a cabinet—before she arrived at the stage of making a decorative panel or picture, which probably included *stump* and *bead* work. There is an excellent record of just such a progression in a child's work in that of Martha Edlin, who was born in 1660. She signed and dated her sampler of coloured *band* patterns and three alphabets, worked in silk on yellow linen—MARTHA EDLIN 1668; in a year's time her sampler of *white work* and *cut* and *drawn* lace patterns, also worked on yellow linen with white linen thread, was finished, signed and dated—16 ME 69: and after two more years, in 1671, her cabinet was completed with her initials M.E. worked in seed pearls on the front panel. This collection of her achievements has been kept together, with her other small embroideries and treasures, in the cabinet and is now on loan to the Victoria and Albert Museum. The work of this child shows a high degree of skill for her age but even so, and although similar records of the period are somewhat few and far between, her talents were not unique; by the age of 11 or 12, most girls probably had passed the sampler stage of their learning. A decade earlier than Martha Edlin and at the age of 'allmost 12 years of age', Hannah Smith had finished her cabinet and put with it the following letter:

> The yere of our Lord b⁰ing 1657 if ever I have any thoughts about the time; when I went to Oxford; as It may be I may; when I have forgoten the time to sartifi myself; I may Loock in this paper and find it. I went to Oxford in the yere of 1654 and my being there; near 2 yere; for I went in 1654 and I stayed there 1655 and I cam away in 1656: and I was allmost 12 yers of age; when I went and mad an end of my cabbinete; at Oxford . . . my cabinet was mad up in yere of 1656 at London. I have ritten this; to sartifi my self; & those that shall enquire about it Hannah Smith.[1]

To 'those that shall enquire' to-day, these two children showed care and fore-sight beyond their years in signing, dating and recording their work at a time about which there is much still to learn. Although the practice of signing and dating samplers became more common after the middle of the century, for many of them where no other records are available, we can arrive at approximate dates only and have to speculate on the age of the worker from observing and comparing with other work that is dated. The amount of work known to be made by children was increasing throughout the seventeenth century, but samplers continued to be made by adults and this is clear by the assured excellence of some, notably that of Elizabeth Mackett, in 1696.[2] With the onus on them of teaching as well as doing their own embroidery, it is more than probable that teachers would have to produce specimens of their work in order to satisfy parents of their ability to teach the young and samplers were a recognised means by which to prove the scope of their repertoire. *Spot* motifs were perhaps best suited to the adult and skilled worker and the repetitive nature of *band* patterns provided the necessary exercise for children, which no doubt accounted for the gradual dying

[1] A. F. Kendrick, *Hannah Smith, Connoisseur,* Volume 85–86, 1930.
[2] Leigh Ashton, *Samplers,* Figure 29. D. King, *Samplers,* Plate 26. P. G. Trendell, *Catalogue of Samplers,* Victoria and Albert Museum, pp. 10 and 11, Plate 11.

out of the *spot* type of pattern and its replacement by continuous patterns in rows.

It is small wonder that some of the inscriptions reflected a wearying of the spirit of the young workers and a longing for freedom 'from all such slavery', typified by an unsigned and undated sampler made in the latter half of the seventeenth century; the lines of the inscription alternate with wide bands of embroidery:

> When I was young I little thought
> That wit must be so dearly bought
> But now experience tells me how
> If I would thrive then I must bow
> And bend unto another's will
> That I might learn both art and skill
> To Get My Living With My Hands
> That So I Might Be Free From Band
> And My Own Dame that I may be
> And free from all such slavery.
> Avoid vaine pastime fle youthful pleasure
> Let moderation allways be thy measure
> And so prosed unto the heavenly treasure.[1]

The three lines in which the words begin with capitals, are worked in letters of a larger scale than the rest and seem to give an extra urgency to the wish.

There is no record of when the school mistress took over the teaching of needlework and probably it was a gradual process over a number of years, but it was a common enough practice by 1639 to be the subject of a comment in the play, *The Citye Match* by Jasper Mayne:

> Your school mistresse, that can expound, and teaches
> To knit in Chaldee, and work Hebrew samplers.

There are also a number of samplers made about the middle of the seventeenth century in which the similarity of the patterns in each, shows them to have come from a common source, such as a school or a popular teacher. Signatures and dates occur more often after the middle of the century and these, coinciding with the increasing amount of school instruction during the same period, probably show that the children were expected to sign their work as a testament to their proficiency, and in many cases acknowledgements to their instructors, whether parents or mistresses, were added. The flowery expressions of gratitude in verse generally offered to parents however, rarely can be compared with the short and practical acknowledgements to the individual mistress or dame, which can be

[1] D. King, *Samplers*, Plate 16.

found on samplers from the middle of the seventeenth century for about 200 years. The similarity in the wording of so many of these acknowledgements, seems to indicate a formula by which it was understood that the resulting work of a teacher's tuition constituted a recognition of her ability, quite as much as of her pupil's skill. Mary Wright was one of the first to end her work with a rhyming inscription (1669) which was copied and adapted until well into the eighteenth century:

> Mary Wright is M(y)
> NAME AND WITH my NE
> DL I wrought the sa
> me and Gooddy Readd wa
> s my dame 1669.

Not every child added the name of her teacher. Other versions of many were those of Ann Fenn:

> Ann Fenn is my name and with
> my hand I made the same.

and of Ann Walters:

> Ann Walters is my name and
> with my needle I mark the same
> That All my Friends may plainly
> See what care my parents took of me.

Ann Bell's tribute to her mother, probably about the middle of the eighteenth century, leaves one in doubt about the parental ability as a teacher. The sampler is undated, small and elementary, with a double alphabet and digits from 1 to 9:

> This my work so
> you may see · what
> care my mother as
> took of me · ann bell[1]

Parents who provided instruction or gave it themselves, first had their help acknowledged in the seventeenth century and an early example in which Margreet Lucus gave her father his due, was adapted and repeated to suit other children and parents for some years:

> My Father Hitherto Hath done hIS Best TO make
> Me A WORKEWOMAN Above the Rest. Margreet
> LVCVH 1681 BeZng ten Year OLd come JULY THE First.[2]

[1] A. W. Tuer, *The History of the Horn-book*, p. 147, Cut 193.
[2] D. King, *Samplers*, Plate 17. P. G. Trendell, *Catalogue of Samplers*, Victoria and Albert Museum, 1922, p. 10.

The same sentiment appears in 1710, this time with the mother as the parent mentioned, although her best in spelling was not outstandingly good. The four line doggerel which followed the couplet was used in scores of samplers throughout the eighteenth and nineteenth centuries:

> my mother hatherto hath don her best to make
> me a work woman as well as the rest
> Anne Iater is my name and England in my nati
> on and south work is my dwelling place and
> Christ is my salvation.[1]

However skilled the teacher, the names of comparatively few are recorded in surviving samplers and of these, each seems to have one only to her credit, which suggests that some may have been family instructors, employed privately in a position similar to that of the nineteenth-century governess. The work of the early schools especially, rarely included the name of the teacher although quite a number of samplers exist which must have had common sources other than printed pattern books, but at a time when initials were more usual than full names, it is possible that some included among the patterns, may have been those of a teacher. There is reasonable evidence, however, that one teacher can be identified by name and initials in several samplers made between 1691 and 1710. In 1691 Hannah Canting inscribed her work:

> HANNAH . CANTING
> IS MY NAME AND WI
> TH MY NEDEL I ROU
> T THE SAME & IUDA
> HAYLE IS MY DAME.

In tablet patterns beneath this, the initials 'H C' and 'I H' were worked and repeated on each side of the date, on the ground under the tablets 'I H 1691 H C', which leaves no doubt as to them being the initials of the pupil and her teacher.[2] Dated 'JUNE 7 1700' Prisca Philips' sampler contained the inscription:

> PRISCA PHILIPS . LOOK WELL
> TO WHAT YOU TAKE
> IN HAND FOR LARNING
> IS BETTER THAN HOUSE OR
> LAND WHEN LAND IS GONE
> AND MONEY IS SPENT THEN

---

[1] F. G. Payne, *Guide to the Collection of Samplers and Embroideries*, p. 66, Sampler no. 91, 1939.
[2] M. Jourdain, *English Secular Embroidery*, Plate facing p. 178.

LARNING IS MOST
　　EXCELLENT JUNE 7 1700
IUDETH HAYL
WAS MY MIST
RIS.[1]

and at the bottom of the sampler, worked within a tablet pattern, the initials 'P P', and outside the tablet 'I H' in capitals similar to those on Hannah Canting's sampler. Making allowances for the uncertainties of individual spelling, especially in samplers, and the fact that the dates do not rule out the possibility, it appears reasonably certain that Iuda Hayle and Iudeth Hayl was the same person. The Canting sampler contains simple elementary work with two alphabets and narrow geometrical *band* patterns suitable for a beginner and the diminutive Iuda for Iudeth, indicates a child's attitude towards a young teacher. The Philips sampler shows more advanced work with *band* patterns exactly similar to those made in three other samplers made soon after—one by Elizabeth Scarles in 1701,[2] another in 1709 by Mary Moyse[3] and a third by Elizabeth Goodday in 1710 [*100*]. The number of patterns in each of the three varies a little; Prisca Philips worked fewer than the other two and Mary Moyse omitted the *pineapple* and one or two others included in the Goodday sampler; the Philips and Goodday samplers both contained the striped stag [*114*] and so on, but the patterns themselves and the same order in which they are placed, identifies them without question with a common source. All contain the same rhyming inscription and Elizabeth Scarles also includes the initials 'I H' with her own, linking her work with Judeth Hayl; Mary Moyse and Elizabeth Goodday embroidered 'R T' with their initials but in larger scale and in a more prominent position and it seems possible that these refer to the name of the school

114　*Striped* stag *in Philips and Goodday samplers.* 1700 *and* 1710

and not that of a teacher in the school, as on the other samplers. Some children acknowledge their parent's and teacher's help with their work, but after the suitable tributes to teachers on other samplers, that of Jane Rimington was cursory to say the least; paying full tribute to all concerned in the work, including herself, she announced:

[1] *Some Pictures and Samplers from the Collection of Lady St. John Hope*, n. 36.
[2] M. Jourdain, *English Secular Embroidery*, Plate facing p. 180.
[3] Leigh Ashton, *Samplers*, Figure 33.

GOD
Hath Laid Up In heaVen For Meacrow
n that WLL neVer Faid the
rIghteIous Judg at the Last daY WILL
Place It on MY head * By thIs YOU
se What MY Parant hath don
FOr Me * Iane rIMIngtOn MarKed
thIs ageed 12 Years the 8 daY of
JanUary With E. Bambrough 1789

Early in the eighteenth century there is evidence of teaching by sampler in institutional schools. Samplers by Elizabeth Clements in 1712[1] and by Mary Derow in 1723[2] were made in the Charity School of St Clement Danes and both show better needle-work and patterns than can be seen in school work done later in the century. Elizabeth Clements' sampler contains the almost inevitable *alphabets* and *numerals* in rows but her other patterns retain traces of some from the seventeenth century; a *swan* [115] similar to one in Sibmacher's pattern book of 1597 and a *boxer* border pattern, occupy most of the top half. Other small patterns are treated as *spot* motifs but are worked in symmetrical pairs in the lower half between two figures,

115   Swan *on Elizabeth Clement's sampler*

one of which must be presumed to be the Matron of the school and the other of Elizabeth herself as a pupil, wearing a 'foundling cap', school dress and apparently, a pair of football boots. The inscription after the alphabet reads:

ELIZABETH·CLE
MENTS·OF·THE·CHARITY·SCHOOL·OF·ST·CLEMENTS
DANES·AGED·TEN·YEARS·BEGUN·THIS·SAMPLER·AVG
VST·THE·TWENTIETH·ANNO·DOM·1712

and two lines which complete her work show her relief at having done so:

[1] *ibid.*, Figure 35.
[2] In the Collection of the Fitzwilliam Museum.

THIS·I·HAVE·DONE·I·THANK·MY·GOD·WITHOUT·THE
CORRECTION·OF·THE·ROD * ELIZABETH·CLEMENTS *

Other school children have voiced their relief, pride, self-encouragement, self-satisfaction and a host of other sentiments and virtues, which no doubt they liked to think they possessed. 'BE NOT WEARY IN WELL DOING' sometimes ends a sampler but sometimes it appears about half way down, as if to spur on a flagging spirit. Signs of a struggle are apparent in others also, without an actual admission:

DELIGHT IN LARNING SOWN WILL BRING
A CHILD TO LARN THE HARDEST THING.

and perhaps the last word in conscious virtue belongs to Sarah Lewis, 14 years old in 1835:

The hour is come i will not stay
But haste to school without delay
Not loiter here for tis a crime
To trifle thus with Precious time.[1]

There is however an appealing honesty in the hardened sinner who troubled neither to sign or date her sampler but ended it:

here a figure there a letter
one done bad another better.

Throughout the eighteenth and nineteenth centuries spelling instruction by sampler continued, but the name of the child's teacher occurred less frequently and that of her school more often. Of the schools which are mentioned, many carry names of places which are now wholly urban but were quiet villages when the samplers were made; others still remain in the cottages where they were made, in villages which have not changed for 200 years. The inscriptions on a few school samplers taken at random show how universally samplers were accepted in the curriculum. 'Sarah Hodgson her work in ye 11th year of her age, *Taught by Mary Wells at Bradford, 1765*'—'Elizabeth Ecklee did this at *Mr Hill's Academy. Kempsey* in the 11th year of her age.'—'Sarah Cherrett aged 12 years, *Winterbourne Telstone and Almer Board School Standard V*

116 *Christ's Hospital scholar. One of a pair in Mary Graves's sampler.*
1851

[1] F. G. Payne, *Guide to the Collection of Samplers and Embroideries*, p. 58, no. 51.

1887.'—'Martha Meech, *Evershot School. 1815*'—'Margaret Whiteside's work. Aged 12 years, 1823, *A. Robert's School. Bolton.*'—'Jane Liddiard Aged 13 years and 3 months. March 10th 1834, *Christs Hospital Hertford*'. Two figures representing Christ's Hospital scholars were among the patterns on Mary Graves' sampler made in 1851 but no mention of a scholar of that name can be traced in the

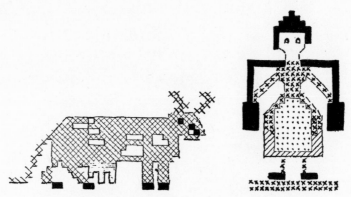

117   Cow *and* milkmaid *from Sarah Fear's sampler*

school records of that period [*116*]. The small Somerset village of Shapwick can boast two schools in which sampler-making was taught, as evidenced by one made by Sarah Fear 'worked at Mr Dyer's School, Shapwick, Aged 13. June the 24, 1760'. from which drawings of her rural choice of patterns are illustrated [*117*] and the other, of silk *cross* stitch on worsted, was made by Hannah Hockey at Mrs Champion's School in 1798. It is entitled 'ON THE DAY OF JUDGMENT' followed by the text 'The end of all things is at hand, be ye therefore sober and watch unto prayer'. The sampler is divided into two halves by a vertical line from the text downwards and 11 verses of a hymn are worked on either side. In the second half, room enough is left for the usual courtesies to the teacher and a little moralising in verse:

> These lines I here present unto the Sight
> Of you, my Friends, to shew how I can wor[k]
> My M[rs] unto me hath shewn her skill
> And here's the Product of my Hand and Need[le]
>
> The Needle, an Instrument tho' small
> Is of great Use and benefit to all
> Trust rather to your Fingers ends
> Then to the Promises of Friends.

Hannah Hockey End this Sampler in The
13 year of her Age in the Year of our Lord
1798 Work'd at Mrs Champion's School Shapwick.

Towards the end of the eighteenth century *map*-samplers became a popular type and there seems little doubt that, if they were not all made by school children, at least their main purpose was educational and children once more were expected to do two things at once—this time to combine geography with their needlework. A number of map outlines probably were drawn by the school mistress, but it is clear that many were made by the children themselves, as their accuracy frequently was too wide of the mark to have been the work of a teacher. Most of those which are known and recorded, date from the 1770s, but Miss Jourdain mentions 'maps of the world, of continents, or of England appear, often bearing dates as far back as 1720, though they are more commonly dated in the later years of the eighteenth century'.[1] Later in her book, a reference is made to one sampler of an early date—'a map bearing the early date of 1720 was lent by Miss Hughes to the Exhibition of Needlework at South Kensington in 1873'[2] but any with a date as early as that must be exceptional and as a rule they were not made until nearer the end of the century.

A popular map represented England and Wales, showed 'Part of Scotland' as far as Edinburgh, and 'Part of Ireland' to include Dublin, and more enterprising ones covered the whole of the British Isles, with surrounding isles and islets in detail. *Europe* and the *Two Hemispheres* were perhaps the next in popularity, but maps of single countries also were made, including *France, Spain, Africa, Ireland* and others; a rather shaky conception of *North America*, much of it marked 'PARTS UNKNOWN'[3] and another showing nine-tenths of *Australia* named 'NEW HOLLAND' and the remaining tenth inserted as a narrow strip for 'NEW SOUTH WALES', raise a doubt as to their educational value as lessons in geography. By the 1780s map outlines were being printed commercially on to the material and in those of England and Wales the county outlines were put in to be filled in with colour, and other details such as towns, usually were worked in black. Maps of single counties are found and these appear always to be commercially produced, as for instance *Wright's Map of Cornwall*, of which a surviving copy was signed 'Anne Gribble her work done in the 12th year of her age at *Miss Warren's School, Truro. 1784*'. A number of examples remain of the popular map of two hemispheres, each with their headings 'The New World' and 'The Old World', under

[1] M. Jourdain, *English Secular Embroidery*, p. 120.
[2] *ibid.*, p. 191.
[3] M. B. Huish, *Samplers and Tapestry Embroideries*, Figure 25.

a general title of 'THE WORLD', and one worked by Selina Attwood in 1798[1] contains also, an inscription:

An Outline
MAP OF THE WORLD
for LADIES NEEDLEWORK
and Young Students *in*
GEOGRAPHY

which leaves no doubt as to the accepted purpose of *map* samplers. But if the outlines were provided ready drawn, the filling in of cities, towns and villages was left to the individual worker and it is rare to find two maps which are identical in these details. County capital towns may be marked but no others, except those which might have been of importance to the worker; Ann Rhodes (1780) emphasised 'York City' and 'Edinburgh City' by embroidering a small *cathedral* pattern at each place but omitted altogether to put London on her map.[2] Ann Gardiner (1792) probably lived at Hawkshead in Lancashire, as her map contained no other place names except London, but on a narrow strip of Lancashire, near

where Hawkshead would be found, six cryptic letters are embroidered:
H W
K S
H D[3]

A comparatively early map [121] made by a member of the Field family, and a descendant of Oliver and Elizabeth Cromwell (p. 165), gives the names of the County Towns and with most of them, the number of miles from London; in general there seems to be agreement between the maker of the map—'M.F.'—in 1778 and the Automobile Association of to-day, on the number of miles given; Caernarvon, Salisbury and Lancaster for instance, were apparently the same distance then as now, but the road to York had shrunk by six miles and that to Harlech had lengthened by as much as seventeen. 'Ann Brown. Aged 11.' seemed to rely on guess work: 'her delineation of Northumberland takes her well down the canvas so that by the time she reached Newcastle, she has carried it abreast of Dumfries and Cork ... Yorkshire grows downwards beyond Exeter and Lundy Island, which last named places have crept up Northward of Manchester and Leeds.'[4] Sarah Boardman completed a geographical marathon in cross stitch in May 1807, but without a map, as she worked:

The Chief Countries of Europe are
Norway, Sweden, Denmark, Russia, Poland, Prussia, Germany,

---

[1] *Some Pictures and Samplers from the Collection of Lady St. John Hope*, no. 40.
[2] D. King, *Samplers*, Plate 46.
[3] In the Collection of the Victoria and Albert Museum, T. 273–1916.
[4] M. B. Huish, *Samplers and Tapestry Embroideries*, p. 75, Figure 26.

The Lords prayer
our Father which art in hea:
ven hallowed be thy name
thy kingdom come thy Will
be done in earth as it is in
heaven give us this day our
daily bread and forgive us
our trespasses as we forgiv
them that trespass against us
and lead us not into Temptati
on but deliver us from evil
for thine is the kingdom the
power and the glory for
ever and ever Amen
Elizabeth Cridland 1752

118   *1752. Silk thread on wool. Cross stitch. Signed, Elizabeth Cridland. 13¼ × 9¾ inches*

119 *Late eighteenth century. Silk thread on Tiffany. Chiefly darning with chain stitch and some French knots. Signed, C. Taylor.* 14 × 13¼ *inches*

120 *1777. Silk and linen threads on linen. Cross, satin and Florentine stitches with some cut and drawn work. Signed, Anne Rollestone Alleyne.* 16¾ × 8½ *inches*

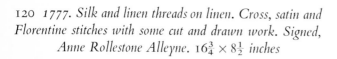

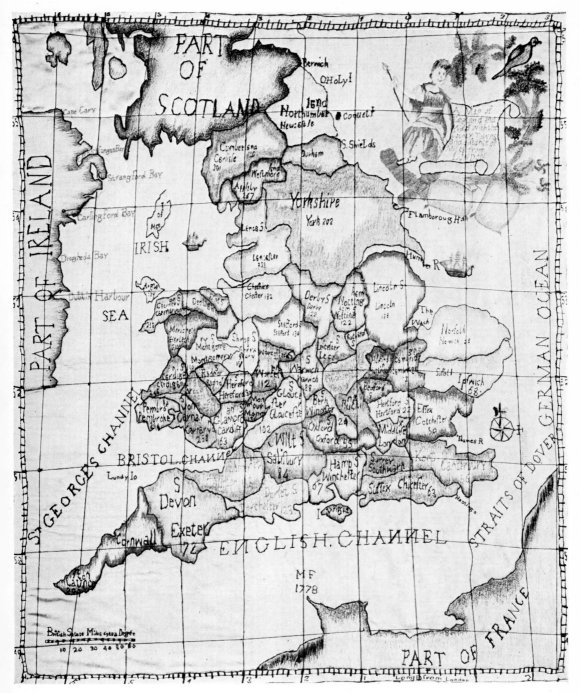

121   *1778. Silk thread on satin, with some hair. Satin, split, stem and back stitches, some French knots. Signed, M.F. $19\frac{1}{2} \times 16\frac{1}{2}$ inches*

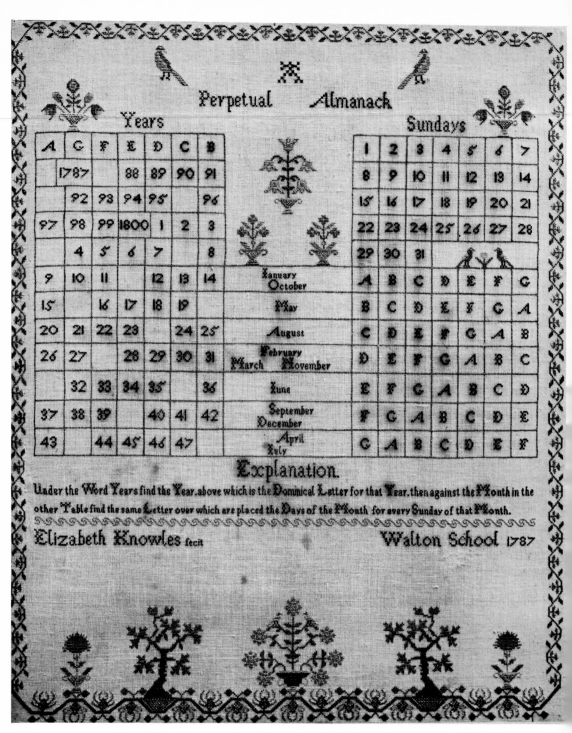

122 1787. Silk thread on linen. Cross stitch. Signed, Elizabeth Knowles. $15\frac{3}{4} \times 13$ inches

123   *1796. Silk thread on linen. Cross, satin, split, chain, stem, tent, back and buttonhole stitches, with some French knots. Signed, Ann Day. 19 × 12 inches*

124 *1799. Silk thread on linen scrim. Pattern darning. Signed, Susanna Pettit Bocking.* 13 × 12 *inches*

125 *Early nineteenth century (detail). Scottish. Cot... thread on fine muslin. Satin, stem, chain (tambour) ... needlepoint fillings. Whole sampler, length 82 inches*

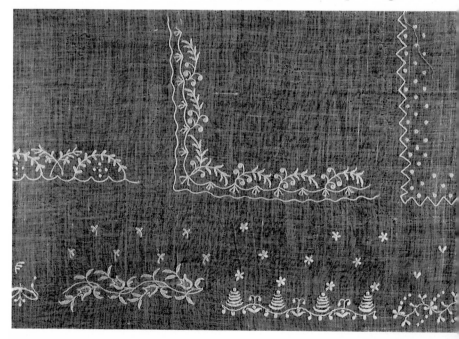

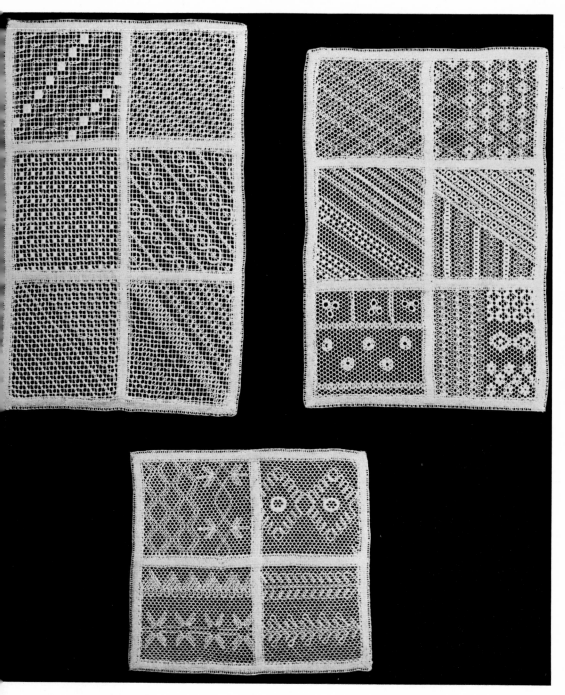

26   *Early nineteenth century. Cotton thread on net. Darning stitches.* 6×4, $5\frac{1}{2} \times 4$, *and* 4×4 *inches*

127 *1803. Silk thread on wool. Cross stitch. Signed, E.T. 8 × 11 inches*

Holland, Netherlands, France, Switzerland, Hungary, Spain,
Portugal, Italy, and Turkey.
            Their Capitals are
Bergen of Norway, Stockholm of Sweden, Copenhagen of
Denmark, Petersburgh of Russia, Warsaw of Poland,
Konigsberg of Prussia, Vienna of Germany, Amsterdam of
Holland, Brussels of the Netherlands, Paris of France, Berne of
Switzerland, Buda of Hungary, Madrid of Spain, Lisbon of
Portugal, Rome of Italy, and Constantinople of Turkey.
            The Chief Islands of Europe are
Great Britain, Ireland, Iceland, Minorca, Majorca, Ivica,
Corsica, Sardinia, Sicily, Malta, Candia, and Cyprus.
            The Principal Seas are
The Baltic, the Mediterranean, The Archipelago, The Black Sea,
The White Sea, The Irish Sea, and the English Channel.
        Sarah Boardman , Her Work , Finished   May   1807.[1]

Geographical details usually found on printed school maps are embroidered on
sampler specimens; points of the compass are included on almost all maps but a
scale of miles on single countries, the British Isles, and English County maps only.
'M F' [121] gives the *British Statute Miles 69 to a Degree* and Ellen Carr [174] the
Scale of Irish Miles. Lines of longitude and latitude are marked, generally in fine *stem*
stitch on the Hemisphere maps and in numbered degrees on the borders of others,
in a variety of stitches such as, *cross*, *back* and *stem*. Sailing ships are represented on
the seas and oceans, apparently always sailing to the west, although Ann Rhodes
(1780) provided an exception to this, with one ship making for Plymouth (stern to
the onlooker) in immediate danger from ramming, by a rowing boat with four
oarsmen.[2]

Silk embroidery on satin or linen was characteristic of eighteenth-century
samplers, but by the nineteenth century it had been replaced largely by linen on
linen or woollen canvas. Silk was the basic thread but in addition, chenille, hair,
metal thread and spangles were used to achieve particular effects and in most
maps no opportunity was missed to add decoration to the background of the
geographical content. Elaborate floral borders with flowing stems and ribbon
patterns in bows and streamers surrounded maps of hemispheres and continents
and the title of each map was inscribed on a scroll or enclosed in a garland of
flowers, leaves or ribbon. In maps of England and Wales or of the British Isles,
the title often was situated in the 'North Sea or German Ocean', with Britannia

---

[1] *Some Pictures and Samplers from the Collection of Lady St. John Hope*, no. 44.
[2] D. King, *Samplers*, Plate 46.

ruling the waves nearby. Within the same ornament the date and maker's name were included, or alternatively they would be found in the sea off the Isle of Wight or perhaps near Lundy Island. The map on Figure 121 is shown with 'M F 1778' in the English Channel and a mile or two north of 'Flamborough H^d', Britannia is seated holding a spear instead of a trident in her hand (with a curious thumb-up grip) and beside her, a scroll bearing the title:

A Map of
England and
Wales With the
County Towns
and distance of
Miles from
LONDON

The map was worked in silk on satin, with the exception of the *ships* which are of hair and the stitches used were *satin, split* and *stem*; *back* stitch was used for the letters and *French knots* for the leaves and the trees, on which an anxious *bird* acts eternally as look-out.

Maps within oval borders appeared from about 1780; a 'MAP OF AFRICA' (1784), 'DONE AT MR ARNOLD'S FETHERSTON BUILDINGS', was surrounded with an oval border of embroidery with spangles,[1] and one by Alice Priest in 1790 was of 'ENGLAND AND WALES' within an oval garland of leaves and berries and the title worked on a scroll of ribbon.[2] 'A NEW MAP OF IRELAND' with an oval border was one of those printed commercially early in the nineteenth century and carries the name of the publisher—'*Published 20th July 1820* R. H. Laurie. *53 Fleet Street. London.'*—'*Where also may be had* England, Scotland & Europe *on the same plan.'* This map is of linen and was worked with silk thread and chenille, the title being enclosed in a *harp* of dark green couched chenille. The County outlines were worked in a different colour for each Province—red for Ulster, fawn for Connaught, brown for Leinster and Munster in green; the border of silk-embroidered flowers was outlined with russet brown chenille and the work was signed and dated *Ellen Carr. Killileagh. July 1825.*

Other types of samplers considered to be suitable exercises in the education of the young, included *Almanacks, Ready Reckoners* and *Darning,* which appeared at about the same time as the *Maps.* Almanacks were of the perpetual kind and a typical example is in the collection of the Victoria and Albert Museum[3]; worked

[1] M. B. Huish, *Samplers and Tapestry Embroideries,* Plate XXIX.
[2] *Some Pictures and Samplers from the Collection of Lady St. John Hope,* no. 42.
[3] D. King, *Samplers,* Plate 42.

in *cross* stitch it is complete with the Dominical letters and the 'Explanation' for finding the required date—'Elizabeth Knowles fecit Walton School, 1787' [122]. The Ready Reckoners can have served little purpose save as an exercise in marking numerals but as reckoners they are not always reliable and an undetected mistake has been known to slip through. *Darning* samplers had more to commend them as exercises in needlework, as many of them were working examples of pattern *darning* needed for the repair of woven textiles and the forerunners of 'invisible mending'. Their origin is believed to be European, as examples of an earlier date than those known to be English, are of German, Dutch and Danish work made about the middle of the eighteenth century and many can be seen in private and Museum collections in this country. The most practical of them contain straightforward examples of various alternatives *web*, *twill* and *damask* patterns which could be achieved by darning [124] and were kept as workbox references, as few of them seem to have been framed. But not content with working samplers, many embroiderers elaborated them with floral borders, and sprays and vases of flower, leaf and ribbon patterns composed of *darning* stitches and outlined with *stem*, *chain* or *back* stitch [119].

Darning patterns demanded a high technical skill, and was a separate subject in the recognised system of needlework instruction followed in the schools, which was considered of enough importance for the girls' class rooms to be adapted to its needs. In 1821 regulations stipulated that 'in the general arrangement time must be allowed for needlework', for the girls' education (which otherwise was the same as that for the boys) and that for this purpose 'the form be five or six inches from the inner edge of the desk to allow freedom to work'. The eighth lesson of the syllabus for sewing was devoted to *darning*, in which the method was to tack paper to a piece of canvas with a hole in it to be filled with the darn— 'The children perform the work in two colours, blue and yellow, on linen that it may appear more distinctly. When a child has completed one of these darns she may practice on a small piece of fine muslin in which a hole has been purposely torn.' Darns on samplers were worked on the same principle, always on a material with threads even enough to be counted, such as muslin or linen, from which a square piece was cut for each darn and the hole filled in again with two or more colours *darned* into a pattern.

School instruction in needlework throughout the nineteenth century was very thorough and in most schools needlework exercise books were kept in which small examples of the children's work were stitched or pinned to the pages; many of them probably were given to the teacher or kept by her, as schoolleaving 'autograph' books. The contents in those which have survived (and there are many of them) are so similar that the standard of each child's work is the only thing which differs. The book itself usually was dated and almost invariably the first page contained a sampler of *cross* stitch with one or several *alphabets*, *numerals*, an inscription and always the child's name and age. Following pages had attached to them examples of many kinds of work in complete articles, miniature in size, in knitting, fine sewing, crochet, Turkey work, patchwork, rug work in wool and so on, so that the books themselves were samplers of school work. A typical example of a book of this kind was made in the Westbourne Union School, Sussex, during the years 1842, 1843 and 1844, with several pieces of work by each child showing her progress year by year. Each page of her work was headed by a strip of canvas bearing the child's name and age in cross stitch, which appears again on the small samplers—measuring about six inches long by four and a half inches wide—worked in silk or wool on scrim or linen, names which included Eliza Zillwood, Ann Betsworth, Harriot Hawkins, Jemima Suett, Eliza Griffin, Ann Benham, Eliza Cobb, Emma Betsworth, Hannah Till, Eliza Dear, Harriet Budd and Emma Brewer. Sometimes a particularly gifted child would fill a whole book with her work; 'a School Sample Book' in the Victoria and Albert Museum contains 'Specimens of Needlework executed by Ellen Mahon, Boyle School'. She included two samplers, the first signed 'Ellen Mahon 1852' and the second by a more mature Ellen was signed 'Elleanor Mahon, 1854'. Her other work consisted of stitch examples used in making clothing, *buttonholing*, *herring bone*, *feather*, *coral* and *fly* stitches and so on and processes, such as making gussets, were shown on small sets of doll's clothes in miniature—three dresses and knickers, and examples of *knitting* in socks, cap, bootee, collar, gloves and mittens. She made also a *knitting* sampler, contained in most school needlework books, consisting of openwork patterns knitted in white cotton thread and intended for children's white socks and stockings. Instructions for similar knitted samplers are given in Caulfeild's *Dictionary of Needlework* with a diagram and a colour plate; the sampler is worked in chequer board style, each section showing a different pattern—nine stitches across and six rows long—intended to be worked 'in knitting silk or fine knitting cotton'[1] (p. 200).

Most of the late nineteenth-century sampler work was done in schools and orphanages and consisted largely of alphabets and numerals enclosed in a simple border pattern, but those made in the Bristol Orphanages were purely business like and no other samplers show a more strict economy in material and space. Made from about 1870, they consist of alphabets, numerals and narrow border and corner motifs worked in red silk on closely woven linen. Sometimes small patterns of household objects, animals, houses, ships as well as Christian names and initials, were included but the *marking* patterns clearly were the most important

[1] Caulfeild and Saward, *Dictionary of Needlework*, Plate facing p. 116 and pp. 531 to 534.

consideration. Rows of three-figure numbers have been mentioned already (p. 113) as a feature of these samplers and occasional groups of initials probably refer to the children also. The sampler illustrated [198] contains not only the name of the chief worker but also the address of one of the Orphan Houses—No 3 Ashley Down— which was to many the most important, as the house where the remarkable founder of the Orphan Houses, Dr George Muller, ended his days.

It is probable that more than one child took part in the work of each sampler and this would account for the inclusion of several names. In connection with the Orphanage samplers, Sir Leigh Ashton records the evidence of a woman who was brought up in the Muller Homes, saying that the girls who did the work were not instructed but learned the patterns one from another [1] and the identical patterns in most specimens bears out this idea, but there is no doubt that nearly all the small figure patterns shown in the sampler illustrated by Sir Leigh Ashton [2] originated in *The Embroidery and Alphabet Sampler Book* (p. 28).

Samplers worked in *cross* stitch continued to be a requirement of children's needlework instruction, especially in country schools, for some 20 years in the early twentieth century. They were of elementary work, usually *marking* samplers consisting of several alphabets and numerals, which included often a set of Roman figures from I to X, with C.D.M. added, surrounded by a simple border pattern. Linen was used for some specimens but double canvas was almost universal for school work and the thread used was either wool, stranded cotton or D.M.C. crochet silk in crude bright colours. The children made one sampler a year from about the age of nine years old until they left school and many of them have been kept by their makers. A selection of school samplers typical of many others was made by Elsie Tye of Heythrop School, beginning in 1917 with simple alphabets and numerals worked in silk on canvas when she was 11, her next showed elaborate capitals worked in red and blue cotton in 1918 and in her last year at school when she was 13, a more comprehensive exercise of capitals, minuscules, numerals 1 to 10 and Roman numerals I to V, worked in buttonhole twist.

As well as the conventional type of sampler, a piece of work showing processes of mending and dressmaking made in schools also was described as a sampler. The pupil-teacher of the late nineteenth and early twentieth centuries was expected to do a considerable amount of needlework teaching among other subjects, and before she could instruct the children she had to prove her technical ability with examples of stitchery and processes. A past head mistress of a London County Council School began her career as a pupil-teacher before she was 17 and worked two samplers in 1905 which 'had to show all stitches used on flannel and cotton

[1] Leigh Ashton, *Samplers*, p. 12.
[2] *ibid.*, Figure 63.

materials' which were necessary processes for making the calico and flannel under-garments then considered to be the hallmark of respectability. Other students training in Domestic Science made these samplers during their time at Training Colleges, being expected to show 'linen, canvas and flannel samplers during House-wifery training'. They all were made on exactly the same pattern; the calico and flannel examples illustrated [*200, 201*] are typical of all the others, but rather finer work is shown on some muslin samplers, notably in the gathered frills, setting on of lace edgings, and a variety of buttonholes and bars. Most are signed and few are dated but they seem generally to have been made from about 1890 until the early 1920s. Samplers showing the same techniques were made by children but usually these are worked on squares of calico and flannel, four or six inches square, which were hemmed round the edges and joined together with *faggoting* by the tidy ones or strung together in a bunch by the not-so-tidy, but in all of this type, the work showed high technical skill born of much practice in making the long seams, tucks and gathers of contemporary garments.

By the 1920s needlework instruction in schools by means of the sampler gradually had died out. Girls at boarding schools where needlework was taught, made stitch samplers of geometrical patterns but this was by no means common to all schools of this kind, and gradually learning and teaching by sampler was discontinued. Schools for adult students, such as the Schools of Art and the Royal School of Needlework with an established tradition of needlework instruction, continued to encourage the use of samplers (p. 226). Three teaching examples from the Royal School of Needlework show stitches and techniques especially for the use of gold thread in embroidery. The example in Figure 216, shows motifs used in church work on a traditional damask ground and in Figure 204 are methods of working solid surfaces in Japanese gold on firm linen, in which the *chevron* block is worked in the ancient method of couching used in the Opus Anglicanum of the thirteenth century. A third sampler of gold work on a ground of purple velvet, shows a section of the pattern embroidered on the robe of Queen Elizabeth II at her coronation in 1953 [*217*].

The educational value of stitch samplers has been re-discovered in recent years by organisations which are concerned, among other interests, with the continu-ance of needlework tradition in the country and through them instruction is made available—followed by examinations in proficiency—for those who are not able to study at the recognised schools of art. For example, examination papers in needlework of the City and Guilds of London Institute, the National Federation of Women's Institutes and others, require stitch samplers for different types of embroidery as proof of technical ability, many of which are used sub-sequently for teaching purposes by the candidates. Two samplers which showed high standards of proficiency in such examinations are illustrated; one contains a variety of traditional *pulled* and *filling* stitches, cords, buttons and tassels worked in linen thread on linen and is signed 'E. Tansley. 1936', the date being that of the examination year [214], and the other, in a different medium, shows no less than 22 processes of fine sewing on cambric and an advance in skill as compared with the same kind of sewing of some 50 years earlier. It is signed and dated 'E.C. 1946' [215]. Work box samplers in traditional *Holbein* stitch, for day-to-day use, were made by a student of the Winchester School of Art early in the 1960s and consisted of a selection of patterns taken from early samplers and embroidery [218]. Individual students working on their own and those in Colleges of Art to-day make not one stitch sampler but numbers of them, some as many as 30 or more, during and after the period of learning and training. Generally these are kept in folders, with corresponding notes on technical points relating to each example of stitchery; border patterns, filling stitches, individual motifs and so on, are worked on 'pages' of suitable material and alternate with the pages of written notes, which are invaluable as reference sheets or aids to teaching after the period of training is over.

Individual teachers outside the colleges and schools are doing a great deal of work at the present time in places which are often in rural areas, where adult students who are not able to take advantage of the instruction given in the institutions, endeavour to learn when and how they can. The demand for local tuition is high and because of it, classes which are given in village districts often are unavoidably large, so use is made of stitch samplers (which are larger in scale than usual) with accompanying instruction charts from which students can learn the application of various traditional stitches until individual attention by the teacher can be given. In a typical sampler of this kind *outlining* and *filling* stitches are illustrated [220]. Screen samplers also are used (p. 230).

Most of the student work of to-day is unsigned and undated. Occasionally work is initialled but rarely dated, and in none is acknowledgement given to a place or person as the source of learning or inspiration. Future research on work which will have survived from to-day—as some of it most certainly will do—can be made more convincing by the presence of recorded origins. The practice of adding names, dates and teachers to samplers and other work of earlier periods, has helped to complete historical records of which research workers otherwise could have had no knowledge and although the relationship of pupil and teacher has changed from the time when all lessons were learned from one person, it is still of interest and importance that work should be signed and dated, if only so that a worker can 'sartifi' herself in later years. Teachers undoubtedly would appreciate a tribute also although probably they would be satisfied with something less than that paid by 'E. Brown.', who made and gave to her teacher Miss C. D. Fair on the occasion of her marriage to Mr Grey on February 20th 1844, a sampler with these verses:

MY TEACHER

When the descending torrents pour,
The Winds and tempest rudely roar
Who ventures out t'instruct the poor
    My Teacher
Who as the object of her care
Conducts me to the house of prayer
And watches o'er my conduct there
    My Teacher
When childish trifles fill my mind
And I to folly am inclined
Who gently chides in accents kind
    My Teacher,

Who cautions me to watch and pray
And points out Christ the only way
To Yon bright world of endless day
    My Teacher.
Oh may I ever grateful be
My much esteemed friend to thee
For all this kindness shown to me
    My Teacher
Instructed by thy pious care
To heaven I'll send my fervent prayer
That its best blessings thou mays't share
    Dear Teacher.

And when this mortal life is o'er
May my blest soul to glory soar
Then shall we meet to part no more
    Dear Teacher.

PRESENTED
to
C. D. FAIR

BY
E. Brown
FEBY. 20th 1844

CHAPTER SEVEN

The Sixteenth Century

The significance of the sampler in the everyday life of the sixteenth century is emphasised by the number of references to it in their works by the poets and writers of the time; there are in fact many more references in prose and poetry than there are actual specimens remaining. So far, there appears to be no surviving English sampler which is considered by expert opinion to belong to the first 60 or 70 years at least, but the written accounts give descriptions of some, as well as invaluable pictures of the occupations, patterns and colours of the women who did the needlework. The writers were all men; as far as we know none of them was an embroiderer and perhaps this, as well as their obedience to the convention of chivalry towards women, may account for their consistently romantic attitude towards samplers in their writings. On the other hand, as men's clothing was adorned with the embroidery—especially the lace for collars, cuffs and ruffs—for which the sampler patterns were made, no doubt a personal interest gave colour to their observations.

There has been a good deal of supposition as to the age and class of those who made samplers and in general it is thought that the early ones were the work of adult needlewomen and that children's samplers were not made until later, in the seventeenth century. The fine quality of the embroidery in the few surviving sixteenth-century examples shows experience but this does not necessarily mean that all the workers were out of the schoolroom. Girls were taught to sew as soon as they were able to hold a needle; signed and dated embroidery, remaining from work of the first half of the seventeenth century, was made by girls with meticulous care and skill and there seems to be no reason why those in the previous century were not equally capable. If the patterns and sewing are not considered to be child-like, neither were the children; they were dressed and brought up to behave like grown-up people and in whatever period they have lived, when children have worked under supervision, it is inevitable that adult help and instruction should be noticeable in their work. In addition to this is a child's instinct to mimic the actions of its elders and to show off.

The social standing of the sixteenth century embroideress generally was that of the leisured upper-class household, and this is shown by almost every written reference, but apart from these records the cost of the material alone would probably put the work out of reach of any but the well-to-do. The earliest mention of an English sampler is found in account books at the Public Records Office and is that of an item in the Privy Purse expenses for 1502, of Elizabeth of York, Queen of Henry VII: 'It^m—the Xth day of July to Thomas Fisshe in reward for bringing of conserve of chreys from London to Windsor . . . and for an elne of lynnyn cloth for a sampler for the Quene, viijd'.[1] From this entry it is clear that sampler making was established at Court early enough in the century, to indicate it as a customary form of embroidery during the last part of the fifteenth century. Mr Ffransis Payne quotes other early records in the works of the Welsh poet Tudur Aled, who died about 1520; a poem which is 'addressed to a woman who is described as 'gwnïedyddes dal' (a tall seamstress) occur the lines:

> Aur wnïadau a'r nydwydd,
> Arfer o'r sampler yw'r swydd,

the literal translation of which reads 'Gold stitchings with the needle, the use of the sampler is the work'. In another poem, the plumage of the hawk is compared with skilful 'sampler work'.[2]

An English contemporary of Tudur Aled was John Skelton, the poet (also renowned as the 'scandalous rector of Diss') who lived from about 1460 to 1529; a colourful character, who in his early years spent some time at Court as tutor to the young prince, later to become Henry VIII. His poetry reflected the way of life around him in different kinds of society and the *Boke of Phyllyp Sparowe* includes a lament supposedly spoken by a child Jane or Joanna Scrope, who was a pupil at the school of the Benedictine Nuns of Carrow Abbey near Norwich, on the death of her pet sparrow, killed by Gib the cat:

> I take my sampler ones
> Of purpose, for the nones,
> to sewe with stychis of sylke
> My sparowe whyte as mylke,
> That by representacyn
> of his image and facyon.

[1] Quoted, M. Jourdain, *English Secular Embroidery*, p. 177, n. 3. Leigh Ashton, *Samplers*, p. 2. D. King, *Samplers*, p. 2. F. G. Payne, *Collection of Samplers and Embroideries*, p. 23.
[2] *ibid.*, pp. 22 and 23.

To me it might importe
Some pleasure and comforte
For my solas and sporte
But when I was sewing his beke
Methought my sparowe did speke
and opened his pretty byll
Saynge, Mayd, ye are in wyll
Agayne for me to kyll,
Ye prycke me in the head.
With that my nedel waxed red,
Methought, of phyllyps blode
My hear ryght upstode
And was in such a fray
My speche was taken away
I kest down that there was,
And sayd Alas, alas
How commeth this to pas?
My fyngers dead and colde
Coude not my sampler holde
My nedle and threde
I threwe away for drede
The best now that I may
Is for his sowle to pray
    A porta inferi
Good Lord, have mercy
Upon my sparrows soule
Wryten in my bede roule.[1]

Skelton's observation on the making of a sampler, notwithstanding the lack of progress on this occasion, shows that it was not unusual work for a child to do; the poem was written in 1504. An incidental interest lies in the mention of the child's pet being an albino sparrow and is probably the earliest record of one in this country. In 1523 Skelton wrote his last long poem, extolling his own great gifts among the poets of the world, in the *Garland of Laurell*, and he recounts how the ladies of the household of the Countess of Surrey were set to contrive 'a coronal of laurell with verdures light and dark' in his honour, and of their activities in different kinds of needlework:

    With that the tappetis and carpettis were layd,
      Whereon theis ladys softly myght rest,
      The saumpler to sow on, the lacis to enbraid;

[1] John Skelton, *Works*, edited by Dyce, 1843, Volume I, p. 57. Quoted 'Samplers' by Dorothy Stevens, *Embroidery*, p. 4, December 1946. D. King, *Samplers*, p. 2, n. 2.

To weue in the stoule sume were full preste,
With slaiis, with tauellis, with hedellis well drest
The frame was brought forth with his weaving pin.
God give them good speed their worke to begin![1]

Towards the middle of the century there was an early instance of the value put upon a family sampler which Margaret Thomson of Freeston in Lincolnshire bequeathed in her will, proved on 25th May 1546, 'to Alys Pynchebeck my systers daughter my sawmpler with semes.'[2] And six years later (1552) in a household inventory of Edward VI, two entries read—'Item, XII samplers'; 'Item, one sampler of Normandie canvas, wroughte with green and black silk . . . and a book of parchment containing diverse patterns'.[3] It is not known whether any of the

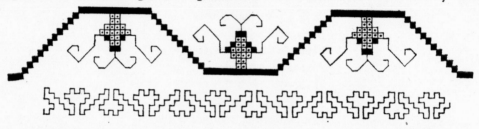

128 *Stylised* carnation *band patterns with double running. Seventeenth century*

samplers were the work of his grandmother, Elizabeth of York but if any of her work had survived the domestic upheavals of Henry VIII, there is a possibility that some at least, might have been made from the 'elne of lynnyn cloth', before she died in 1503. The last two records are the first known occasions in which definite features of contemporary samplers are given—in the Thomson will, the sampler is described as having 'semes', probably referring to straight rows or bands of patterns across the sampler; and in the Edward VI inventory where colour is described, probably indicates embroidery worked in *Holbein* or *black* work, which decorated so much of the clothing of the Tudor period and derived its name from the number of times it appeared on clothes portrayed in paintings by Holbein. It has been known also as 'Spanysshe' work because it was believed, mistakenly, to have been introduced into this country by Catherine of Aragon, but this kind of work now called *double running*, was done here in the fifteenth century, before she came to England [*128, 129*].

[1] John Skelton, *Works*, edited by Dyce, 1843, Volume I, p. 393. Quoted, F. G. Payne, *Guide to the Collection of Samplers and Embroideries*, p. 23. Leigh Ashton, *Samplers*, p. 2. D. King, *Samplers*, p. 2. M. Jourdain, *English Secular Embroidery*, p. 178, n. 2.

[2] Quoted, *Essex Review*, Volume xvii, 1908, p. 147. Leigh Ashton, *Samplers*, p. 2. M. B. Huish, *Samplers and Tapestry Embroideries*, p. 13. D. King, *Samplers*, p. 3.

[3] British Museum, Harl. MSS. no. 1419, pp. 419, 524. Quoted Bury Palliser, *History of Lace*, p. 9. M. Jourdain, *English Secular Embroidery*, p. 178, n. 1. Leigh Ashton, *Samplers*, p. 2. D. King, *Samplers*, p. 3 and n. 3.

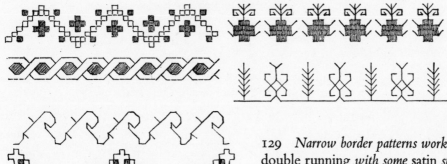

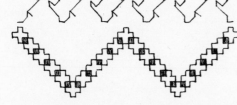

129 *Narrow border patterns worked in* double running *with some satin* stitch

Other literary references to samplers occur during the 1570s and onwards. Some verses by Reginald Scot in 1574 entitled *The Perfect Platform of a Hop Garden*, contained a reference to a sampler and also Sir Philip Sidney's *Arcadia*, in the words:

> And then, O Love, why dost thou in thy beautiful sampler set such a work for my desire to take out?[1]

In his book on samplers Mr Donald King relates what he truly describes as one of the most graphic accounts of samplers in use, which is 'found in a passage describing the pastimes of a rich man's wife in Barnabe Riche's tale *Of Phylotus and Emilia* (1581):

> Now, when she had dined, then she might go seke out her examplers, and to peruse which worke would doe beste in a ruffe, whiche in a gorget, whiche in a sleeve, whiche in a quaife, which in a caule, whiche in a handcarcheef; what lace would doe beste to edge it, what seame, what stitche, what cutt, what garde: and to sitte her doune and take it forthe by little and little, and thus with her nedle to passe the after noone with devising of things for her owne wearynge.'[2]

Shakespeare's observance of social customs included that of sampler making, and it is clear that he was familiar with the subject by the references in two of his plays. In *Titus Andronicus*, supposed to have been written in 1588, he recalls the story of Philomela, who had her tongue cut out by Tereus, the husband of her sister Procne, so that she could not tell how he had betrayed her. From the prison where she was hidden, she worked and sent to her sister the story of her wrongs on a piece of embroidery. It is in the words of Marcus to his niece Lavinia, who had had 'her hands cut off and her tongue cut out', that he recalls her likeness to Philomela:

[1] Quoted, M. B. Huish, *Samplers and Tapestry Embroideries*, p. 13.
[2] D. King, *Samplers*, p. 3.

Fair *Philomela* she but lost her tongue
And in a tedious sampler sew'd her mind;
But, lovely niece, that mean is cut from thee:
A craftier *Tereus*, cousin, has thou met,
And hath cut those pretty fingers off,
That could have better sew'd than *Philomel*.[1]

Allegorical and narrative picture patterns were popular in sixteenth-century embroidery, but samplers containing them are not known before the seventeenth century. In 1594, a quite different aspect of a sampler is shown in *A Midsummer Night's Dream*, when Helena pleads with Hermia:

O is all forgot?
All school-days friendship, Childhood innocence?
We, *Hermia*, like two artificial gods,
Have with our needles created both one flower,
Both on one sampler, sitting on one cushion,
Both warbling of one song, both in one key,
As if our hands, our sides, voices, and minds,
Had been incorporate.[2]

A feature of some seventeenth-century samplers is that the patterns were worked from both ends of the sampler and the idea that probably they were made by two people using the same material is supported by Helena's words (p. 107).

Throughout the history of samplers in the sixteenth century, conjecture has to fill in not only short gaps, but the long periods from which no samplers remain, by extracting the most out of written records and descriptions. Five English and two Continental examples appear to be all that have survived; at any rate, up to the present time these are all that are known. The foreign samplers are two undated examples—one German and one Italian—in the collection of the Victoria and Albert Museum and are believed to belong to the early half of the century; both contain patterns taken from books of the period 1523 to 1530.[3] In referring to these samplers, Mr King mentions also the existence of two others, as being the only known examples of the same period.[4] One of them in the collection of Lord Middleton was noted shortly by Lady Marion Alford and illustrated as a small unfinished specimen, which she dated as 'Time, Henry VIII'.[5]

The difficulty of dating an unmarked sampler is great and one which can be met only with a certain amount of inspired guessing and a sound knowledge of

[1] *Titus Andronicus*, Act II, Scene 5.
[2] *A Midsummer Night's Dream*, Act III, Scene 2.
[3] D. King, *Samplers*, p. 4.
[4] 'The earliest dated sampler' by D. King, *Connoisseur*, p. 234, April 1962.
[5] Lady Marion Alford, *Needlework as Art*, pp. 379–380, Fig. 27.

period dress. The fashion of the time has always had a strong influence over the character of embroidery connected with clothing and domestic interests. In addition to the *black* work used so freely on sixteenth-century dress, work with bead ornament and silk and metal thread also was used extensively from the middle of the century. Elizabethan costume was loaded with embroidery in gold, silver and silver-gilt, as well as silk thread, with spangles and jewels added to enhance the richness, and patterns containing all these are pointers to the date of the work. Lace in costume created the need for the *cut* and *drawn* patterns and here it seems there may have been a good deal of rivalry in producing new patterns, as two identical examples are rare, although many are closely similar. Samplers consisting of lace patterns only are more difficult to date, even approximately, than those which contain coloured or white work. One of the earliest of these—in the London Museum—is worked in lace patterns altogether and is quite the most beautiful of its kind [54].[1] Measuring over a yard long and only six inches wide, it is signed but undated and consists of bands and panels of lace patterns, all except two of which are worked in white linen thread. The topmost *band* has a *rose* and 'S' patterns in red silk and gold thread—the second, a heart and a star worked in silver with black silk; the fourth is a panel containing the Royal Arms of Queen Elizabeth I and her initials 'E R', with the signature of the maker SUSAN NEBABRI below. The other *bands* consist of typical lace patterns, some of birds and animals, and in the last three, flower patterns which may have been chosen for their symbolical meaning in association with the name of the Queen—the *lily, iris, acorn, pomegranate* and *fleur-de-lis* as symbols of Virginity, Royalty, Strength and the Promise of Eternity. The general character of this sampler is Elizabethan and although the date is estimated to be late sixteenth century, it may well have been made earlier, possibly inspired by a spirit of patriotism after the accession of the Queen. Royal emblems appear frequently in decorative textiles to commemorate a coronation or other events of a national character.

The small undated sampler illustrated in Sir Leigh Ashton's book, measures six by seven and a half inches only and also shows patterns which are 'closely allied to the work on late sixteenth-century caps, and the raised work is very typical of the fashion of the time'.[2]

The most important addition to sampler history in recent years is that of the only dated sampler known to have survived from the sixteenth century—made by Jane Bostocke in 1598—which came to light in 1960 and is now in the Victoria and Albert Museum [53].[3] It is larger than the small undated sampler but similar

[1] Leigh Ashton, *Samplers*, pp. 4 and 5, Figure 2.   M. E. Jones, *British Samplers*, Figure 1.
[2] Leigh Ashton, *Samplers*, p. 6, Figure 3.
[3] 'The earliest dated sampler' by D. King, *Connoisseur*, April 1962, pp. 234 and 235.

in shape and proportion, being 14 inches wide and sixteen and three-quarter inches long and, naturally, contains a larger collection of patterns and stitches. The patterns consist of *spot* motifs and borders, a collection of all-over and diaper patterns, a capital alphabet, in which the round Q is used and J, U and Z are omitted, and an inscription as well as the signature and date. The top section of the

130 Daisy *pattern. Sixteenth century*

work consists of a plain ground with *spot* patterns of two *dogs*, a chained *bear*, a *hind*, an heraldic *leopard*, a *cowslip* and two trees containing birds—one has an *owl* within the branches and the other supports a *squirrel* and contains a *pelican in piety* within branches of leaves and a fruit, which resemble the formal *pomegranate*. The *pelican* and *tree* pattern, without the *squirrel* and the second *bird*, is similar to one on the early German sampler (p. 148) and the *daisy* pattern which appears beneath the *chained bear* occurs also in the same sampler [*130*], except that two *carnations* are added to the daisies.

The *alphabet*, signature and date follow the *spot* motifs and then a two-line inscription recording the birth of Alice Lee:

ALICE:LEE:WAS:BORNE:THE:23:OF:NOVEMBER:BE
ING:TWESDAY:IN:THE:AFTER:NOONE:1596

Beneath this a row of narrow arcaded border patterns is worked in short sections, showing a greater sense of economy than that in later samplers, in which borders are continued for the width of the sampler. The other patterns which complete the sampler are planned to fit neatly with the minimum of dividing space between them; all are of the repetitive type and enough of each is shown to make the method of follow-on clear. The fruits and flowers are forerunners of those in seventeenth-century patterns, *rose* [*131*], *carnation* [*132*], *strawberry* (with fruit and flower), *honey-suckle*, *acorn* and *leaf* [*134*], the *vine* [*133, 135*] and the *pome-granate* [*25*]. Some other patterns can be distinguished only by the stitch holes left in the linen, from which the silk has not

131 Rose *motif in* Jane Bostocke's *sampler*

disappeared; an *elephant*, carrying a small *castle* on its back, another *bird* on the tree with the *squirrel* and *pelican* and a small *hare*. Some of the stitches in the *bear* are missing also. The larger of the two *dogs*, which is somewhat heraldic in manner—*collared* and *lined*—can be traced to a Flemish sampler pattern of 1826, which Mr King considers to have 'been based on some printed model which

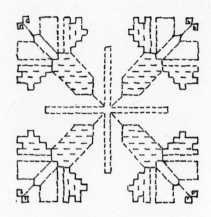

132   Carnation *pattern. 1598*

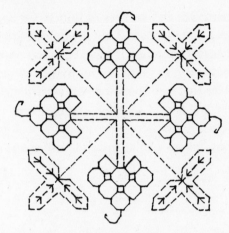

133   Grape *and* vine *leaf pattern. 1598*

134   Acorn *and* oak leaf band *pattern. 1598*

has not yet been traced'[1]; the smaller spotted *dog* was not an aristocratic specimen but nevertheless was important enough to have his name, 'IUNO' embroidered over him and probably was the pet of the child Alice.

The number of stitches and techniques used are equal in importance to the variety of patterns. Silk and metal threads with seed pearls and black beads were used on the linen ground with *tent, back, cross, arrowhead, chain* and *satin* stitches; metal thread was used for *plaited braid* stitch and again with silk for the *pattern couching* or *laid* work, and *coral* and *detached* stitches, *French knots* and *needlepoint* fillings with *eyelet holes* for patterns such as the *strawberries* and *pomegranates*. Part of the surname 'BOSTOCKE' is worked in seed pearls, and black beads are used as the alternate colours in an interlacing pattern on the bottom row. Jane Bostocke was a versatile and gifted worker and ahead of her time according to the present evidence of samplers which remain from the late sixteenth century. From them, it has been thought that inscriptions were not introduced until almost 100 years later; that samplers were not dated until the first quarter of the seventeenth century and were not signed until a few years after that. From the earliest record of 'lynnyn' (1502) as the foundation material and the recommendations for

[1] 'The earliest dated sampler' by D. King, *Connoisseur*, April 1962, p. 234.

'patternes and workes of linnen' (p. 20) at the end of the century, it seems reasonably certain that all sixteenth-century samplers were worked on linen only, but
theories on samplers have been so consistently upset for the last 60 years and more,
that it is unwise to be dogmatic on any aspect but be prepared for anything. It is
clear that any shape or size was made according to the worker's need. The long
narrow *banded* sampler was the most practical for short examples of lace edgings
or motifs, whether in white or coloured thread, but for the aide memoire for
patterns on a solid ground, any shape or size of linen available could be used and

135 Grape *and* vine *leaf all-over pattern.* 1598

this is what was done. The silks in coloured samplers of the sixteenth century
generally are light in tone. The exceptions, including black, are a crimson or
dark ruby colour, and some mid-browns and greens but these are seen also in
paler shades as well as pinks, blues, yellows, cream and buff colours. No doubt they
have mellowed a little in time in the well-preserved examples, but on the whole
the colours have altered very little, when the right side of the work is compared
with the back; this is especially so in the Bostocke sampler, which is in excellent
condition.

CHAPTER EIGHT

The Seventeenth Century

The seventeenth century was the Golden Age of English sampler making. Those considered to be the earliest specimens were unsigned and undated, but approximate dates have been arrived at by comparing the patterns and materials, and to avoid making too optimistic claims, a later rather than earlier period usually has been surmised for each. Styles in embroidery during the last years of the Elizabethan period and the early part of the reign of James I, are almost continuous and certainly no differences mark the end of one century's needlework and the beginning of the next; it is likely too, that a number of samplers begun in the sixteenth century were not completed until a year or so after the beginning of the seventeenth.

The sampler bearing the earliest known date in the 1600s is German, made and

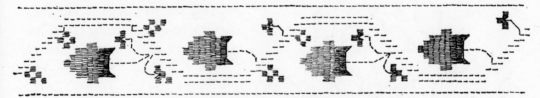

136 *Seventeenth-century* strawberry *band pattern*

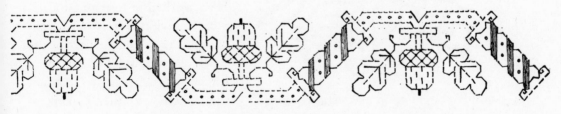

137 Acorn *and* oak leaf band *pattern. Mid-seventeenth century*

138 *Arcaded* honeysuckle band *pattern. Seventeenth century*

signed by 'Lucke Boten' in 1618 and now in the Victoria and Albert Museum[1]; the next two surviving specimens with dates are one signed 'Elizabeth 1629' [56] in the collection of the Fitzwilliam Museum and the other, dated 1630, is the property of the Dorset County Museum in Dorchester; all are well preserved. After 1630, dated samplers became more frequent, until from the last half of the century, it is now almost as unusual to find a *band* type of sampler [95] without a date, as it is to come across a *spot* motif specimen which is signed or dated [97]. So far three only have come to light—the 1630 sampler already mentioned [57], one made by 'Elizabeth Cromwell' which is signed but not dated [62] and another in Dr Goodhart's collection which is both signed and dated 'Elizabeth Branch 1670' [97]. Elizabeth Cromwell's sampler, although really a *spot* motif sampler, does in fact contain a narrow heading above her signature and a short section of border, both in the style of *band* patterns. Joyce Leedes's well packed sampler was signed and dated, after her alphabet had been worked in horizontal *bands* which divide the *spot* patterns composing the major part of the work. It was quite usual for a signed sampler also to contain the initials of the maker in

139 Rose spot *motif. Seventeenth century*

[1] Leigh Ashton *Samplers*, Figure 64. D. King, *Samplers*, Plate 61.

another part of the work, often within a tablet pattern, showing a different method of working or another type of embroidery; Elizabeth Potter initialled hers at the top and signed it at the end [*96*] and Joyce Leedes signed hers and added initials in a *tablet* at the bottom [*98*]. A number of seventeenth-century samplers are initialled, however, and one so marked enabled the probable maker to be identified because her family's coat of arms was among the embroidered patterns[1] (p. 75).

Recorded references to samplers in literature and inventories can be found throughout the century but few descriptions in detail are given. Perhaps the earliest mention comes from *The Crown Garland of Golden Roses* of 1612, reprinted in a collection of *Old Ballads* in 1725 in 'A short and sweet Sonnet made by one of the Maids of Honour, upon the death of *Q. Elizabeth*, which she sewed upon a Sampler, in Red Silk to a new tune or "Phillida Flouts Me"':

> Gone is *Elizabeth*
>   whom we have loved so dear,
> She our kind Mistress was
>   full four and forty year.
> *England* she govern'd well,
>   not to be blamed
> *Flanders* she govern'd well,
>   and *Ireland* famed.
> France she befriended,
>   Spain she had toiled.
> *Papists* rejected,
>   and the *Pope* spoiled.
> To Princes powerful,
>   to the World vertuous,
> To her Foes merciful,
>   To subjects gracious
> Her Soul is in Heaven
>   The World keeps her glory;
> Subjects her good deeds,
>   and so ends my story.[2]

Thomas Milles had no time for sampler making and exhorted young women to:

> Fear God and learne women's huswifery
> Not idle samplers or silken follies.

[1] Leigh Ashton, *Samplers*, pp. 3 and 8, Figure 7.
[2] Quoted, A. Tuer, *The History of the Horn-book*, p. 423.

in his *Treasure of Ancient and Moderne Times* in 1613, in contradiction to the views of William Hawkins (1627) who approved the value of the sampler as a means of learning for the young (p. 112). A brief reference was made by John Milton in *Comus*, written in 1634:

> Coarse complexions
> And cheeks of sorry grain will serve to ply
> The Sampler, and to tear the housewife's wool

Also in 1634 in a 'true and perfect Inventory of all such goods, Cattle, Chattles, as were the Right Honoble Lettice, Countesse of Leicesters . . . taken the vii day of January, 1634' were 'certain samplers divers parcels of curious needlework with much unwroughte silk . . . twoe and twenty papers of sleeve silk, some workinge canvas'.[1] Robert Herrick's poem *The Wounded Heart* from *Hesperides* (1648), contains an observation on the working of a pattern:

> Come bring your sampler, and with art
> Draw in't a wounded heart:
> And dropping here, and there:
> Not that I think that any dart,
> Can make yours bleed a teare
> Or pierce it anywhere;
> Yet do it to this end: that I
> May by
> This secret see
> Though you can make
> That heart to bleed, your's n'er will ake
> for me.

Although patterns in *The needle's Excellency* were taken from Sibmacher's book (p. 22), the verses introducing them were John Taylor's own and add not a little to the records of embroidery in his time. The patterns came, he said:

> From the remotest part of Christendome
> Collected with much paines and industrie
>
> . . . .
>
> Thus are these workes farre fetch'd and dearly bought,
> And consequently good for ladyes thought.

displaying much the same kind of salesmanship as that to which we are expected to succumb to-day. He added to his persuasions on the virtues of the book, with further rhymes cataloguing the patterns:

[1] Quoted, M. Jourdain, *English Secular Embroidery*, p. 178, footnote 3.

140 *Three seventeenth-century* pansy spot *motifs*

> Flowers, Plants and Fishes
> Beasts, Birds, Flyes, and Bees
> Hills, Dales, Plains and Pastures
> Skies, Seas, Rivers, Trees.
> There's nothing near at hand or farthest sought
> But with the needle may be shap'd and wrought.

and listed appropriate stitches for the work:

> For Tent-worke Rais'd-worke, Laid-worke, Frost-worke, Net-worke,
> Most curious Purles, or rare Italian cutworke,
> Fine Ferne-stitch, Finny-stitch, New-stitch and Chain-stitch,
> Braue Bred-stitch, Fisher-stitch, Irish-stitch and Queene-stitch,
> The Spanish-stitch, Rosemary-stitch, and Mowse-stitch,

The smarting Whip-stitch, Back-stitch and the Crosse-stitch,
All these are good and we must allow
And these are everywhere in practise now.

The names of several stitches have not changed but regrettably many others are forgotten in to-day's embroidery and there seems no way of recognising them in any of the multitude of names now used, as stitches which appear similar on the front of the work, frequently have acquired different names to identify them with different methods of working, which can be seen on the back only.

Linen continued to be the foundation on which the patterns were embroidered throughout the century, some of it bleached, some unbleached and occasional examples were yellowed in colour, at a time when it was fashionable for collars, cuffs and handkerchiefs to be this colour, so no doubt it was for this reason that samplers took on the same tint, from about the 1620s.

The fact that the loom-width was used as the length measurement of a number of samplers, may have accounted for the comparatively uniform length of a large number of those containing the *band* type of patterns; from 20 to 24 inches seems to have been an average and popular length but more industrious workers needed from 30 to 36 inches and instances of even longer measurements of 40 and 43 inches are known, but these are exceptional.[1]

Irrespective of the length, widths ranged from six and a half inches to 12 inches, which allowed sufficient space for several repeats of a *band* pattern of average size and at least one example of a larger pattern [56]. As usual there are exceptions, some samplers being more nearly square, as in the *cut* work example illustrated [60] and others exist which are smaller. Samplers of *spot* motifs often— but by no means always—are wider on average and many of these probably are professionally drawn specimens [59], with less need for economy than in the individual samplers kept in the workbox and added to when necessary [64], some of which show great ingenuity in the use of available space [98].

Types of thread used throughout the century were linen, silk and some metal according to the kind of embroidery. Linen, whether white or natural, was used for the *cut* and *drawn* work, *needlepoint* lace stitches and the flat stitches in *white work*; coloured silks for all other embroidery with the addition from time to time, of silver or silver-gilt thread, spangles

141 *Diaper pattern with stylised* rose *motif and inter-lacing border worked in metal thread. Seventeenth century*

---

[1] *English Secular Embroidery*, p. 184. D. King, *Samplers*, Plates 10 and 26.

and beads. Metal thread is found in *spot* motifs especially, *flower* and *fruit* stems often are worked in *plaited braid* and similar stitches, also the *pyramids* and many of the interlacing patterns [53, 57, 58, 59, 64, 65, 97, 141, 148].

Band samplers contained a great variety of types of embroidery and the majority included *cut* work, *drawn* work, *white* work, *needlepoint* lace and coloured embroidery in silk but some examples were devoted to one type only, especially those worked with linen thread, although most of those composed of *cut* and *drawn* work patterns, included also some *needlepoint* stitches [54, 55, 60, 61, 63]. There is no doubt that the demand for lace-edged ruffs, caps and so on kept alive the interest in lace patterns on samplers, but however great the worker's pride in achievement the *cut* work and fine *needlepoint* fillings must have been somewhat tedious work to perform, especially to the young, and the prospect of making sufficient to be used on a ruff must have been daunting to the faint hearted. Lace fashions showed little change during King James's reign and the sin of idleness certainly must have been 'banished from the land' if each ruff worn had been made in the wearer's household, and although not all were as large or as elaborate as those seen at Court, items from various household inventories and wardrobe accounts probably give as fair an idea as any, of the number of yards of lace needed for some pleated ruffs. An account in September 1603, contains 'A memorandum of that Misteris Jane Drumonde her recyte from Ester Littelye, the furnishinge of her Majesties Linen Cloth' with the following items among others:

> It. one piece of fine lawin to be a ruffe, 5l.
> Item, for 18 yeardes of fine lace to shewe
>   the ruffe, at 6s the yarde, 5l. 15s. 4d.[1]

(It is to be hoped that this rather odd accountancy went undetected.) Other references mention 25 yards being needed for a ruff, and 150 yards for '6 extraordinary ruffs' on another occasion, but these were out of the ordinary requirements and produced by professional lace makers, not necessarily the amount in ruffs for which home-made sampler patterns were recorded; most family portraits of the time show less elaborate examples as being more common. Not all ruffs were edged with fine lace and much was imported from the Continent, 'ruffs and cuffs of Flanders lace' being in great demand, as well as English *bone* lace, for which patterns no samplers exist. Smaller articles of clothing, such as cuffs, caps for day and night wear, handkerchiefs, cravats and fans all worn by men as well as women, seem more likely to have been popular with the family embroiderer and continued after the pleated *ruff* and *cuff* went out with the accession of King Charles I. After 1625 deep collars or 'falling bands' of lace took their place and

---

[1] Quoted, Mrs Bury Palliser, *The History of Lace*, p. 285, footnote 31.

142 Carnation *border patterns showing* painted lady *and* speckled *varieties.*
Seventeenth and eighteenth centuries

every conceivable adornment to dress was made of lace, a fashion which lasted almost until the end of the century; even during the Commonwealth when the wearing of lace was frowned upon (in theory at any rate) lace patterns continued to appear in samplers. With the accession of William III imports of Flanders lace increased and fine bone lace was more in demand, so gradually the white sampler work of *cut* and *drawn* lace patterns declined, although *needlepoint* lace flourished with *hollie point* for some years after the end of the seventeenth century.

Coloured patterns in *band* samplers consisted of geometric and formal floral border patterns [*136–8, 154, 155*] which, after the middle of the century generally were worked in brighter, richer and more varied silks, and in stitches such as *tent* or *satin* stitch, to produce a solid and colourful effect not known in the outline patterns of some earlier samplers, although both kinds continued for many years, often in the same work. Patterns which basically were very much alike, contained a number of individual interpretations, especially in the flower patterns. Botanical and garden varieties with peculiarities of form or colour seem to have been the inspiration behind *roses* worked with *petals* of detached *buttonhole stitches* and worked in double layers to give the effect of a double flower—a comparatively new fashion in garden roses at the time [*99*]. The *Painted Lady* carnation was highly favoured among professional flower growers and its unique colouring with the under side of the petals white and the upper side red, appeared in carnation patterns showing just such characteristics; the 'flaked' and 'speckled' varieties

143 Pansy *motif used in* band *and* spot *motif samplers of the seventeenth century*

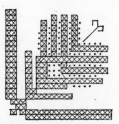

144 *Stylised* carnation *motif for a corner.* *Seventeenth century*

also were represented and were shown in *band* and *spot* patterns, usually worked in bright or dark red, and over stitched with short stitches in white silk [*142*]. Groups of flowers were shown in the arcaded patterns, often with one large centre *flower* and smaller sprays of different flowers and leaves branching from a main stem; the *pansy* was especially popular for this kind of motif [*143*]. Stylised flower shapes were used for corner patterns also [*144*].

Although stump work was universally a popular pastime of the century, it does not appear to have invaded samplers in England and examples of detached or raised work on *pavilion, flower, figures* and other small motifs, which are characteristic of patterns done from the reign of Charles I, seem to be as far as the sampler maker would allow herself to go. As well as the slight padding put in to raise the *boxer* figures, occasional examples are found in border motifs [*99*], but the sampler did not lend itself to anything which prevented folding or rolling and this may have been a practical reason for the omission of any patterns in *stump* work. White work was done only in *band* patterns consisting of wide and

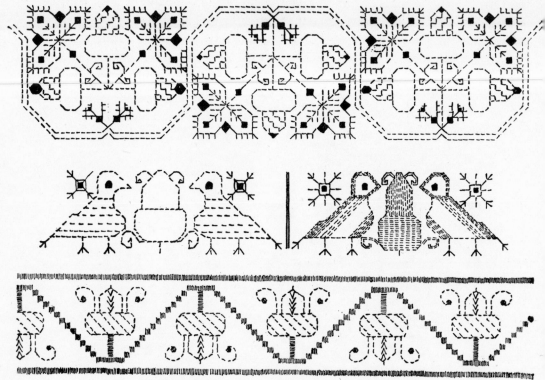

145 *Stiffly formal* acorn band *patterns. Seventeenth century*

146 Acorns *in a double border pattern. Seventeenth century*

narrow borders in which the most characteristic stitch was *satin* worked in white linen thread; *drawn* work, *buttonhole*, *eyelet* and *hem* stitches are commonly found with it and the patterns are predominantly geometric, with stiffly formal *flower* motifs and *acorn* border patterns which are almost inseparable from white work samplers [*164*]. An unusual addition to one example is that of royal blue beads in the *drawn* work motifs of the illustrated sampler [*95*].

Until comparatively recent years *spot* motif samplers were thought to be a rare and exceptional type of early work, as few examples only were known in private and Museum collections, but Dr Douglas Goodhart's interest in this type of seventeenth-century samplers has resulted in his collection, which continues to grow, adding to the know-ledge already acquired about them. The type certainly is the most lively and decorative and contains motifs which may be divided into two kinds; the 'sundry sorts of spots as *Flowers*, *Birds*, and *Fishes* etc.', as described by Richard Shorleyker in '*A schole-house, for the needle*', were distinct from the smaller heraldic and formal devices which were included in the *diaper* and *all-over* patterns [*11, 13, 19, 21, 23, 26, 141, 147, 148*]. It has been thought

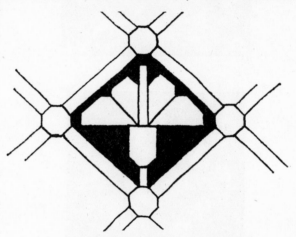

147 Carnation *motif in a diaper pattern.*
Seventeenth century

that the *spot* motif sampler was the earliest type; Sir Leigh Ashton considered it 'possible that in this form a Tudor type is repeated' and it may well be that an authentic example of that period will yet be found to bear out this opinion.[1]

A characteristic of the *flower*, *fruit* and *animal* motifs was the attempt to represent them in their natural colouring and this included shading of colour in the achievement of the desired effect, a feature not found in formal *band* patterns. The small *flower*, *fruit* and other motifs of the *all-over* patterns generally were worked in paler or brighter colours than the ground—often of a rich dark green—a type of pattern which calls to mind the words of Sir Francis Bacon: 'Wee see in Needle-workes, and Imbroideries, It is more pleasing, to have a Lively Worke upon a Sad and Solemne Ground; than to have a Dark and Melancholy worke upon a Lightsome Ground: Judge therefore of the Pleasure of the Heart, by the

[1] Leigh Ashton, *Samplers*, p. 4.

Pleasure of the Eye.'[1] Although these words were published finally in 1625 they were written in 1597 and were therefore observations on embroidery of Queen Elizabeth's time which could well apply to many of the motifs on samplers ascribed to the seventeenth century [148].

148 *'Lively worke upon a Sad and Solemne Ground.'*

According to present evidence, patterns in outline only or with small amounts of solid stitchery were uncommon in *spot* samplers as compared with the numbers composed almost entirely of the heavier type of work. An occasional *spot* motif in outline is found among the other kind of patterns [149][2] and in some *band* samplers a section at the beginning or end was devoted to a few small *spots* of heraldic *beasts, flowers* and so on.[3] *Elizabeth Cromwell's* work is the only one of its kind so far, which reasonably can be said to belong to the middle of the century, although its date cannot be fixed. It is known that the sampler was made by a member of Oliver Cromwell's family and has remained with her descendants

[1] Francis Bacon, *Essays.* 'Of Adversitie.' Essay V, p. 17.
[2] Leigh Ashton, *Samplers,* Figure 16. Now in the Fitzwilliam Museum.
[3] M. B. Huish, *Samplers and Tapestry Embroideries,* Plate V.   D. King, *Samplers,* Plate 12 and 13.

since the time it was made, but no records have been discovered as yet, to show as to which of the Elizabeth Cromwells it belonged. Oliver Cromwell's mother was an Elizabeth, a widow when she married Robert Cromwell in the late sixteenth century; his wife was Elizabeth, a young woman of 22 when they married in 1620: his daughter born in 1629, also was Elizabeth and his daughter-in-law Elizabeth, married to Henry Cromwell in 1653, was the great, great grandmother of Anne Cromwell who married a John Field in 1733, and whose direct descendant is the present owner of the sampler. Of these Elizabeths, the first named is unlikely to have made it; Oliver's wife, described as 'a careful mortal, who struggled hard with honours to which she had not been born and tried to forget the great lady in the prudent housewife',[1] probably had no time for any but essential needlework during the years from 1621 in which her eight children were born, but their upbringing would not have been neglected and her daughter's education in needlework almost certainly would have included making a sampler. Assuming that the child made it

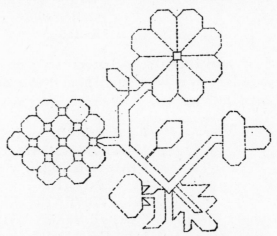

149   Flower *and* fruit spot *motif in outline only.*
Seventeenth century

at about the age of eight, it would have been possible for her to have made the sampler in question [62]; the choice of some motifs speak of a youthful taste— the *fish* swimming in the *water*, below a sailing *swan*, the families of four of their young accompanying the *hare* or *rabbit* and the *goose*, do not suggest an entirely adult interest but until some reasonable proof is found, we can speculate only as to which is the right Elizabeth. The colours are those of the first half of the century; greens, pale yellow or cream, and browns, a little blue and some red, black and dark purple detail to a few motifs; the thread used is silk with no metal at all.

The advent of alphabets, numerals, signatures and dates among the patterns of schoolroom samplers, was followed almost inevitably, by other information about the worker—her age, her aspirations and so on and by inscriptions containing pious or improving sentiments. Martha Salter's work contained her name and the date 1651, and possibly is the earliest example of this kind of inscription:

[1] John Buchan, *Oliver Cromwell*, p. 511.

MARTHA SALTeR
THe FeARe OF GOd IS AN eXCel
LeNT GIFT[1]

Mr Huish illustrated Mary Hall's sampler and quoted her inscription with her age, which up to then had not been thought to be of interest:

MaRy
HaLL IS My NaMe AnD
WHen I WaS THIRTeen
yeeRS OF AGE I ENDED THIS
IN 1662.[2]

Four years later Rachel Loader was more ambitious than either of these and recorded part of her inscription in rhyme, of which the second line is worked in *eyelet* stitch and the remainder in *satin* stitch:

I AM A MAID BVT YOUNG MY SKILL
IS YeT BVT SMALL BVT GOD
I HOP WILL BLeS Me SO I MAY LIVe
TO MeND THIS ALL RACHEL LOADeR
WROVGHT THIS SAMPLeR BeING
TWeLVE YEARS OVLD THE TENTH
DAY DeSeMBeR 1666 HL[3]

A possible reference to her work as a 'sam' was made by Ann Wattel in 1670 at the end of her work: 'Ann Wattel is my name, with my neddle and thred I ded this sam and if it hath en(ded) better I wold b–' but unhappily her inscription never did end, better or otherwise, so it will never be known what she 'wold b'. and perhaps her spelling was at fault and she meant to say 'I ded this same'.[4] Inscriptions such as the tribute paid by Margreet Lucus to her father in 1681 (p. 119), and those with acknowledgement to the teacher, became more popular with the years, and by the end of the century were common to most samplers, especially those extolling the moral virtues and the advantages of learning. The verse already given as being associated with Judeth Hayl's teaching (p. 120) is recorded first as having been used by Judith King on 'Oct. 2. 1684'[5] and two years later by Elizabeth Creasey in 1686 with an additional couplet:

[1] D. King, *Samplers*, Plate 14.
[2] M. B. Huish, *Samplers and Tapestry Embroideries*, Plate VIII.
[3] In the Collection of the Fitzwilliam Museum. Reference T. 39–1928.
[4] M. B. Huish, *Samplers and Tapestry Embroideries*, p. 21.
[5] In the Collection of the City Art Gallery, Bristol.

LooK WeLL tO that thoV taKeSt IN H
HaNd ItS Better WOrth TheN hoUse
Or LaNd WheN LaNd Is GONe aNd M
MoNeY IS SPeNt TheN LearN
INg IS MOSt EXCeLeNT
Let Vertue Be Thy Guide and it will kee
p the out of pride Elizabeth Creasey.
Her work Done in the year 1686.

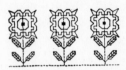  

150 *Two seventeenth-century and one eighteenth-century* rose *border patterns typical of the transition period*

Half the rhyme is worked in narrow *bands* of *cross* stitch alternating with floral *band* patterns which compose the top section of the sampler in colour, the remaining words are embroidered in white *satin* stitch and the rest of the patterns are of *white* work with some *cut* and *drawn* motifs, the whole being embroidered on yellow linen.[1]

Shortly after this work was done, Mary Minshull used the same verse on her sampler but her chief inscription was an account of an earthquake:

THERE WAS AN EARTHQUAKE
ON THE 8 OF SEPTEMBER 1692
IN THE CITY OF LONDON
BUT NO HURT THO IT
CAUSED MOST PART
OF ENGLAND TO
TREMBLE[2]

and a year later another account of contemporary history was used for the sampler of Martha Wright:

The Prince of Orang landed in the West of England on the 5th day of November 1688 and on the 11th day of April 1689 was crowned King of England, and in the year 1692 the French came to invade England and a fleet of ships sent by King William, drove them from the English seas, and took, sunk, and burned twenty-one of their ships.   Martha Wright, March 26th 1693.[3]

[1] M. B. Huish, *Samplers and Tapestry Embroideries*, Plate XII.
[2] *ibid.*, Figure 24, p. 71.
[3] *ibid.*, p. 71.

The most noticeable development in sampler making during the seventeenth century was the gradual change in style and quality of the needlework; lace patterns, metal thread and beads had all but vanished, *spot* patterns had been reduced to a few inches allowed to them in *band* samplers and outline stitches were giving way to those which produced a smoother, more solid surface to the embroidery. Also the early work with all its diversity of stitches, patterns and threads, was more honest in purpose and less pretentious in all respects, than the repetitive sameness which was the keynote of much of the work after the middle of the century. The early *spot* motifs had an air of warmth and charm due to being the spontaneous recordings of ideas and patterns—whether inspired ones or failures—which were kept in the secret seclusion of the workbox. Even those which might be called the second-earlies, when the trend was towards more orderly arrangements of the patterns, experimental essays in colour and stitches, often and intentionally half finished, gave them a more individual character than the neat, closely worked band patterns, one following the other without intervening spaces. These rarely were left uncompleted, and suggest show pieces which were considered more worthy of critical inspection and the light of day, without the loss of prestige which might attach to out-of-sight working specimens. The development of school work undoubtedly accounted for the growth in numbers of *band* samplers (p. 117) but it would be incorrect to take it for granted that all made in the last part of the century were specimens by the teacher or the pupil and no longer used as pattern records. A number of surviving examples show adult experience and there is written evidence that the first purpose of the sampler still was considered of importance in Thomas Brookes's *Paradise Opened* of 1675, in which he notes that 'Such as begin to work with the needle look much on their sampler and pattern: It is so in learning to write and indeed in learning to live also'.

CHAPTER NINE

The Eighteenth Century

Within the first quarter of the new century the character of the sampler showed more changes than it had done in the hundred years from 1600. Traces of patterns which had become part of the conventional repertory of that time can be seen, although at lengthening intervals, throughout the eighteenth century, especially *carnation* and *honeysuckle* motifs in the reversed patterns on *band* samplers, but other floral patterns with brighter colours and of a freehand type in which each leaf and flower motif was different, began to take the place of the repetitive patterns [*101, 119, 123, 150–3, 155*]. This difference, which affected all embroidery of the period, largely was due to the influence of the imported Indian printed cottons in which trailing flower and leaf patterns were the chief characteristics and their rapid growth in popularity is shown by their appearance in samplers made before the end of Queen Anne's reign. The methods of working many of the patterns included wider spacing with less need for economy in material, curving instead of angular lines and real signs of a change of purpose from the pattern record to an example of decorative needlework. It was kept no longer in the workbox

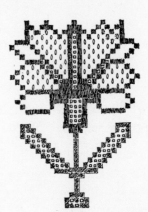

151 Carnation *motif used in* band *patterns. Seventeenth century*

but considered worthy of display in a frame as a picture; gradually the shape changed also to more conventional proportions for this purpose, until most samplers were almost square; the motifs were arranged symmetrically and surrounded by a border of floral or geometrical patterns.

Alphabets were included in nearly every sampler and it was at the beginning of the century, in 1711, that John Brightland's *Grammar of the English Tongue*

152   *Eighteenth-century* carnation *motifs, resembling those of the seventeenth century*

included the model 'Sampler Alphabet' clearly to satisfy the demands of school-room education (p. 110); sampler numerals matched the letters [*109*] and the inscriptions became longer and more elaborate, with moral precepts, prayers, verses from the Bible and hymns accompanying the now habitual names and dates. In 1700 Susanna Ingram worked a *band* sampler in which the alphabet and a rhyme took up nearly half of her work:

> Dear ChILd DeLaY NO TIMe
> BUt WIth ALL Speed AmeND
> The LONger thOU DOSt LIVe
> The Nearer TO ThY END
> YeSterdaY IS GONe TO MorrOW
> IS None OF ThiNe ThIS DaY
> The LIFe TO VertUOUS ACts
> INCLINE.[1]

which encouraging view of the future typifies many similar rhymes on contemporary samplers. By the 1720s the *Lord's Prayer*, the *Creed*, the *Ten Commandments*, or *The Sum of the Ten Commandments* took up the centre of many samplers, sometimes surrounded by a floral border[2] and sometimes enclosed in a *tablet* which either was square in shape or rectangular, or within *columns* as shown in Dr Lucas's sampler [*103*]. The Ten Commandments usually appear in verse form, although once at least they are quoted from the twentieth chapter of the *Book of Exodus*[3] but the words from Dr Isaac Watts's *Divine Songs* were more suited to the size of the sampler and the worker:

153   *Eighteenth-century* honeysuckle *motif*

[1] Leigh Ashton, *Samplers*, Figure 31. Now in the collection of the Fitzwilliam Museum.
[2] D. King, *Samplers*, Plate 29.
[3] M. B. Huish, *Samplers and Tapestry Embroideries*, Plate XVII.

1. Thou shalt have no more Gods but me.
2. Before no idol bow thy knee.
3. Take not the Name of God in vain:
4. Nor dare the Sabbath-day profane.
5. Give both thy parents honour due.
6. Take heed that thou no murder do.
7. Abstain from words and deeds unclean.
8. Nor steal, though thou art poor and mean.
9. Nor make a wilful lie, nor love it.
10. What is thy neighbour's dare not covet.

Other improving verses were taken from the same source.

In the preface to *Divine and Moral Songs for Children*, first published in 1720, the key is provided to the popularity of the many hundreds of this kind of inscription which appeared throughout the eighteenth century. Dr Watts addressed it 'TO ALL THAT ARE CONCERNED IN THE EDUCATION OF CHILDREN', wherein they are admonished with 'the awful and important charge that is committed to you . . . and therefore whatever may conduce to give the minds of children a relish for virtue and religion . . . aught to be proposed to you', which proposition amounted to the necessity for 'learning truths and duties' in verse, as a means of ensuring that 'what is learned in verse is longer retained in memory and sooner recollected'. Dr Watts added also: 'This will be a constant furniture for the minds of children that they may have something to think upon when alone and sing over to themselves. . . . Thus they will not be forced to seek relief for an emptiness of mind out of the loose and dangerous sonnets of the age.' The principle of learning in verse was adopted wholeheartedly by the schoolmistress in teaching needlework and with so much ready-made verse from which to choose, there was also the thought no doubt, that the embroidered reminder on the wall might well be more constant than memory, however well learned the lesson. Although Dr Watts's verses seem to have been the most popular, he was the first of three eminent eighteenth-century hymn writers who flooded religious teaching with their work, and with that of Philip Doddridge and John Wesley following Isaac Watts, it was inevitable that the influence of Methodism should be felt in all aspects of school work to which it could be applied.

The constant stress laid on the unimportance of the transitory earthly state and the imminence of death on either hand, even in the nursery, came out in the work of the very young, whose samplers include the most dire and gloomy of the forecasts, by which they must have been frightened to death, or so surrounded by the thought of it, that they accepted the words of their inscriptions without comprehension. Even in the days when a high rate of infant mortality was a matter of

154   Honeysuckle *border. Eighteenth century*

course, it is hardly possible to believe that Charlotte Robertson could have completed her verse, worked in black silk thread on coarse linen, if she had realised its meaning:

> The soul by blackning defiled
> can never enter Heaven
> Till god and it be reconciled
> And all its sins forgive.
> Charlotte Robertson. Aged Six.
> Time Flies. Death Approaches.

Nor the child of seven years whose anonymous work contained a similar thought:

> And now my soul another year
> Of thy short life is past
> I cannot long continue here
> And this may be my last.[1]

Others were concerned that their work should be preserved and with it, the memory of the maker, and the thought in the lines of Ann French in 1766 was common in samplers until well into the nineteenth century:

> This handy work my friends may have
> When I am dead and laid in grav.[2]

155   *Reversed* carnation *and* honeysuckle *border. Typical of the eighteenth century*

[1] M. B. Huish, *Samplers and Tapestry Embroideries*, p. 53.
[2] *ibid.*, p. 56.

The same idea is included in a longer inscription of 1736, of which the first half appears frequently as a single verse:

> When this you see remember me
> And bear me in your mind;
> And be not like the weathercock
> That turn att evry wind.
> When I am dead and laid in grav
> And all my bones are rotten,
> By this may I remembered be
> When I should be forgotten.[1]

Some took a gentler view, by comparing life's span with that of a flower; such words as 'decay' seem to have been brought in to suit the rhyme rather than to emphasise the fate of the worker and Mary Wakeling's sampler of 1742[2] contained an arcaded *band* of reversed *flower* patterns between the *alphabets* and inscription, as well as a surrounding border of *carnations* and *honeysuckle*, thus making the threat within seem less potent:

Go dainty flowers go swiftly to decay, poor wretched Life's short portion flies away we eat, we drink, we sleep; but lo, anon, old age steals upon us never thought upon.

Elizabeth Raymond achieved the ripe old age of eight in 1789 and expected a wintry end to her life:

> Lord give me wisdom to direct my ways
> I beg not riches nor yet length of days
> My life is a flower, the time it hath to last
> Is mixed with frost and shook with every blast.[3]

But many children were drawn to choose Song III of Dr Watts's *Moral Songs* entitled 'The Rose' and seemed to find more comforting thoughts in its verse:

> Then I'll not be proud of my youth or my beauty
> Since both of them wither and fade;
> But gain a good name by doing my duty:
> This will scent like a rose when I'm dead.

Historical records occur from time to time during the eighteenth century. Queen Anne is a recognisable *figure* pattern in the early years without the need for the initials 'A R' embroidered beside the *figure* [*101*] and inscriptions referring

---

[1] *ibid.*, p. 55.
[2] D. King, *Samplers*, Plate 33.
[3] M. B. Huish, *Samplers and Tapestry Embroideries*, p. 54.

to or mentioning, the first Kings of the House of Hanover are not uncommon. The association with King George I was incidental to the finishing of one sampler:

> Elizabeth Humphry her Sampler
> October the 29th 1714 in the
> first year of the reign of
> King George the first. whom
> God preserve.

Elizabeth Dick towards the end of his reign had a more rousing sense of patriotism with:

> God bless King George
> Preserve the Crown
> Defend the Church
> Cast rebells down.
> aged 10 years. Elizabeth Dick, 1726.

But Mary French let down the side once more and referred to King George II in the briefest manner possible:

> Mary
> French end
> ed this work
> in the tenth ye
> ar of her age o
> ne thousand sev
> en hundred for
> ty one in the f
> ourteenth
> year of t
> he RKG2.

A commemorative inscription of an historical occasion, was enclosed in an oval *leaf* garland on an oval sampler—a shape which had become popular especially for *map* samplers towards the end of the century, made by Caroline Lepel Fuller and dated 1789. The occasion was the state entry into Dublin of the fourth Earl of Bristol, Bishop of Derry at the time when he hoped to be elected President:

> Hibernes Sons let this Auspicious day
> To Bristol's Earl your grateful tribute pay
> Let Ireland's records consecrate his name
> Proclaim his worth Immortalise his name
> Whose generous sould aspires to make you free
> Prevent your chains and give you Liberty.[1]

[1] In the collection of the Fitzwilliam Museum.

Caroline Fuller was a great-grand-daughter of the first Earl of Bristol, of whom the fourth Earl was a first cousin, and she was ten or eleven when she made the sampler; she died unmarried on the first of April in 1867 and was buried at Wargrave, where her age is recorded as being 88 on the brass mural in the church, but given as 89 on the gravestone.

The growing number of inscriptions, alphabets and numerals on a sampler so reduced the space available for other patterns that the number and variety of

156 *Eighteenth-century* heart *patterns, in* cross, eyelet *and* satin *stitches*

stitches used decreased also. For the first 50 years *eyelet* and *satin* stitches were the most popular for letters, whether in alphabets or inscriptions, but from 1750 onwards *cross* stitch took their place, with a few exceptions, as when one alphabet of two in a sampler was, perhaps, worked in *eyelet* (the other inevitably in cross stitch), or in *map* samplers which contained place names, a scale of miles, and so on, where the letters were worked in *back, stem* or *double running* stitches. Other more adventurous patterns and stitches continued to be used in work which had shorter or no inscriptions, of which Dr Lucas's sampler by Ann Day is one example [123]. And the reversed *flower* patterns introduced among the scattered but orderly assortment of her motifs must be one of the last traces of the arcaded *band* patterns which had been popular for about 200 years; the *flower pot* pattern is much in evidence and two *fruit bowl* motifs also are shown. Realistic *tree* patterns were popular during the end period of the eighteenth century, of which there is no lack in this sampler and these, as well as the formal motifs, *animals, birds, hearts, flowers* and the *strawberry* border, typified many hundreds of others belonging to work of the period [154–60]. The maker cannot be accused of a wholly conventional attitude in the choice and arrangements of some other patterns, which give an air of enjoyment to the work rather than that of drudgery which seems to cling to other samplers at times.

Possibly because of the insistence on moral versifying ruling at the time, few

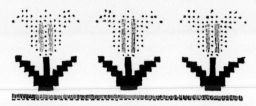

157　*Eighteenth-century tulip border pattern*

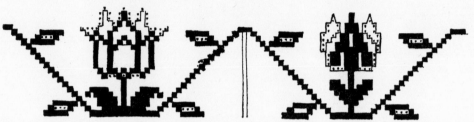

158　*Two variants of a late eighteenth-century tulip arcaded border pattern*

inscriptions of the eighteenth century have needlework as a subject and those which do, reflect a feeling of irksome duty rather than pleasure:

> In this work
> you may plainly see
> what care my parents
> take of me.

appears so many times that it is rather like a chorus which is repeated after each verse in a popular song. A sampler verse near the middle of the century shows an appreciation of some virtue in sewing by Mary Miller in 'her work finished February 6th 1735':

> No surplice white the priest could wear
> Bandless the bishop must appear
> The King without a shirt would be
> Did not the needle help all three.

but Eleanor Speed concluded her sampler in 1734 with 'Be not weary in well doing', after having worked the *Ten Commandments*, three moral precepts, and a verse which it is to be hoped she did not deserve:

> Return the Kindnesses you receive
> As far as your Ability gives leave
> Nothing is more unmannerly and rude
> Than that vile temper of ingratitude.[1]

[1] D. King, *Samplers*, Plate 31.

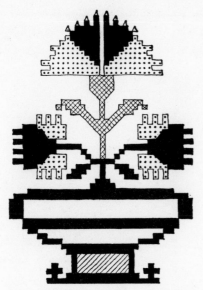

159   Carnation *flower pot pattern.*
Eighteenth century

160   *Late eighteenth-century* tulip *flower pot*

After all this well-doing it is not inconceivable that she was weary of her sampler. Mary Cole worked another verse in 1759:

> Better far for me
> Than all the Sempster's art
> That God's commandments be
> Embroidered on my heart.

and the following was 'wrought by Frances Purdy. 1761':

> Young ladies fair whose virtuous minds incline
> To all that's Curious, innocent and fine
> With admiration in your works we read
> The various textures on the twining thread
> Then let your fingers whose unrival'd skill
> Exalts the needle, grace the noble Quill.[1]

Perhaps Dr Johnson reflected the reluctance of some young people at this time when he wrote: 'Our girls forsake their samplers to teach Kingdoms wisdom.'[2]

Several different kinds of samplers which evolved during the eighteenth century have already been mentioned, the *puzzles, acrostics, arithmetical charts, map*

[1] M. B. Huish, *Samplers and Tapestry Embroideries*, Title page.
[2] In 'The Idler', *Weekly Gazette or Universal Chronicle*, 1758–1760.

and *darning* samplers were all popular, but except for the *maps* and the *darning* patterns, none had a long period in favour. Another kind of sampler of which a number of examples have survived and which show a higher degree of technical

161 Heart *pattern worked in* hollie point

162 Crown *worked in* hollie point

163 Acorn *motif with a* heart *border in* hollie point

skill than most, was the comparatively small linen sampler which appeared first during the 1720s containing motifs in *hollie* or *holy point*, the *point lace* stitch used in Church work of the religious houses of the Middle Ages, whence the name was derived; it was known also as nun's work. The patterns were made by the spaces left in the close fine stitching which formed the ground [*102, 161, 162, 163*] and the work was used especially for decoration in baby clothes, such as caps, christening clothes, carrying cloths, mittens and so on. It was worked always on linen with a linen thread and the motifs alternated with small panels of *cut* work and *band* patterns of *white work*, many of them running from edge to edge of the sampler which was finished with simple *buttonhole* stitch, but some specimens are surrounded with borders of *white work*, such as the *acorn* or geometrical repetitive patterns, as shown in samplers from the collections of the Museum of

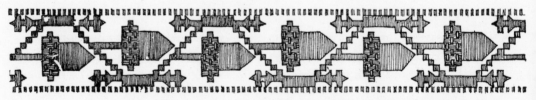

164 Acorn *border in* white work, *typical of those in* hollie point *samplers*

Antiquities of Scotland in Edinburgh [*102*], signed and dated 'Jenny Grant 1725' and the Fitzwilliam Museum, Cambridge [*105*], signed 'S B' and dated 1737. Jenny Grant was the daughter of an eighteenth-century Scottish Judge, Lord Elches.

Most of the *map* samplers undoubtedly were school work, so also were the simple *pattern darning* samplers, but some of the elaborate floral patterns in this stitch must have been the work of adults as the quality was above the schoolroom average of the time in which they were made. This period probably began about 1770, but not a great number of *darning* samplers are dated and of those which are, none as early as 1770 has been identified so far. Details in *darning* stitch frequently were added to sixteenth- and seventeenth-century samplers, but in them the stitches were more widely spaced than in the work of the eighteenth century and were used for *filling* and *veining* patterns in leaf, flower and other motifs seen in the work of those periods [*165*]. The

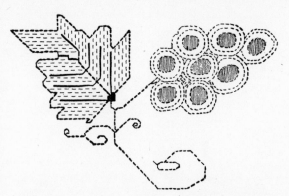

165 Grape *and* vine leaf *motif showing the use of darning stitches for* veining. *Seventeenth century*

simple darns in a **+** shape and worked in two colours [*124*] (and p. 195) rarely contain any other stitch except where initials, signatures or dates occur and then *cross* stitch is used for the letters and numerals only, but in the floral patterns *darning* is supplemented with *stem* and *chain* stitches used to outline the *leaves* and *flowers* and so on, and to work the flowing *stems*; *French knots* are used also, often to add detail such as *flower stamens*, and of course, *cross* stitch for letters when they occur, but inscriptions, verses and the like are not included with *pattern darning*. Some of the few signed and dated specimens have been recorded; Elizabeth Trollope signed a slightly lop-sided *floral* pattern in 1790 when she was eleven[1] and in 1777 E. Cousens signed and dated her 'Darning peice':

E Cousens

27

1777

[1] D. King, *Samplers*, Plate 44.
[2] *ibid.*, Plate 45.

An initialled and dated specimen, with 'M C 1778' worked with darning into one of the *cross* darns, and of singular excellence,[1] with another made by Sarah Everitt in 1777,[2] were unlikely to have been the work of very young children however gifted and 'C Taylor' [*119*] probably was young but out of the schoolroom;

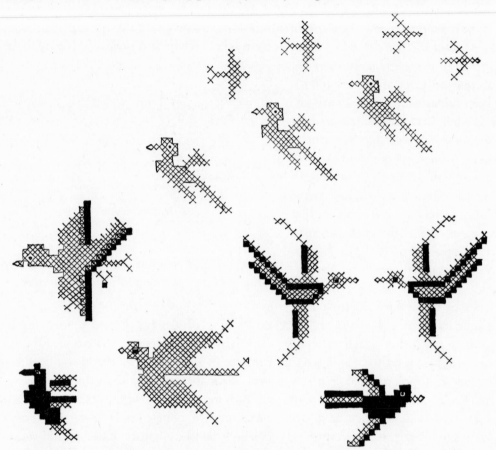

166   *Some* bird *patterns found in matching pairs. Eighteenth and nineteenth centuries*

slightly irregular shapes, such as the *butterflies*, do not suggest adult work but the sampler as a whole shows a firm competence which is not at all juvenile.

After the middle of the century *band* patterns virtually had disappeared and samplers which contained them were exceptional among the growing numbers of those consisting of small scattered patterns which covered the ground, not as in the seventeenth-century *spot* motif samplers, but in balanced, orderly arrangements, with the patterns often in matching pairs. Elizabeth Cridland's sampler,

[1] M. B. Huish, *Samplers and Tapestry Embroideries*, Plate LVI.
[2] Leigh Ashton, *Samplers*, Figure 49.

signed and dated 1752, shows this very well [118]; the *Lord's Prayer* worked within a *tablet* pattern supported by four flying angels headed the work and beneath it another inscription:

The   hand
of the diligent shall
bear rule but the slothfull
shall be under Tribute.

Pairs of *flower pot*, *fruit basket* and *tree* patterns, both formal and naturalistic were fitted in neatly; *bird* patterns followed the heraldic tradition but more imagination than heraldry is evident in several *stags* [169]; single *strawberries* appear with regularity among the motifs [167]. The *landscape* spanning the bottom of the sampler shows a type of pictorial pattern of which this must have been an early example of the hundreds to be found in later work. *Landscapes*, small scenes with a *house*, *human* and *animal* figures and patterns of pictorial character rapidly became popular[1] and were introduced into samplers in whatever way the worker's fancy led her; a central position was popular and some took up a considerable amount of space on the sampler.

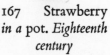

167   Strawberry *in a* pot. *Eighteenth century*

With the *landscapes* and *houses*, *figure* patterns became more common, although not as many representing biblical characters, as there had been in the seventeenth-century work. Many illustrate *family* figures, such as the Philips family (p. 70)[2] the figure labelled 'This is my dear Father' (p. 70)[3] and the *milk maid* and her *cow* in Sarah Fear's work [117], clearly were figures associated with the child's rural life; a sampler of 1750 contains figure patterns which illustrate a contemporary story,[4] and a few patterns recall biblical scenes, of which one is the *Return of the Spies from Canaan* [170] and another, irresistible to sampler makers, *Adam and Eve*. This pattern appeared with regularity after the mid-eighteenth century regardless of the size or number of other patterns and motifs on a sampler and obviously was thought to be a highly suitable subject for the young; it was worked nearly always in *cross* stitch but only rarely with a relevant inscription, although some patterns have appropriate initials 'A' and 'E' embroidered by the figures. A worker of 1757, and clearly of tender years although her age is not given, scorned cross stitch and chose satin stitch for her pattern, which probably she

[1] *ibid.*, Figures 48, 50 and 53. D. King, *Samplers*, Plates 40, 41, and 43. M. B. Huish, *Samplers and Tapestry Embroideries*, Plates XXII and XXVII.
[2] M. B. Huish, *Samplers and Tapestry Embroideries*, Plate XXII. Leigh Ashton, *Samplers*, Figure 48.
[3] D. King, *Samplers*, Plate 43.
[4] *Samplers and Tapestry Embroideries*, Plate XXIV.

168   *An early nineteenth-century* stag

169   *Eighteenth-century stags*

drew for herself [171]; however, any artistic deficiencies were compensated by an unusually generous supply of leaves, including two bracelets each and complete girdles of them instead of one leaf. The pattern by Margaret Rammage and dated 'October the 3 1798', was embroidered on a hussif equipped with four

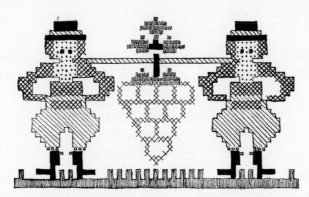

170   *Return of the Spies from Canaan. 1781*

pockets and was intended to serve also as a workbox sampler, with the usual patterns arranged symmetrically as on a sampler—*flower pots, fruit baskets, flowering plants*, single *flower* motifs, a *house, crowns, dogs, hearts* and *butterflies*, as well as verses eight and nine from the third chapter of the *Book of Genesis*:

> And they heard the voice of the
> Lord God walking in the garden in the cool
> of the day: . . . and the Lord
> God called unto the man and said unto him
> Where art thou?[1]

The figures of *Adam and Eve* were embroidered in a curious shade of mauve silk which made them appear to be blue with cold and fright; whether intentional or not, it is curiously effective in the context.

The universal preoccupation of the age for turning the expression of every sentiment, thought, or moral story into rhyme overwhelmed even *Adam and Eve* by the 1770s and some extraordinary compositions appeared:

> Adam alone in paradise did grieve and thought
> Eden a desert without Eve until God pitying
>   his lonesome state crowned all
> his riches with a lovely mate what
> Reason then has man to slight or

---

[1] In the Collection of the Fitzwilliam Museum, 38–137.

flaught her that could not live in
paradise without her
Fly sin be sure live goodly still
Then welcome death come when
it will
Margaret Batty finished this work in the
ninth year of her age 1777.

Four years later in 1781 the following lines were divided to lie on each side of the
figures and the *Tree of Knowledge*, in the work of Mary Simpson:

Adam and Eve whilst innocent
In Paradise were placed
But soon the serpent by his whiles
The happy pair disgraced.

The simplicity and brevity of this jingle did not lose their appeal for nearly a
hundred years and it can be found in numbers of samplers in company with the
Adam and Eve pattern during the nineteenth century also. The ingenuity with
which the religious and moral sentiments were translated into nursery rhyme
language was remarkable, and that much abused thing poetic licence, was

171   Adam and Eve *pattern in* satin *stitch. 1757*

stretched to its limits in many of the rhymes of eighteenth and nineteenth centuries (Chapter Twelve). Virtues of Obedience, Duty, Learning, and above all Humility, received the most attention and good as were the sentiments and intentions behind the verses, all too often the words or even the spelling reduce them to the level of absurdity; three almost contemporary inscriptions illustrated the degree of this level. In 1770 Ann Hunt dealt with the evils of this world:

> Bad Company As Deadly Poyson Shun
> thousands by It Are ruin'd And Undon
> the giddy Multytude Stil gose AStray
> turn From the broad And tuse the
> Narrow Way.[1]

and eight years later Sarah Beckett looked forward to the joys of the next life when she 'Finished this Piece Decemb[r] 24 in the eighth year of her age 1798':

Omay thy powerful word,	Omay we all improve
Inspire a breathing worm	The grace already given
To rush into thy kingdom, Lord,	To seize the Crown of perfect love
And take it as by Storm!	And scale the mount of heaven.[2]

Who but someone very young could have embroidered Esther Tabor's short lines (dated 1771), with its subtle and undisclosed implications:

> Our days, alas, our mortal days
> Are short and wretched too
> Evil and few the patriarch said
> And well the patriarch knew.[3]

These inscriptions were, perhaps, slightly worse than the average but only slightly, and when they, and numbers of others in the same vein, were set in a 'giddy Multytude' of *birds, crowns, hearts, animals* and *flowers* the youthfulness of the makers was emphasised. By the end of the eighteenth century the average age of the sampler maker was lower than that at the end of the seventeenth and this was reflected in words defining youth put into the mouth of Hastings in *She Stoops To Conquer* (1773),—'For instance, miss there, would be considered as a child, a mere maker of samplers'.[4]

The words spell also, the epitaph of the sampler, as one of the most fundamental changes which had taken place in the years of the eighteenth century was the final disappearance of its original purpose as a pattern record. The demands of

---

[1] In the Collection of the Victoria and Albert Museum, T. 43–1917
[2] Leigh Ashton, *Samplers*, Figure 53. Quoted, M. B. Huish, *Samplers and Tapestry Embroideries*, p. 52.
[3] M. B. Huish, *Samplers and Tapestry Embroideries*, p. 55.
[4] Oliver Goldsmith, *She Stoops To Conquer*, 1773, Act II.

fashion were responsible for the disappearance of some patterns when, at the beginning of the century, they dispensed with the *cut-work* laces so popular in Tudor and Stuart periods and during the reign of William and Mary, and by degrees many of the embroidered textiles went out in favour of the new colour-printed cottons.

The advantages of teaching by means of the sampler were many and the method was developed as far as the wit of the school mistress would take it, until the variety of subjects seems to have absorbed more attention than the needle-work with which they were recorded. The quality of the stitchery and the artistic merit of the patterns were reduced to the level of the pupils' ability and the com-petitive rivalries of the schoolroom resulted in such eccentricities as the *puzzles*, *acrostics*, *calendars* and *maps* to which the name sampler truly should not belong. Samplers with *hollie point* lace and *pattern darning*, gave practice in patterns and skills which could be put to practical use in needlework of the time, that is to say, in ornamenting baby clothing or in repairing worn fabrics, but other kinds had some sentimental and decorative values and little else. It is even doubtful in some cases as to whether the knowledge of the subject, in such things as arithmetical problems, the dominical year, or geography, was quite equal to the strain.

Materials increased in variety; the use of linen continued for all types of sam-pler and the yellow colour, introduced in the 1600s continued for a time. Early in the 1720s a fine, even, woollen canvas or tammy cloth became popular, but a Welsh sampler of this material dated 1709 is recorded,[1] so it is possible that it came into limited use before 1720, but owing to its susceptibility to damage by moth, earlier work perished. Of other materials, cotton was used for the *Almanack* made by Elizabeth Knowles in 1787 and satin was popular for *maps*, especially for those with commercially-drawn outlines, but many *maps* were worked on linen. Some of the finely worked samplers made towards the end of the century were on a thin glazed gauze known as tiffany, but generally speaking, linen had returned to popularity and general use by the 1790s, due no doubt to the dis-advantages of the woollen canvas.

The need for economy in material seems to have gone with the end of the seventeenth century and the selvage edges to samplers were no longer left; instead, raw edges were *hemmed* or *oversewn* and *hollie point* samplers sometimes were finished with *buttonholed* edges. Raw edges in surviving samplers may be accounted for at times by the original hems having been fastened into the frame and the fabrics rotted with age and rust from pins or nails; others in a better condition, occasionally had been sewn roughly to a tape or strip of linen at the edges which had taken the wear from the sampler.

[1] F. G. Payne, *Guide to the Collection of Samplers and Embroideries*, p. 30.

172   *1818. Silk thread on wool. Cross stitch.*
Signed, Mary Ann Ansen. 13 × 11 *inches*

173   *1823. Silk thread on linen. Cross stitch.*
Signed, Hannah Fieldhouse. 13 × 13 *inches*

174   *1825. Irish. Silk thread and chenille on linen. Satin and cross stitches and chenille couching. Signed, Ellen Carr. 21 × 16 inches*

THE words of Agur the son of Jakeh, even the pro-
phecy: the man spake unto Ithiel, even unto Ithiel
and Ucal, Surely I am more brutish than any man,
and have not the understanding of a man. I neither
learned wisdom, nor have the knowledge of the holy.
Who hath ascended up into heaven, or descended?
who hath gathered the wind in his fists? who hath
bound the waters in a garment? who hath establish
ed all the ends of the earth? what is his name, and
what is his son's name, if thou canst tell? Every
word of God is pure; he is a shield unto them that
put their trust in him. Add thou not unto his words,
lest he reprove thee, and thou be found a liar. Two
things have I required of thee; deny me them not
before I die: Remove far from me vanity and lies:
give me neither poverty nor riches; feed me with
food convenient for me: Lest I be full, and deny
thee, and say, Who is the LORD? or lest I be poor,
and steal, and take the name of my God in vain.
30th of Proverbs, the first 9 Verses. ＼＼＼＼

The Lord is gracious, and full of compassion; slow to
anger, and of great mercy. the Lord is good to all;
and his tender mercies are over all his works. ＼＼＼
Psalm. CXLV. Verses 8th 9th. ＼＼＼＼＼＼

Emily Jane Brontë Finished this Sampler. March 1st 1829

YE saints on earth, ascribe, with heaven's high host,
Glory and honour to the One in Three;
To God the Father, Son, and Holy Ghost,
As was, and is, and evermore shall be.

175 'March 1st 1829.' Silk thread on wool. Cross stitch.
Signed, Emily Jane Brontë. $12\frac{1}{2} \times 7\frac{1}{2}$ inches

176   *183 . Silk thread on wool. Cross and satin stitches. Signed, Sophia Stephens.* $21 \times 20\frac{1}{4}$ *inche*

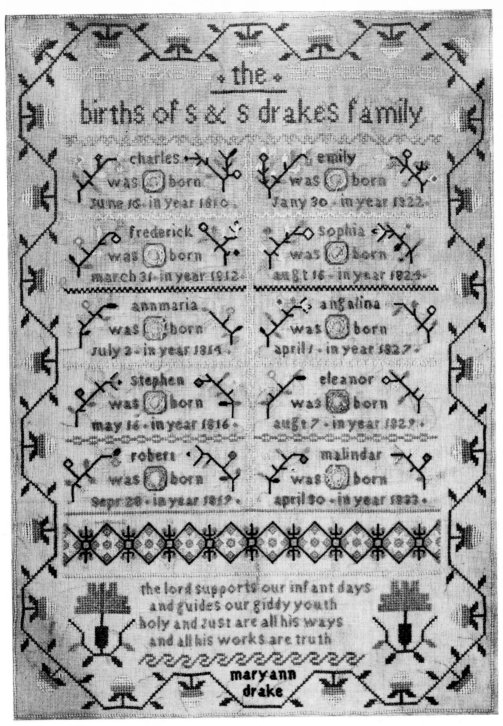

177   *c. 1834. Silk thread on linen with some hair. Cross stitch.*
Signed, Mary Ann Drake. 17× 12½ inches

178   1837. *Silk thread and bead-work on linen. Cross stitch. Signed, Elizabeth Harrison.* 14 × 13 *inches*

179   1837. *Silk thread on wool. Cross stitch. Signed, Austin Frederic Tidy.* 8½ × 13 *inches*

Jesus permit thy gracious name to stand.
As the first efforts of an infants hand.
And as her fingers on the sampler move.
Engage her tender heart to seek thy love.
With thy dear children may she have her part.
And write thy name thyself upon her heart.

The Church

Round these lone walls.
Assemblig neighbours meet.
And tread departed friends.
Beneath their feet.

And new made graves.
That prompt the secret sigh.
Show each the spot.
Where he himself must lie.

Ann Britton
Aged 14 1842
Cock Road
Daily School

180   *1842. Silk thread on linen. Cross stitch. Signed, Ann Britton.* $13\frac{1}{2} \times 14$ *inches*

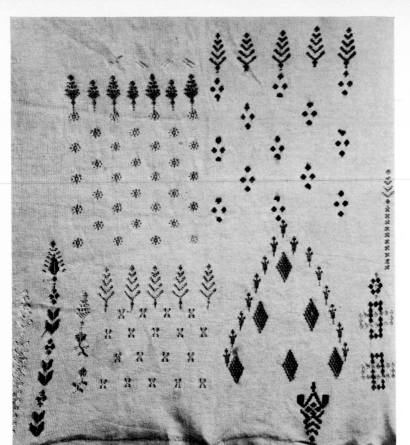

181 *Mid nineteenth century. Silk thread on stocking web. Satin stitch, worked on the woven stitches and known as Chevening*

182 *1845. Silk thread on linen. Cross stitch. Signed, Sarah Roberts. One side of a bag, $7\frac{7}{8} \times 7$ inches*

Comparison with measurements of samplers in the previous century shows that those of the eighteenth century had shortened to an average length of between 13 and 18 inches, and a width of from 10 to 13 inches, but some long, narrow specimens were made also during the first fifty years. A number of small samplers measuring from about two to five inches square have been found from time to time, which contain a few small motifs and occasionally are initialled but rarely dated. They appear nearly always to be worked with silk on linen, occasionally the thread is linen also, and a suggested use for them has been that they were practice samplers for the motifs to be embroidered on larger samplers, as these had acquired the status of embroidered pictures and were no longer exercises in themselves. Many of them also were 'friendship' samplers, made as small gifts and often contain inscriptions and initials as 'D H to A H' (p. 92), and sometimes are dated. Soon after the middle of the century such things as needle and letter cases were made, which in effect were small-scale samplers. Of those which have survived some are unused, others are in various stages of disintegration, but the decorative patterns are all those familiar to the sampler makers—the *flower pot, bird, animal, Adam and Eve* and so on in proportion to the size of the work, some of which is finely sewn on gauze.

Linen or silk thread continued in use on linen samplers; silk appears only on woollen, cotton and gauze specimens which have survived, but metal thread virtually died out at the beginning of the century, except for a few samplers which contained a little. Beads also were no longer used; a few samplers in the later years contained some *couched* chenille for *tree* and other patterns included in the *landscapes* (p. 85), and its use continued for some time in the nineteenth century; human hair also found a place in sampler patterns but somewhat in advance of the rage for its use at the end of the century which lasted into the 1900s (p. 93). Linen thread was always white, as in earlier samplers, but the silks were brighter in colour than those used in the seventeenth century, and in greater variety of shades.

A characteristic of the *darning* samplers is the delicacy and restraint of colour in the embroidery; the discipline imposed on the choice of two colours or shades only in the cross-shaped darns, seemed to create what amounted to a fashion, if not a tradition in all darning patterns, for half tones and subtle pairing of colours— purple and pale gold, dark red with faded pink, dark moss green and a pale blue are typical of all cross shaped *darns*, and delicate natural colours, sometimes outlined in black, dark green or white, were used for the floral patterns; *ribbon* patterns or *bows* often are introduced also and these seem always to have been blue in colour.

The number of different stitches in use had dropped considerably by the middle of the century and by the 1790s nearly all kinds had been abandoned in favour of *cross* stitch.

Numbers of samplers show signs of alteration and repair to the fabric and embroidery, especially when the work had become a prized heirloom of the maker's descendants, and the later work is evidence of loving care. Susannah Pryor's sampler, signed and dated 'April 6th 1779', has a note written in ink on the back of the frame which reads 'Taken out and cleaned May 30th 1835. Thos Royde' but as a rule, cleaning and repairs have been done anonymously. In the matter of alterations, however, samplers, as with other works, have not escaped the hand of the forger. A sampler now bearing the name of 'Eleanor Speed' has had the Christian name altered and the two dates which should have read 1733 and 1734, were altered to 1783 and 1784, presumably a later relative of the maker wished to claim her grandmother's work as her own.[1] An even more dastardly act took place in the nineteenth century when the date on the sampler of 'L. Hart', now appearing as 1627, was substituted for the real (and later) date; the forger (possibly a dealer) had overlooked the significance of the embroidered pattern which represented three lines of music from a tune called '*St Peter*'—and the tune was not published until 1830.[2]

Before the century ended the educational aspect of the sampler was used by two painters, in each of whose pictures the importance attached to sampler making in different kinds of girls' schools of the time, was illustrated. The well-known *Visit to the Boarding School* by Morland, in the Wallace Collection, shows the school which was patronised by the well-to-do and a sampler being shown as evidence of the pupil's progress; the other is of the Dame's School of the village, with boys and girls of all ages, the cat, and the sunny window, filling the picture, every child in a different occupation and one girl waiting for the inspection of her sampler with an *alphabet*, by the dame, who is the central figure in Frances Wheatley's *The Schoolmistress*.

[1] D. King, *Samplers*, Plate 31.
[2] In the collection of the Fitzwilliam Museum, 38–69.

CHAPTER TEN

The Nineteenth Century

It has been said that the nineteenth century was the Age of Anyhow, a description that could well be used to describe the period in sampler making also. A good deal of the work on the conventional samplers was indifferently done and the idea of pattern recording had spread from coloured *cross* stitch to a number of different kinds of needlework. Not all of these were the work of children, and two small groups were made in connection with the commercially-produced articles, in which sample patterns were needed for hand embroidered finishes essential to the manufactured product; these samplers were used in connection with the *white*

183 Tulip *motif.*
1801

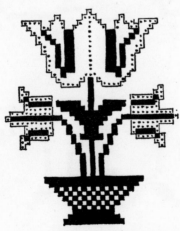

184 *Mid nineteenth-century*
tulip *flower pot*

185 *Early nineteenth-century*
all-over tulip *pattern*

186   Strawberry *border patterns of the eighteenth and nineteenth centuries*

work done on muslin known as *Ayrshire* embroidery and for the silk *clocks* or *clox*, used in the hosiery trade. Other kinds of purely domestic samplers were made for fine sewing and mending processes, knitting, beadwork and patchwork.

During the first 25 years or so, as in earlier centuries, none of the conventional samplers showed any great change in the kinds of patterns or stitches; *cross* stitch had become settled in as the height of all aspiration in the workers and the most popular patterns continued to be *flower pots, birds, animals* and verses or inscriptions as before. Nearly every sampler contained a border pattern on four sides, generally of *carnation* or *strawberry* patterns and sometimes of both, as when *carnations* were used for the two end borders and *strawberries* at the sides and so on. *Urns* and *weeping willows* were popular after the death of Princess Charlotte [*50*, *178*].

A distinctive type worked entirely in cross stitch, however, should perhaps have been included in the eighteenth century, as one example at least is known to have been made then and, recorded by Sir Leigh Ashton, was signed and dated 'M Quertier, 1799'.[1] Examples of this type consist of a series of formal or natural *flower* and *leaf* patterns, and some geometric motifs enclosed in *garland* or *tablet* patterns and arranged as neatly spaced motifs worked in silk on woollen canvas. The example illustrated was made by Eliza Trusted and signed 'E T 1803' [*127*], and contains a number of similar, and some identical patterns with those on the 1799 specimen; both are worked in silk *cross* stitch on worsted, M. Quertier's in black, and Eliza Trusted's in red thread. Many of the motifs are exactly similar to those found on the

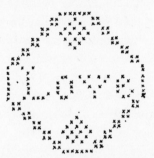

187   Cross stitch *pattern for a gift pincushion. Nineteenth century*

small mattress type of pincushion which was so popular during the nineteenth century, of which the covers were made of knitting in fine silk. It is a simple matter to adapt a *cross* stitch pattern to one for knitting, and a knitted pincushion made by a member of Eliza Trusted's family contains an identical pattern with one on her sampler, but with the undated initials 'E T' substituted for 'E S'. Another pincushion from the same family, has on one side a *carnation* pattern which is almost identical with one on the Quertier sampler and on the reverse of the pincushion are the words, also in knitting, 'From Ackworth School'. These pincushions were made as tokens of friendship, and by several initials and dates found among the sampler patterns, it seems clear that they may have been intended for this purpose. The sampler of 1799 includes a floral *wreath* enclosing

[1] Leigh Ashton, *Samplers*, Figure 54.

'M Q to M N 1799' and this is more likely to have been the pattern for her gift pincushion, than the inscription on a gift sampler. Another pattern of a *leaf* and *berry* garland surmounted by a *crown*, reads 'A T 1799' and doubtless was the pattern for a pincushion intended for 'A T'.

Samplers of patterns of knitting have been mentioned already (Chapter Six, p. 138) and these were especially numerous in school sampler books. Most were of open work patterns knitted with white cotton thread, in vertical lines intended for children's sock and stockings and others worked in white wool and of closer patterns, probably were used for small vests, petticoats and under bodices. The name given to the patterns in the key to the sampler in Caulfeild's *Dictionary* are *rectangular, box, Stromberger, diamond, dotty, small diamond, German, herring-bone, lemon, lozenge, bryony, pettifer, shell, hemstitch, coral* and *ladder*, most of which have gone out of use now, although some of the patterns are used for fine shawls.

A small group of samplers, consisting of needle-made lace patterns worked on net foundation, belongs to the early nineteenth century although none has been signed or dated. Darning on net was one of the early forms of lace making in which patterns of all kinds were worked, but although examples of the work itself are comparatively numerous, especially in European work, no English samplers of this kind of pattern making seem to have been made until 1800 or just before and they were of the simplest kind. Manufactured net was not made until the early 1800s, until when there had been the laborious necessity of making fine net by hand and the set of three illustrated are worked on machine-made net [*126*]. A slightly earlier, larger and more elaborate specimen in the same chequered arrangement but on hand-made net, is in the collection at Gawthorpe Hall, Burnley,[1] and another of about the same date, in which the arrangement of border or insertion patterns is in two columns, resembles that of the *band* samplers.[2]

Another and even smaller group of samplers is that concerned with motifs and patterns used in Ayrshire embroidery, so called from the name of the County with which it was associated and where it flourished for about 50 years and more in the 1800s. A few specimens only seem to have survived from the numbers made and the patterns they contained were of the *flowers* and *sprigs* worked in white on muslin, which were called for by the fashion for embroidered muslin dresses of the late eighteenth and early nineteenth centuries. The fashion was yet another born out of the enthusiasm for the imported Indian textiles, this time for the embroidered muslins from Dacca which were copied first in domestic embroidery, but the demand outgrew this limitation and the work was taken up by the trade.

---

[1] 'Laces on Net' by Rachel B. Kay Shuttleworth, *Embroidery*, Autumn 1960, p. 83.
[2] 'Netting for the Embroidress' by Sylvia Groves, *Country Life*, August 11 1960, Illustration 2.

Mrs Margaret Swain has written on the results of her research into the history of Ayrshire embroidery[1] and part of a sampler of muslin containing examples of *flowered* and *sprigged* patterns used for handkerchief borders and corners, discovered in the course of her work, is illustrated [125].[2] The whole sampler measures 82 inches in length and is 28½ inches wide; dress patterns are contained in it, also at one time all the patterns in the sampler were numbered and separated by a waving line in red cotton. Unfortunately these markings have been taken out but the stitch holes remain and the numbers still can be deciphered.

When the dress materials were to be embroidered, the patterns were drawn in outline (by hand at first but later were printed) and the material then was put out to skilled women and girls—the 'flowerers'—who completed the details working in their homes. The stitches used were *chain, satin* and *darning, needlepoint* fillings being added about 1814, and the embroidery was done with the muslin stretched on a tambour or hoop frame. An account of how the work was organised in the trade was written by Mr Cyril Wallis in 1951: 'The material, cut up into lengths for the making of various articles, was despatched to the agents resident in different parts of the country. Each piece of cloth was printed with a stereotyped pattern bearing a number, the amount of time required for the work, and the sum to be paid for it on completion.'[3]

188   *Flower motifs from border patterns in manuscript pattern book 1840*

[1] M. H. Swain, *The Flowerers*, 1955.
[2] 'Two rare Scottish Samplers' by Margaret H. Swain, *Embroidery*, Spring 1960, Figure 6.
[3] 'The History of Scottish Embroidery' by W. Cyril Wallis, *Embroidery*, Summer 1951, p. 6.

Another Scottish sampler found by Mrs Swain, contains eighty small motifs of needlepoint fillings worked on linen; each is numbered in figures written in ink and is thought to have been a worker's reference sampler.[1] A sampler worked by Miss Agnes Martin in 1850 in the possession of the Belfast Museum and Art Gallery contains examples of filling stitches also. Commercial samplers such as these are rare now and obviously were needed only when manufactured work had to be put out to be finished by hand away from the factory. No English samplers of flowered muslin exist; white work however, was done on fine cambric and a manuscript pattern book, probably compiled during the 1840s, was found in 1951 by Miss Isobel Minto, in which a collection of pen and ink drawings of embroidery patterns had been made.[2] This delightfully personal notebook was the equivalent of a sampler and contained motifs and border patterns for many types of embroidery including Broderie Anglaise, whitework and braiding; some of the motifs were intended for the reticules which had to be carried by the wearers of muslin gowns of too fragile and transparent material to allow of pockets [188–90].

189   Jasmine *spray. 1840*

The embroidery known as *chevening* was the trade name given to the work of adding the *clocks* to manufactured stockings, 'half-hose', gloves and mittens. Clocks embroidered on the Court stockings of George III were made 'by the actual transfer by hand of the appropriate loops during the course of manufacture',[3] but throughout the nineteenth century the more usual method was for the stockings to be put out to women who did the work in their homes, taking the patterns from a sampler on woven stocking web. The work generally was distributed by a representative of the firm concerned, who travelled round to the

190   *Small motifs from 1840 pattern book*

[1] 'Two rare Scottish Samplers' by Margaret H. Swain, *Embroidery*, Spring 1960, Figure 7.
[2] 'A Nineteenth Century Pattern Book' by Isobel Minto, *Embroidery*, Winter 1951, p. 11.
[3] 'Chevening' by Maisie Currey, *Embroidery*, Autumn 1951, paragraph 5, p. 24.

cottages giving out the stockings and collecting and paying for the finished work of the previous week, a woman taking two or three dozen pairs at a time. In some districts they were collected from the warehouses by individuals who did the distribution and sometimes children collected the work before school. Distribution by the manufacturers was done weekly—'The day for distribution and collection was always on a Monday—it was the custom that the cottagers never worked on that day, known as "Stockingers' Monday".' [1] The clocks were embroidered with coloured silks in satin stitch using the woven loops of the fabric as a guide and some were more complicated than others—'I did it on leaving school, until I was fifteen. . . . I only did the clox as you call them but was starting to learn the fancies; cheveners always spoke of them as straights and fancies.' [2] The name *clock* was supposed to have been given to the pattern because of its resemblance to the pendulum of a clock. The building of machines which could add *clocks* automatically in the process of stocking weaving did away with the need for hand work and a dying industry was killed finally when the machines were taken over by the Government for the making of 'half hose' for the Army, on the outbreak of war in 1914.

Beads have been found in sampler work of every century but generally were used to highlight a pattern or to give emphasis to the letters of initials or a signature [53]. A number of nineteenth-century samplers contain one or two patterns in coloured bead work but one illustrated in Mr Huish's book contained all the conventional *flower pots*, *birds*, *trees* and so on, worked entirely in this way; it is signed 'Jane Mills' and is undated but the patterns are similar to those of the silk embroidered patterns of the early nineteenth century. [3] Bead work had been especially popular in the embroidery of the seventeenth century from the time of the Restoration and numbers of bead work pictures have survived from that time but if samplers with patterns of beads only were made during the following centuries, none has been discovered in recent years, or recorded. The centre pattern of a well preserved nineteenth-century sampler, commemorating the death of Princess Charlotte, consists of a memorial *tablet* and *urn* worked entirely in brown, black and white beads [178]; the trunk of the *weeping willow tree* springing from the top of the *urn* is of brown beads and the inscription on the white bead *tablet* is worked in small black beads:

Prs CharLotte
Died NOVEM
ber 6 1817
Aged 22

---

[1] 'Chevening' by Maisie Currey, *Embroidery*, Autumn 1951, paragraph 4, p. 24.
[2] *ibid.*, paragraph 1, p. 23.
[3] M. B. Huish, *Samplers and Tapestry Embroideries*, Plate XXXII.

The sampler was not made until 1837 but nevertheless it contains a memorial inscription of two verses, embroidered side by side:

ON THE DEATH OF HER ROYAL HIGHNESS THE PRINCESS CHARLOTTE OF WALES & SON

Weep on Britannia, o'er thy Princess tomb
Now sunk in death and wither'd in her bloom
Within the breast exist a deadly wound
Thy shield and sceptre neglected on the ground
Fall night's black curtain o'er the cheerful day
Let mirth subside and perish all that's gay.

An angel sleeps whose sweet angelic mind
Was generous gentle dignified refined
A God like prince with tears bedew her urn
And mourn those charms that never can return
Th' Almighty wo'd the virtues he had given
And called her gently to her kindred heaven
Elizabeth Harrison's Work 1837.

Beads were included in sampler patterns of Berlin wool work and from the middle of the century were used in increasing quantities for decorative embroidery especially on dresses, purses, 'Gentlemen's watch chains', and for 'hanging baskets, lamp shades and dinner rings' and in these connections it may not be wholly irrelevant to note a comment of 1882 that 'Large quantities of coarse beads are sold to America and Africa, for embroidering their garments &c., and the taste these savages display over their work puts to shame that of more civilised nations'.[1] Necklaces of beads made on small table looms were fashionable at the end of the century, a fashion which lasted into the early years of the 1900s and the example illustrated was found in a chest of bird's eye maple, containing a number of trays fitted with glass topped boxes full of beads; the necklace must in fact have been used as a pattern sampler for work on a bead loom [197].

Samplers, of which many more probably were made but discarded as of no importance, have survived in which various stitches needed for making and repairing household linen were set out. Very few bear a date or signature, probably for the same reason that so many of the earliest samplers were anonymous—that they were added to as a particular stitch or process was needed for a reminder. A repair sampler dated 1894 and signed 'GEFB', must have come from a capable and competent housewife; it is worked on linen with linen and cotton

[1] Caulfeild and Saward, *Dictionary of Needlework*, p. 24.

thread, showing open hems of several kinds, fastenings—hooks and eyes, buttons and buttonholes and loops—repair patches and some pattern darning. The worker was a member of the Barnardiston family [202]. The school samplers of dressmaking and repairing processes made from about 1890 and during the first quarter of the nineteenth century have been described in the chapter on school work (p. 139). They must have been made by every young woman who intended to teach, as they have survived in quantity but some workers broke ranks and used blue cotton for some of the *faggotting* and *herring bone* stitches, instead of the more usual white; initials and dates also, sometimes were added in pink or blue thread.

Patchwork of great complexity and especially that made of silk, was popular from the middle of the nineteenth century, with each worker trying to out-patch her neighbour in ingenuity, and so it is not surprising to find a sampler of patch-

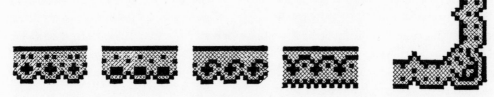

191   Canvas lace work *patterns in Berlin wool work. Mid nineteenth century*

work every now and then, with collections of geometrical patterns. Unfinished attempts exist which appear to have been abandoned in the middle of the struggle, but other examples can be found in a more or less presentable state. The sampler illustrated [196] is anonymous and probably was made about 1870; the materials are all silk, some of twentieth-century date which have been put in to replace worn patches; the lining of glazed calico and the silk fringe at the edges, have helped towards the preservation of this sampler. A somewhat unusual relationship between patchwork and samplers can be found in a large coverlet made of small square patches joined to make patterns imitating those on the conventional sampler; each patch represents a *cross* stitch and the pattern was built up to make a central panel containing letters of the alphabet, surrounded by the usual types of *bird, animal* and *flower* motifs. It is dated 1847 but time has mellowed this masterpiece and probably it is a good deal less startling now than it was when it was new.

Another group of samplers made approximately between the years 1830 and 1880, was that representing or influenced by Berlin wool work [1] [193, 195]. The samplers were made on linen, worsted or canvas in bright colours and naturalistic shading of the patterns, which are characteristics of the work; all of them that is,

[1] F. G. Payne, *Guide to the Collection of Samplers and Embroideries*, Plates XVIII, XIX; no. 5, plate XX. D. King, *Samplers*, Plates 57, 58.

except the patterns in imitation of lace edgings, insertions and motifs, which were worked always in black silk and known as *canvas lace* work. Various thicknesses of silk were used to produce the lace effects [*191*].

The stitches used for samplers of Berlin wool showed greater variety than in other types, and although a good deal of the work was done in *cross* stitch, some samplers contain also *tent*, *satin* and *Florentine* stitches with some *couching*, *laid* and *plush* work. The completed specimens usually were bound at the edges with silk ribbon or braid and one measuring over 50 inches in length and about six inches wide, has a padded cylinder covered in tartan silk attached to one end for rolling when not in use.[1] A mid nineteenth-century example measures over ten feet long and is four inches wide[2] and another smaller specimen was made into a housewife [*193*]. The patterns were composed of floral and geometrical motifs and arranged neatly somewhat in the manner of the *spot* motif samplers, but with little serious attempt at economy of space. The samplers have not survived in great numbers nor do they appear to have been school work, but are considered possibly to have been the work of 'skilled needlewomen to serve as models for amateurs, in the same way as the coloured charts'.[3] Many of these samplers have suffered considerably from damage by moth and not to put too fine a point upon it, a number are considerably less clean than the conventional and more decorative samplers which have spent the years behind glass. The problem of keeping wool embroidery clean must have been a concern of the workers at the time when the work was reasonably new, as a contemporary recipe for 'Cleaning Wool Work' was given in Caulfeild's Dictionary, but effective as it may have been for nineteenth-century embroidery, it is hardly likely to be widely used in the 1960s; if the wool work 'is much soiled, wash it with gin and soft soap, in the proportions of one quarter of a pound of soft soap to half a pint of gin'.[4]

Inscriptions were not included in Berlin wool work, but many of the floral, pictorial and architectural patterns on the conventional type of sampler were worked in Berlin wools and these also contain inscriptions, dates and signatures. More than one pattern on a sampler in wool work can be traced or compared with patterns in embroidered pictures—the view of Penrhyn Castle shown on a Welsh sampler [*195*] occurs also on a wool work picture in the National Museum of Wales.[5]

Much the same subjects for inscriptions, popular in the eighteenth century, continued to be chosen, possibly with the emphasis laid even more heavily on

[1] In the collection of the Fitzwilliam Museum, T. 72–1938.
[2] D. King, *Samplers*, Plate 57. Barbara Morris, *Victorian Embroidery*, Plate 11.
[3] D. King, *Samplers*, p. 10.
[4] Caulfeild and Saward, *Dictionary of Needlework*, p. 80.
[5] F. G. Payne, *Guide to the Collection of Samplers and Embroideries*, Plate XX, no. 5.

abject humility, resignation to the perpetual presence of sin and death, dread of the hereafter, and deep gloom. Lamentations on the death of the Princess Charlotte were numerous and popular from 1817 onwards [178] but an earlier commemorative sampler in patriotic verse, contained lines on the Peace of Amiens in 1802[1]; the patterns were worked in silk and silver thread on worsted and consisted of floral sprays and crossed swords bearing the crosses of Saint George and Saint Patrick. The sampler is bound with dark red ribbon and the verse takes up the middle of the work:

> Past is the storm and o'er the azure sky serenely shines the sun
> With every breeze the waving branches nod their Kind assent.

ON PEACE

> Hail England's favour'd Monarch: round thy head
> Shall Freedom's hands perennial laurels spread.
> Fenc'd by whose sacred leaves the royal brow
> Mock'd the vain lightnings aim'd by Gallic foe
> Alike in arts and arms illustrious found
> Proudly Britannia sits with laurel crown'd
> Invasion haunts her rescued Plains no more
> And hostile inroads flies her dangerous shore
> Where'er her armies march her ensigns Play
> Fame Points the course and Glory points the way.
>
> O Britain with the gifts of Peace thou'rt blest
> May thou hereafter have Perpetual rest
> And may the blessing still with you remain
> Nor cruel War disturb our land again.

The Definitive Treaty of Peace was signed March 27th 1802 proclaimed in London April the 29th 1802 Thanksgiving June the 1st 1802.

> Mary Ann Crouzet
> Dec[br] 17 1802.

In a letter to *The Times* in June 1935, mention was made of a sampler containing a record of 'notable landmarks in social progress and scientific advances in knowledge appertaining to the nineteenth century' and those which had impressed the worker of the sampler were: 'The Nineteenth Century. Reform Bill passed. Steam Engines. Railways. Penny Postage. Steam Navigation. Friction Matches. Telegraph. Telephones. Gas and Electric Lighting. Money and Postal Orders.

---

[1] M. B. Huish, *Samplers and Tapestry Embroideries*, p. 71. Now in the collection of the Fitzwilliam Museum, 38–52.

Bicycles. Photography. The Phonograph. Free Education. Typewriting. Parcels Post. Rontgen Rays. O Wondrous Age.'

The long inscriptions of the eighteenth century became even more popular in the first half of the nineteenth, some taking up so much of the sampler space, that

192 'The Church.' 1842

there was room only for a narrow surrounding border. One hundred years after their publication, extracts from Dr Watts' *Songs* still were being used for rhyming inscriptions; 'The Sluggard' from *Song I* of *Moral Songs* (20 lines long), and *Song XX* 'Against Idleness and Mischief' (16 lines beginning with the familiar 'How doth the little busy bee'), are examples, and inscriptions in prose and rhyme found several times in surviving specimens include such subjects as, 'An Invocation to Gratitude', 'Desire', 'On Youth', 'On Death', 'On Virtue'; 'To Young Ladies', 'Advice', 'The Church', 'To Spring', 'Consider Your Ways', 'Mind superior to

Body', and many others (Chapter Twelve). Different rhymes sometimes had the same title, 'Advice' and 'The Church' especially, both being subjects capable of adaptation to different points of view. A verse on 'The Church' is illustrated on Ann Britton's sampler of 1842 [*180*]:

The Church

Round these lone walls
Assembling neighbours meet
And tread departed friends
Beneath their feet.

And new made graves
That prompt the secret sigh
Show each the spot
Where he himself must lie.

The subject of the grave, introduced into so many of the sampler verses, seemed an incongruous choice when surrounded by *flower pot*, *bird* and *butterfly* motifs and a *strawberry* border but such was the case, and some verses which approached the gruesome in detail, were the most likely to be accompanied by a frivolous assortment of patterns.

Margaret Morgan swept 'a thousand children' into eternity with her in her sampler:

There is an hour when I must die
Nor can I tell how soon twill come
A thousand children young as I
Are called by death to hear their doom[1]

with a border of honeysuckle, pansies and rosebuds surrounding the verse, quoted from Dr Watts' 'Solemn Thoughts on God and Death', *Divine Song* X, as well as three scenes from the Bible (Elijah fed by the Ravens, the Finding of Moses, the Flight into Egypt), a balloon with two passengers, some trees and a number of other patterns.[2] A more casual attitude to the idea of death seems to have been taken in 1820:

The grass is green, the rose is red
Where is my work when I am dead.[3]

The thought of the worm as a symbol of humility and self abasement is inherited also from verses of the eighteenth century and this is the gist of Mary Elsey's verse:

Alas and did my Saviour die
For such a worm as I?[4]

[1] F. G. Payne, *Guide to the Collection of Samplers and Embroideries*, p. 59, no. 77.
[2] F. G. Payne, *Guide to the Collection of Samplers and Embroideries*, Plate XVII.
[3] In the Collection of the City Art Gallery, Bristol, catalogue no. 32.
[4] In the Collection of the Guildford Museum, Guildford, no. G 519.

and no one could go further in the practical application of her principles than an anonymous young worker of the 1820s:

> Sweet it is to see a child
> Tender, merciful and mild
> Ever ready to perform
> Acts of kindness to a worm.

Many verses however have a fresh and welcome outlook on humility like that of Caroline Mason, aged ten in 1877:

> Lord look upon a little child
> By nature sinful, rude and wild,
> O lay thy Gracious hand on me
> And make me all I aught to be

and perhaps confession was good for the soul of Jane Grey:

> The trees were green,
> The sun was hot,
> Sometimes I worked,
> And sometimes not.
> Seven years my age
> My name Jane Grey
> And often much
> Too fond of play.

But of all the verses one appears more often than any other. It can be seen on Ann Britton's sampler [*180*] and it has been said that the lines were written by Dr Isaac Watts for his niece to embroider on her sampler,[1] but there appears to be no example of it in eighteenth-century samplers. Dr Watts died in 1748 and the first appearance of it as a sampler inscription seems to have been during the first ten years of the 1800s. In writing of this verse Mr Ffransis Payne quotes from *Notes and Queries* for 1871 to say 'The lines were composed by the late Rev. John Newton for the sampler of his niece, Miss Elizabeth Catlett', and of the two suggested authors and nieces, the latter seem to be the more likely. Mr Payne adds also: 'It is startling to realise that the author of the . . . lines was none other than Cowper's evangelical friend, the erstwhile African slave trader.'[2] There are of course several slight variations in the wording but Ann Britton's is the most common:

> Jesus permit thy gracious name to stand.
> As the first effort of an infants hand.

[1] Leigh Ashton, *Samplers*, p. 1.
[2] F. G. Payne, *Guide to the Collection of Samplers and Embroideries*, p. 38.

193 *Mid nineteenth century. Silk and wool threads on canvas. Cross, tent, plush and Florentine stitches.* 18 × 4 *inches*

194 *c. 1850. Silk on canvas, mounted on flannel. Cross and chain stitches. Maker, Mrs Scott.* 2 × 2 *inches*

PERHYN CASTLE NORTH WALES

Sarah Morgan, Aged 15 Years.

195 *Mid nineteenth century. Welsh. Silk thread on canvas. Cross, satin and chain stitches. Signed, Sarah Morgan. 24½ × 21 inches*

196   *c. 1870. Silk, taffeta, satin and ribbon. Oversewn on wrong side. 34 × 40 inches*

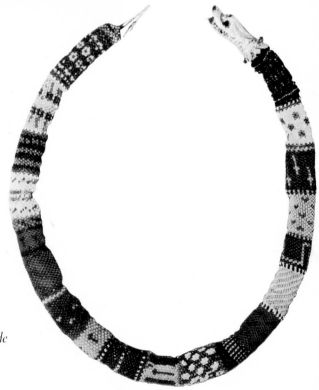

197   *Late nineteenth century. Loom-made bead patterns on cotton thread. Length 16¼ inches*

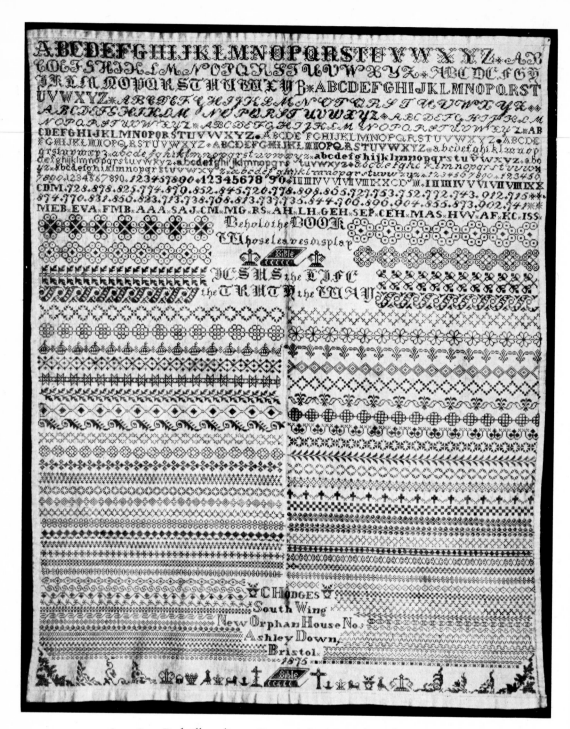

198   *1875. Red silk on linen. Cross stitch. A Bristol Orphanage sampler.*
Signed, C. Hodges. 19½ × 15¾ inches

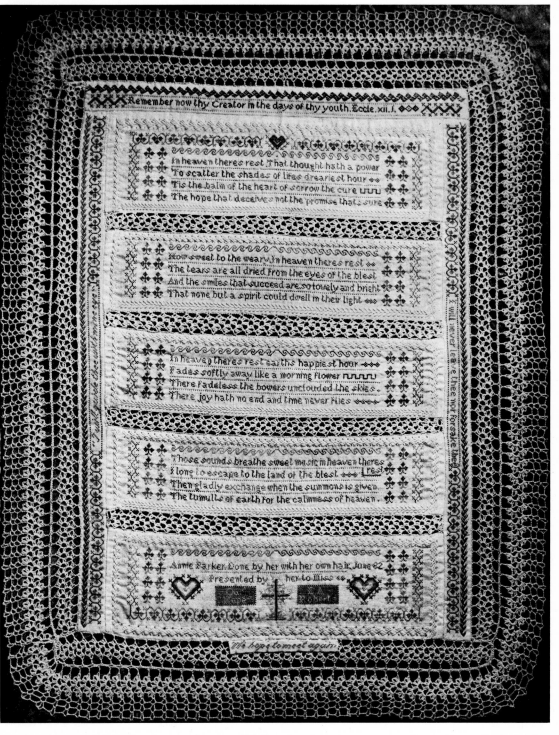

199 *'June 82' (1882). Hair, with some silk thread and crochet cotton on linen. Cross, feather and double feather stitches. Signed, Annie Parker. 14 × 10 inches*

200 *c. 1900. Cotton and silk threads on flannel with some calico. Dress-making processes using running, hemming, herring-bone, feather, double feather, back, cross and buttonhole stitches, also French knots. Signed, M.F. 18½ × 14 inches*

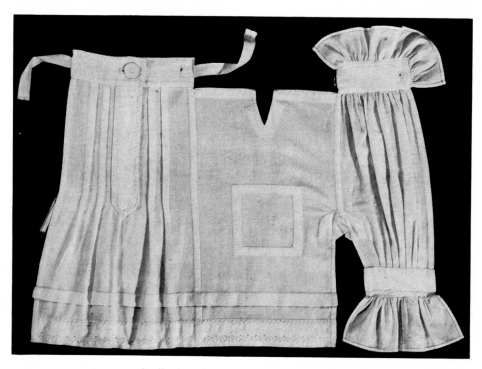

201 *c. 1900. Cotton and silk threads on cotton. Dressmaking processes using, running, hemming, back, feather, double feather, cross, eyelet and buttonhole stitches, also French knots. Signed, M.F. 13¾ × 11½ inches*

*1894. Silk and cotton threads on linen. Processes used for
[hou]sehold linen showing hem, open hem, cross, drawn work,
[feat]her, satin and darning stitches, buttons and other fastenings.
Signed, G E F B*

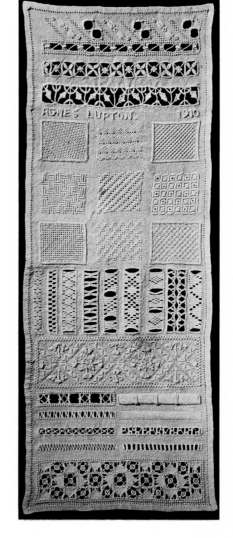

*1910. Linen thread on linen. Cutwork, eyelet, satin,
[rais]ed stem, fish-bone, detached overcast, needleweaving and
drawn work filling stitches. Signed, Agnes Lupton.
$7\frac{1}{2} \times 19\frac{1}{2}$ inches*

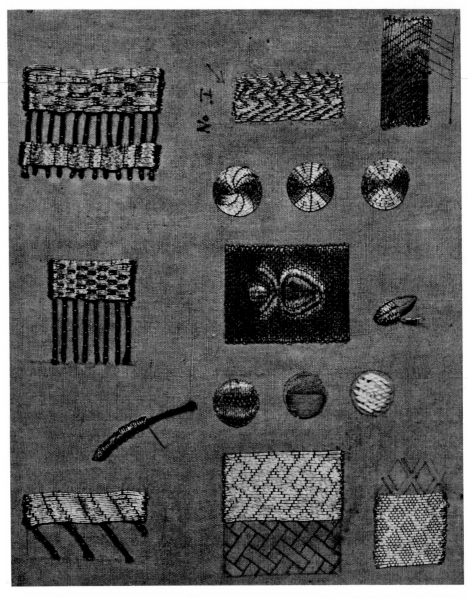

204   *c. 1910. Silk and gold thread on linen, with some cord. Methods of working solid surfaces in gold.* 11 × 9 *inches*

And as her fingers on the sampler move.
Engage her tender heart to seek thy love.
With thy dear children may she have her part.
And write thy name thyself upon her heart.

Inscriptions in prose cover a number of subjects but those with verses or extracts from the Bible are the most numerous. Hannah Fieldhouse chose verses from the *Epistle to the Ephesians* beginning, 'Children obey your parents in the Lord...' for her sampler which recorded her family by their initials [*173*]; others found the *Psalms* more to their choice and the *Ten Commandments*, the *Lord's Prayer* and *Agur's Prayer* can be seen in so many surviving samplers that count of them is lost. A unique collection of samplers, however, containing this type of inscription should be recorded because of its connection with the Branwell and Brontë families and which is now housed in the Brontë Parsonage Museum at Haworth; those made by the children having gone back to the house where they were made, after having been in private collections for some years.

The earliest of the samplers belong to the eighteenth century and were made by Mrs Brontë when she was Maria Branwell and aged eight, and by her sisters Ann, Margaret and Elizabeth, the last being the eldest and Aunt Branwell who went to care for her sister's children after their mother's death in 1821. All are worked in dark green silk on canvas and contain alphabets, texts and simple geometrical patterns; Maria Branwell's sampler, signed and dated 'April 15th 1791', has an additional pattern at the bottom, worked in pink and ginger brown wool. Ann Branwell, later Mrs Kingston, signed her sampler, Margaret signed and dated hers 'March 23rd 1799' and Elizabeth's, also signed, is dated 'October the 11th   ', the year of making having been lost when the corner of the sampler was torn.

The Brontë children, Maria the eldest at the age of eight and Elizabeth aged seven, must have made their samplers under the eye of Aunt Branwell as they were dated 1822, the year in which she went to Haworth; both are worked in brown wool on canvas. Charlotte's first sampler was made in 1882, when she was six years old, and also is of wool on canvas, but has been restored, and the present pink wool is not the original; her second sampler, linen thread on grey canvas, contained verses from the *Book of Proverbs* and was made in 1829 (p. 243). Emily and Anne each made two samplers also; Emily's were dated 'April 22nd 1828' and 'March 1st 1829' [*175*] (and p. 244) and Anne's 'November 28th 1828' and 'January 23 1830' (p. 244). If it were not for their associations one would be inclined to think of them as having little interest. They are worked on grey canvas, all contain texts or extracts from the Bible, the last three have the same geometrical border pattern; the interest lies in the differences. The names of the workers, and the choice of their texts so in keeping with their characters and the well-known background of

205   Peacocks *with the tail 'close'. Eighteenth and nineteenth centuries*

their lives, in which every moment was fully occupied, make these samplers one of the most interesting of family collections.

A number of inscriptions were worked in languages other than English and in general, clearly were school exercises. Those in French are the most common and other occasional examples are found in Latin, Hebrew and in Welsh. Referring to small number of inscriptions in the Welsh language Mr Payne writes that 'a reason sometimes given for the comparative rarity . . . is that sampler working was one of the many means of making children familiar with English'.[1] A verse in French worked by an English child, Ann Henley in 'Mai 1843', was typical of others:

La Charité

Que je vois de vertue
Qui brillent sur la trace
Charite, fille de la Grace
Aves toi marche la douceur
Qui suit avec in air affable
La patience inseparable
De la paix, son aimable sœur.

[1] F. G. Payne, *Collection of Samplers and Embroideries*, p. 35.

The nineteenth-century reluctance of a woman over 21 to reveal her age can be seen in sampler dates in which the last two figures have been unpicked by the maker, when she had come to realise the shocking disclosure made in her early innocence; some workers of the 1830s, narrowed down the guess-work of their acquaintances to a span of ten years and many samplers made within that time make the concession of leaving '183 ' [176].

Sampler patterns such as *birds, flower pots, flower* motifs and borders [183–6, 205–7] were used to decorate small things in daily use, husifs, spectacle and letter cases, small work bags [182] and so on, on which patterns were arranged in sampler fashion even to the name and date. Maps and darning samplers virtually had disappeared with the eighteenth century; an occasional specimen was made at the beginning of the nineteenth century, such as the darning sampler dated

206 Rose *flower pot.*
Nineteenth century

1802 illustrated by Mr Huish, which carried three sets of initials and probably was a schoolroom sampler worked by three children[1]; a repair sampler with darning patterns of 1894, already mentioned, was unique for its time [202].

Towards the end of the century little remained of the sampler as it had been up

207   Rose *motifs. Nineteenth century*

[1] M. B. Huish, *Samplers and Tapestry Embroideries*, Plate LV.

to 1850. Few specimens were made on linen, most of them were worked on woollen canvas and in the later years a coarse mesh canvas was used; wool was more commonly used for the embroidery than silk, especially with the increase in the use of the open mesh canvas, although some work in black or red silk (or both) was done. *Cross* stitch had become so common that it was known as *sampler* stitch, although *tent* stitch was used occasionally. The *dogs*, *trees*, *birds*, flower *pots* and even the tortoiseshell *cats* sitting or sleeping on cushioned stools, were dying out fast [172]; printed pattern books and charts, Art needlework and fancy work had taken the place of sampler making and although the words of Thackeray were written in 1848, they foreshadowed the fate of the sampler by the end of the century; during a visit to Queen's Crawley, 'the home of the dirty, cynical old Sir Pitt Crawley', Becky Sharp surveyed the room from her bed: 'The mantelpiece cast up a great black shadow over half of a mouldy old sampler, which her defunct ladyship had worked no doubt'.[1]

[1] W. M. Thackeray, *Vanity Fair*, Chapter VII.

CHAPTER ELEVEN

The Twentieth Century

The first 20 years of the twentieth century were as barren of good sampler work as those of the last half of the nineteenth, when nearly all of it was done in school and of elementary standard. Two major wars within the first 50 years of the 1900s accounted for two negative periods in the development of embroidery and although sampler making had declined to such a low level at the beginning of the century, a small number continued to be made (other than school work), but they dated from the years before and after the war periods of 1914 to 1918 and later between 1939 and 1945.

As well as the fact that the sampler as a popular form of needlework had died by 1900, numbers of needlework magazines were published at low prices, which supplied patterns and instructions for all embroidery needs. Advertisements for various brands of canvas and embroidery threads, advocated the making of samplers with these products by illustrating already-made examples, showing patterns worked in *cross* and *satin* stitches, all a little larger than life size, which included a 'signature' of the advertiser's trade name.

Other commercial inventions included a 'sampler series' of coloured cards with transfers and appropriate instruction for working the patterns of *leaf* and *flower* motifs in natural colours, which would result from the use of thread manufactured by the advertising firm. At the time of the coronation of King Edward VII a ready stamped sampler was sold, to commemorate the event, of which a number were embroidered and still exist. The patterns were stamped on a narrow strip of linen about six inches deep and 24 inches wide, to be viewed horizontally, and consisted of five small panels containing *figures*, *landscapes* and other patterns resembling illustrations in fairy tale books. Each panel contained a rhyming caption describing the contents:

This is Edwardes
Crowning yeer
See his Crowne
I sew you heer.

This is his Palace
Where he bides
He has many
More besides

This is the Garden
Full of trees
Where Kind Edward
Takes his ease.

This is his coro
nacione gowne
In which he walketh
Up and down

This is all
I have to say
For King Edward
Let us pray.

With these and other inducements of a similar kind, it is surprising that the traditional sampler survived at all.

Until 1920 the school type of sampler was of coarse *cross* stitch worked in wool, stranded cotton or crochet silk, generally on an open mesh canvas which was sometimes of a curious dingy yellow and did not improve their appearance, and sometimes on linen. The patterns consisted almost entirely of rows of *alphabets* and *numerals* in the manner of a *marking* sampler [208], often with a single line of simple stitches on the hems which hardly deserved the description of a border pattern; names, dates and ages nearly always were included. The lifeless result of this work, to a great extent was due to the teaching and not so much to the children, as numbers of samplers showed good technical ability and very little else, while many of the small specimen sampler books which were the fruits of comprehensive teaching, showed how good other work could have been, if direction in the matter of colour and pattern had been given. Small *figure* patterns were put into their samplers by some children, and simple *bird, animal, flower* and *fruit* basket patterns also were included from time to time; those worked in cotton or silk produced better results than others in wool, which were all too common.

208   *Type of letters in an alphabet. 1909*

Inscriptions were not as popular as they had been in the nineteenth century and those which were used were not as lengthy; none appears to have consisted of anything like the *Ten Commandments*, Dr Watts' *Songs* or any of the recurring inscriptions of the 1800s, although verses from school hymns were worked on samplers where space allowed. Two samplers made by sisters while at Broad Clyst school in Devon in 1909 and 1911 contain alphabets, verses and patterns worked in red and green cotton in *cross* stitch on linen. A small figure pattern in one [*209*] could have represented one of the children, in her bonnet and dress; another pattern was of an *owl* [*210*] accompanied by a verse from a somewhat unusual source, but otherwise was more appropriate to the pattern than many inscriptions:

> A clear March night,
> The moon is up—the sky is blue,
> The owlet in the midnight air
> Shouts from nobody knows where;
> He lengthens out his lonely shout
> Halloo, halloo, a long halloo.
> The Idiot Boy.

Another verse came from the school song book, of which the tune is still remembered by the worker:

> Catch the sunshine, don't be grieving
> O'er that darksome billow there
> Life's a sea of stormy billows,
> We must meet them everywhere.
> Pass right through them, do not tarry
> Overcome the heaving tide,
> There's a sparkling gleam of sunshine
> Waiting on the other side.

209 *A small figure pattern. Twentieth century*

210 Owl *motif. 1909*

In a letter about the samplers, one sister has 'recollections of copying from an old sampler, as our dear old schoolmistress used to produce them from a drawer where they were all carefully kept'; this method of school copying was maintaining a teaching tradition for samplers, which has accounted for the persistence of so many patterns over long periods of time.

School instruction in needlework by means of sampler making continued until the 1920s, although gradually it was dying out and the work done by Elsie Tye at Heythrop (p. 139) must have been an exception rather than the rule. It is probable that the decline was in some measure due to much of the teaching being left to the pupil teachers, as however good they may have been they could not have had the experience of older instructors. Series of first, second and third grade *cross* stitch samplers of the conventional kind were made by these girls, as well as by the younger children, and also the flannel and calico samplers showing *tucks*, *hems* and other sewing processes (p. 139) but most of the embroidery stitch samplers came from students doing serious study of the subject in the schools and colleges of art. A certain amount of information about them has to be taken on trust, as early examples have proved hard to come by, but apparently they were strictly practical with no attempt at decorative or pictorial motifs and were made and kept as stitch reference samplers. Some distinctive examples of students' work were made during the early years of the First World War by students at the School of Art at Edinburgh; from available examples, they were worked in dull blue linen with silk thread, in selected and well-disciplined colours and a good variety of stitches. Several samplers made by students at the Royal College of Art 1918 and 1919 under the tuition of Mrs Christie are shown as illustrations in her book and a number of other stitch samplers made by Mrs Christie also are shown containing decorative and pictorial patterns as well as practical stitch samplers.[1]

A sampler made in the early years of the century, about 1910, which has been mentioned already (p. 140), was made at the Royal School of Needlework and kept for demonstrating the various methods in the use of gold thread [204]. The sampler showing a section of the gold embroidery to be worked on the coronation robe of Queen Elizabeth II, was one made for a special purpose and is unique in that way [217]. Probably because of the cost, stitch samplers showing the use of gold do not seem to have been made outside the embroidery schools.

Individual workers with interests in special types of embroidery, have always made and kept samplers as working pattern and stitch charts, whatever the current changes in embroidery fashion, and an example of traditional *white work* on linen was made by Miss Agnes Lupton in 1910 [203] on which she worked the *cut* and *white work* stitches which were found in seventeenth-century samplers [95].

[1] Mrs Archibald Christie, *Samplers and Stitches*, Plates V, XI, XIX, XXIII, XXIV.

Others of her samplers contain coloured as well as white embroidery on linen made in the early 1930s, at a time when she was running what was in fact, almost a village industry at Cattistock in Dorset, for sets of hand-embroidered household linen worked in traditional patterns and stitches. Miss Lupton's early sampler was unique in its time and so also was a sampler of *drawn* and other stitches made by Miss Gertrude Moxon about 1920 [212]. It was worked on fine scrim with linen thread and contains 127 patterns in a chequered arrangement, each being separated from the next by an open hem worked in pale blue thread. A similar sampler containing a number of patterns much the same as Miss Moxon's, is of Danish work in the collection of the Victoria and Albert Museum, but the delicate precision of the English sampler was exceptional for its time, and none other appears to have been attempted.[1]

The 1920s saw, also, the first stages in the resurrection of the sampler as part of the equipment of the embroiderer's workbox, a resurrection which arose directly out of the teaching in the schools of art over the years, by instructors with foresight and skill as well as knowledge and experience in embroidery, which was out of reach for the school teacher who had to grapple with all the many sides of general education, in addition to needlework.

Miss Louisa Pesel was one of those teachers who was a great believer in the value of the sampler and much of her embroidery and her books were based on patterns and motifs taken from early English samplers. After her return to England from Athens, where she was director of the Royal Hellenic School of Needlework, she was commissioned to make a series of stitch samplers showing stitches in use in early English work, and others from Eastern and Western embroideries, for the Victoria and Albert Museum where they are kept. Valuable as are these samplers for students of embroidery, the embroidery for which Miss Pesel was best known was that in connection with Winchester Cathedral, which is still called 'Winchester work'. Her earliest work there was the collection of kneelers, and stall and chair cushions made for the private chapel of the Bishop of Winchester at Wolvesey, and for the designs Miss Pesel adapted a number from seventeenth-century samplers.[2] Soon after these were completed, in 1931, Miss Pesel undertook the work in connection with the Cathedral itself, organising about 200 workers of the 'Winchester Cathedral Broderers' in a task which took nearly five years to complete. The designs were taken or adapted from various sources within the Cathedral—such as the carvings, illuminated books and floor tiles—by Miss Sybil Blunt and the coloured wools for the work were selected by Miss Pesel. The largest part of the work probably was that of embroidering

[1] D. King, *Samplers*, Plate 73.
[2] Louisa F. Pesel, *English Embroidery* II.

nearly 400 kneelers and for these and the seat cushions, alms bags and so on, workers who undertook each item worked from patterns and stitch samplers. Mrs Catherine Little of Compton was closely associated with the work and the sampler illustrated was made by her in 1934 [*213*].

Miss Pesel's Cathedral embroidery was one part only of her work and in Twyford where she lived, she organised the Yew Tree industry, where she taught the workers the traditional stitches on linen, including *white work* and *Holbein* or *double running* stitch in black for which seventeenth-century samplers provided many of the patterns. Illustrations in embroidery pattern books compiled by Miss Pesel were taken from samplers, in private and Museum collections, of the same period.

In Winchester itself, traditional linen embroidery has been taught by Miss Etta Campbell at the School of Art for many years and samplers made by her students during the years 1930 to 1933 were used to illustrate her book.[1] The pair of small samplers of *double running* stitch worked in black silk on linen were made by another student, Miss Valerie Lovell, in 1955 and 1960 while working at the School of Art with Miss Campbell [*218*].

The work begun by Miss Pesel at Winchester was to result in a revival of ecclesiastical embroidery in this country. The period of 1939 to 1945 was of years virtually lost to embroidery and it was not until the 1950s, with the end of war-time shortages, that materials became plentiful enough and of sufficient quality, for many local ambitions all over the country to be realised. Working guilds of embroiderers came into being, on similar lines to that organised in Winchester, in connection with many of the cathedrals and large churches; country parishes as well as those in cities and towns have been, and are being, refurnished with embroidery to an extent unknown for more than a century. Much of the work in smaller parishes is being done by people, men as well as women, who have been unaccustomed to any work of the kind before, but where a leader of experience has been found the results are as appropriate and as highly successful as any of the cathedral work. Pattern and stitch samplers made with the canvas and wool, or with whatever materials are being used for the embroidery, make it possible for inexperienced workers to continue much of the work at home. In some villages completion of the work could have been a matter of years, if it had not been for the use of working samplers. In spite of this, individual detail is never absent from the corporate work; initials and dates have been included, usually where and how the worker chose, on his or her piece of the work; and other variations which do not alter the character of the work as a whole are accepted by an inspired leader, to the extent in one instance of welcoming a suggested inscription on the sides of a

[1] Etta Campbell, *Linen Embroideries*, Frontispiece, Plates III, IV, V.

kneeler, instead of the conventional pattern which had been planned. The worker was a retired Admiral and the inscription ran 'GOD SAVE THE QUEEN'. Two working samplers which are shown on Figure 219, are examples of those which were used for the embroidered kneelers in the parish church of the village of

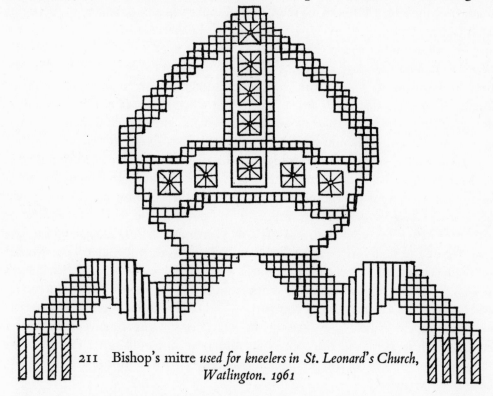

211   Bishop's mitre *used for kneelers in St. Leonard's Church, Watlington. 1961*

Watlington near Oxford; the work was of wool embroidery on canvas, designed and directed by Mrs Oscar Truscott [10, 211].

Needlework guilds and societies concerned wholly or partly with needlework, have given much encouragement in recent years to sampler making. Examination requirements for types of needlework as well as embroidery—traditional quilting, patchwork, fine sewing among them—have included stitch and pattern samplers (p. 140) and competitions, confined to members of the organisations concerned, have been organised on a national scale. In 1961 the Scottish Rural Women's Institutes held a competition for a sampler of wool embroidery on canvas, in which the opportunity to show modern treatment and experiment in stitches, patterns and arrangement was emphasised.

Part of a *screen* sampler made by the North West branches of the Embroiderer's Guild which was entered for a competition, also in 1961, is illustrated [221, 222].

The competition was for a small six-fold screen sampler suitable for standing on a table, to be made by a group of workers, and several of those sent in contained a single pattern for which a different kind of treatment was used on each panel. The pattern on the sampler on Figures 221 and 222 was taken from a drawing, made by Miss Helen Rhodes, of the Guild's London headquarters at 73 Wimpole Street; the methods used in two of the illustrated panels are of *black work* on linen, and of *darning* on net in two shades of red with some grey and white, and *double running* stitches in black to represent the ironwork. Embroidery used on the other four panels was of *drawn* work and other stitches, in green and grey thread on linen; of *drawn*, *satin* and *double running* stitches on cream linen in natural coloured linen thread; of *applied* work with hand embroidered detail, and of *applied* work with machine stitching and a little hand-worked detail.

As the revival of church embroidery in the 1930s was due to the inspired work of Miss Pesel, that of domestic embroidery in the same period was due in no small way to the encouragement given to it by the Needlework Development Scheme in Glasgow. Operating originally in Scotland, the work of the Scheme, after the interval between 1939 and 1945, was carried on from Glasgow in England also. Among its many services, such as loan collections of embroidery, the Needlework Development Scheme commissioned work from contemporary embroiderers as well as building up collections of work from earlier periods of British and foreign embroidery, for the purpose of comparison and study, and a number of samplers, including recent work, were among the collections. Unfortunately the Scheme closed down in 1961 and the collections dispersed, but with other embroideries, the samplers are now in the permanent collections of the Embroiderer's Guild in London.

Screen samplers appeared first in the 1930s and since the end of the 1940s have been popular for class teaching. Classes for adult education in needlework have suffered from overcrowding as much as other subjects and the problem of devising ways to help both instructors and students resulted in the use of stitch and pattern samplers mounted on a support which would stand on a table, so enabling one or more students to use the same 'visual aid'. The advantages of the same type of presentation for displaying samplers, at exhibitions and so on, were obvious and the screen sampler has proved useful also, for showing the progressive stages of developing patterns and stitches.

Although the pictorial type of sampler of the eighteenth and nineteenth centuries is made rarely nowadays, decorative panels recording various ways of applying traditional stitches to modern work, such as the *houses* on the screen sampler, are becoming popular. *Darning* on net and *black work* are particularly so. As well as one of the *houses*, an example of recent work on a working sampler of *darning* on net was illustrated in *Embroidery* in 1961,[1] for patterns to be worked on a christening gown of net over a silk foundation. *Black work* stitches in a pattern of *shells*, *seaweed* and *fishes* on an oval decorative panel is in the collection of samplers at Gawthorpe Hall; it is signed 'FRANCES KAY. 1961'.

As a subject for prose or poetry it is significant that twentieth-century samplers have inspired no one. Men's fashions undoubtedly inspired much of the praise for samplers by the sixteenth- and seventeenth-century poets (all men) as they were dependent on the makers for the good appearance of their dress, but men's clothes have been affected hardly at all by embroidery for the last 60 years or more. The Edwardian carpet slipper worked in *cross* stitch did not need a sampler; and the occasional embroidered waistcoat which crept in did not grow into enough of a fashion to warrant a new vogue for *sampler* making, so until an unlikely demand arises for 'falling bands' of lace or other hand embroidered adornments for men's clothes, it is consequently unlikely that the poetry of the century will turn to samplers for inspiration.

A sampler of another age was the subject of what appears to be the only poem with this choice; it was written by Mary Webb in 1928 and is entitled *Anne's Book*:

> And so, Anne Everard, in those leafy Junes
> Long withered; in those ancient, dark Decembers,
> Deep in the drift of time, haunted by tunes
> Long silent; you beside the homely embers,
> Or in some garden fragrant and precise
> Were diligent and attentive all day long!
> Fashioning with bright wool and stitches nice
> Your sampler, did you hear the thrushes sing
> Wistfully? While in orderly array,
> Six rounded trees grew up; the alphabet,
> Stout and uncomprising, done in grey;
> The Lord's Prayer, and your age, in violet;
> Did you Anne Everard, dream from hour to hour
> How the young wind was crying on the hill,
> And the young world was breaking into flower?
> With small head meekly bent, all mute and still,
> Earnest to win the promised great reward,
> Did you not see the birds, at shadow-time,
> Come hopping all across the dewy sward?
> Did you not hear the brittle bells of Faery chime

[1] *Embroidery*, Winter, 1960–1961, Figure 99.

Liquidly, where the brittle hyacinths grew?
Your dream—attention; diligence, your aim!
And when the last long needleful was through,
When, laboured for so long, the guerdon came—
Thomson, his *Seasons*, neatly bound in green—
How brightly would the golden letters shine!
Ah! many a petalled May the moon has seen
Since Anne—attentive, diligent, ætat nine—
Puckering her young brow, read the stately phrases.
Sampler and book are here without a stain—
Only Anne Everard lies beneath the daisies;
Only Anne Everard will not come again.[1]

Perhaps the contemporary sampler has its day in literature still to come. To-day's needlework books and magazines illustrate a nineteenth-century sampler from time to time, in connection with articles on embroidery, but none of the advertisements dealing with embroidery materials emphasises in any way the necessity for their use in sampler making.

Strange to say, an advertisement did appear in a daily paper in 1960, in which a conventional sampler was represented, but the advertised product was a brand of petrol, and the sampler patterns and an inscription, related to motoring and petrol pumps. American magazine advertisements, on the other hand, offer 'sampler kits' which contain everything needed to complete the printed design provided, and are intended for adult workers, as well as those younger ones, who are reluctant to think for themselves. Examples include the 'Pledge of Allegiance Sampler Kit' ('a patriotic sampler for Girl Scouts and Camp Fire Girls') or the 'Kitchen Sampler Kit' ('the cross stitch design is highlighted with a little outline . . . to give rounded form to the lush colourful vegetables') or the reproduced copy of an old sampler can be provided, ready stamped on linen with the embroidery silks supplied in 'authentic time-faded colours'.

Cross stitch always will retain a place in sampler work, but the number and variety of other stitches in regular use can be seen from present-day working samplers, whether they are made by students and fully or partly occupied embroiderers; all are based on traditional stitches with many variations which have grown up with the work. They are worked in silk, wool or cotton, on linen and single or double canvas of different kinds; the synthetic untarnishing gilt thread, lurex, is now used for effects given by the silver or silver gilt thread of the sixteenth- and seventeenth-century work.

[1] Mary Webb, *The Spring of Joy*, p. 79.

The record of the twentieth century must be left unfinished. There are another 35 years or so to go before it can be completed, but the last 35 have seen the sampler change from an undistinguished piece of elementary school work, to its original standing as a stitch and pattern record of an experienced embroiderer. Having thus come full circle, it is to be hoped that the days of the 'mouldy old sampler' are over.

CHAPTER TWELVE

Inscriptions and Verses

Inscriptions are of interest still, to owners of samplers of the eighteenth and nine-teenth centuries, whether these were inherited or acquired in other ways, which have inscriptions with slight differences in the wording, spelling or phrasing. Some rhymes were repeated on so many samplers, such as 'Jesus permit thy gracious Name to stand . . .' (p. 210) that all possible variations ran out, but others which, for a number of reasons, seem a little out of the ordinary in these days, may be worth recording. The *Bible* extracts on the samplers of Emily, Charlotte and Anne Brontë are similar to those on others of the nineteenth century, but the samplers are not vaguely anonymous as many hundreds of others and because of what is known of their background, the inscriptions on all three are quoted. Very little is known of the makers of samplers which have been cherished by their descendants; sometimes a portrait or a miniature gives an idea of what she looked like, but although the choice of the patterns may seem ordinary enough, the choice of some of the inscriptions does not and what prompted a child of 15 to make the extraordinary choice of the lines beginning, 'You took me Robert, when a girl, into your home and heart' (p. 254), will never be known.

The comparatively few inscriptions in this chapter are in addition to those earlier in the book. They are arranged, as far as possible, according to the subject of each, regardless of dates and a few only of the very long ones are given. Most have been copied from samplers in private houses but a number have come, with permission, from samplers in Museums or quoted from books, some of them now out of print. Where it is known, the date of each inscription is added and in some, where an identical verse has occurred in several samplers over a period of years, the earliest and latest dates which can be found are given; a number of Dr Watts' *Songs* have been embroidered on undated samplers and of the few which

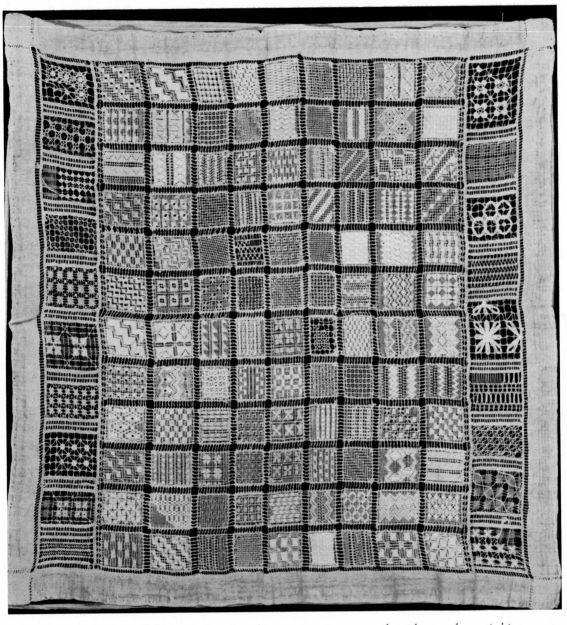

212   *c. 1920. Linen and silk thread on linen scrim. Drawn work with some hem-stitching. Maker, Miss Gertrude Moxon.* $14\frac{1}{4} \times 14\frac{1}{2}$ *inches*

213 *1934. Wool thread on linen. Rice, cross, long and short tent, satin and eyelet stitches. Sampler for Winchester Cathedral work.*
Signed, F.C.L. 10 × 20 inches

214   *1936. Linen thread on linen. Eyelet, sheaf, satin, detached overcast, bullion, drawn work filling stitches and needleweaving, with cords, button fastenings and tassels, also insertions and picot ring edges. Signed, E. Tansley. 14 × 7½ inches*

5   *1946. Cotton and silk on cambric. Fine sewing mpler showing running, hem and open hem, feather and ible feather, blanket, eyelet, buttonhole, back, petal hem, in and whipping stitches with some applied work and picot ring edges. Signed E.C. 23 × 10¾ inches*

216   *c. 1920. Silk and gold threads on figured silk damask, with jewels, laid work and couching in motifs for church embroidery. Worker, Mary Nevitt. $8\frac{1}{2} \times 20\frac{1}{2}$ inches*

217   *1952–1953. Silk and gold thread with spangles on purple velvet, showing the style of design and methods for the embroidery on the Coronation Robe of H.M. Queen Elizabeth II. $22\frac{1}{2} \times 12$ inches*

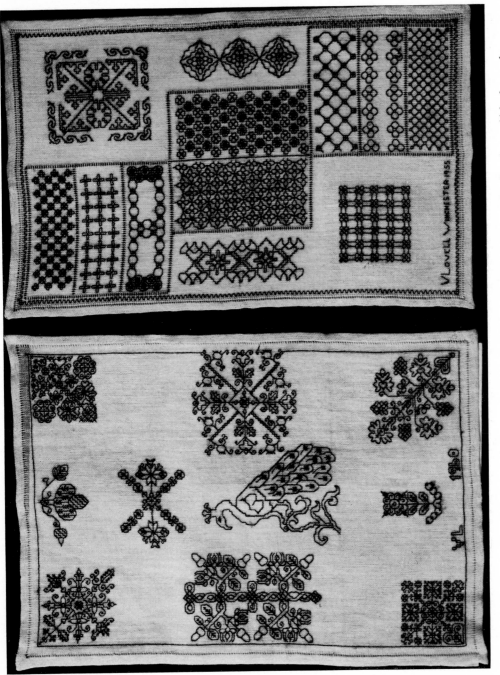

218　1955. 1960. *Silk thread on linen. Two workbox samplers in double running stitch of traditional black work patterns. Signed, V.L. 1960, V. Lovell Winchester 1955. Each sampler $12\frac{3}{4} \times 7\frac{3}{4}$ inches*

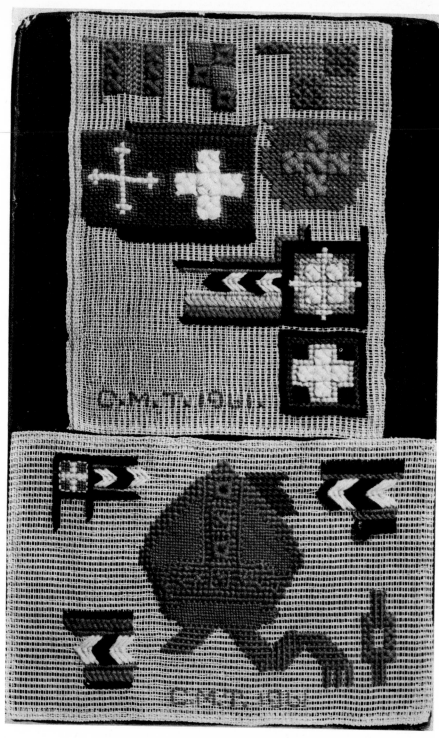

219   *1961. Wool thread on double canvas. Two working samplers for kneelers*
in the parish church of St. Leonard's, Watlington.
Signed, C.M.T. Each sampler, 4 × 6 inches.

220   *1961. Silk thread on linen. Sampler for class teaching in outline and filling stitches. Signed, S.S-A. 27 × 22 inches*

221   *Black silk on Evenweave linen. Double
running in traditional black work.
Worker, Mrs C. Marsden.* 13¾ × 5½ *inches*

222   *Red, grey, white and natural silk thread on
square mesh net. Darning stitches with some double
running in black silk. Worker, Mrs Timperley*
13¾ × 5½ *inches*

1961. Two panels from a six-fold screen sampler

are quoted in this chapter one date only is given, 'Obedience to Parents' being the exception.

Inscriptions of a religious nature are probably the most common, and they include texts, hymns, moral songs and prayers. Rhymes containing moralising sentiments, generally on the consequences of Sin and the advantages of Virtue are numerous and others on the themes of Death and Hell come a close second in popularity. Usually one verse or two contented the makers, but others must have felt compelled to go on to the bitter end, especially with such things as Dr Watts' 'The Sluggard', 'Good Resolutions', and 'Obedience to Parents' with all the gruesome details of the 'dreadful plagues' lying in wait for the disobedient.

All eccentricities of spelling and grammar which occurred in the originals have been left in.

Verses from the Bible

A House divided against itself can't stand.

Better is a dry morsel and quiet-
ness therewith:than a house full of
sacrifices,and strife.Prov 17. ver I.

He loveth transgression that loveth strife:and he that exalteth his
gait seeketh destruction. ver 19.

He that hath a froward heart findeth no good: and he that hath a per-
vers spirit falleth into mischief ver20.

A reproof entereth into the heart
of a wise man more than an hundred stripes into a fool. ver 10.

He also that is slothful in his
work is brother to him that is a
great waster. Proverbs 18: 9 ver.

The fear of the LORD tendeth
to life:and he that hath it shall
abide satisfied:he shall not be
visited with evil. Prov. 19 ver 23.

Charlotte Brontë finished this sampler April the 1 1829.

Honour the LORD with thy sub-
stance and with the first-fruits of
all thine increase:So shall thy barns
be filled with Plenty, and thy Press-
es shall burst out with new wine.
My child despise not the chastening
of the LORD;neither be weary of
his correction:For whom the LORD
loveth he correcteth, even as a father the son in whom he delighteth.
Happy is the man that findeth wisdom, and the man that getteth under-
standing.For the merchandise of it is
better than the merchandise of silver,and the gain thereof than fine gold
She is more precious than rubies:and
all the things thou canst desire are
not to be compare unto her.Length
of days is in her right hand,and in her
left hand is riches and honour.Her
ways are ways of pleasantness,
and all her paths are peace.She is a
tree of life to them that lay hold upon
her:and happy is everyone that re-
taineth her. Proverbs 9–18 verses,

ANNE BRONTË : January 23 . 1830.

THE words of Agur the son of Jakeh, even the pro
phecy:the man spake unto Ithiel,even unto Ithiel
and Ucal,Surely I am more brutish than any man,
and have not the understanding of a man.I neither
learned wisdom,nor have the knowledge of the holy.

Who hath ascended up into heaven, or descended?
who hath gathered the wind in his fists? who hath
housed the waters in a garment? who hath establish
ed all the ends of the earth? what is his name, and
what is his son's name,if thou canst tell? Every
word of God is pure,he is a shield unto them that
put their trust in him. Add thou not his words,
lest he reprove thee,and thou be found a liar.Two
things have I required of thee;deny me them not
before I die: Remove from me vanity and lies:
give me neither poverty nor riches:feed me with
food convenient for me:Lest I be full,and deny
thee,and say,Who is the Lord? or lest I be poor,
and steal,and take the name of my God in vain.
30th of Proverbs,the first 9 Verses.

The LORD is gracious, and full of compassion:Slow to
anger,and of great mercy. the LORD is good to all:
and his tender mercies are over all his works.
Psalm. CXLV. Verses 8th 9th

Emily Jane Brontë: Finished this Sampler. March 1st 1829.

YE saints on earth,ascribe,with heaven's high host,
Glory and honour to the One in Three;
To God the Father,Son,and Holy Ghost,
As was,and is,and evermore will be.

THE PLEASURES OF RELIGION
Tis Religion that can give
Sweetest pleasures while we live
Tis religion must supply
Solid comfort when we die
After death its joys will be
Lasting as eternity
Let me then make God my friend
And on all his ways attend.   1810 to 1835

An alternative to the last two lines are given sometimes as:

Be the Living God my friend
Then that Bliss will never end.   1835

Defend me from mine enemies O God
Defend me from mine enemies that
rise up against me.   1701

O worship the Lord in the beauty of holiness.   1792

God is Love
Still waters run deep   1889

God is Love
Abide with us
Time is short   1888

Love the Lord and he will be
A tender Father unto thee.   1694 to 1835

Zaccheus short of stature fain would see
his saviour pass and climbs into a Tree,If we
by Faith would see this glorious King,Our
thoughts must mount on contemplations wing.   1774

ON THE CRUCIFIXION OF GOOD FRIDAY

No songs of Triumph now are sung
Cease all your sprightly airs
Let Sorrow silence every tongue
And Joy dissolve in Tears.   1801

EASTER

The Holy Feast of Easter was injoined
To bring Christ's Resurrection to our mind.
Rise then from Sin as He did from the Grave
That by His Merrits he Your Souls may save.   1800

Prayer in Rhyme

During the time of life allotted me
Grant me good God health and liberty
I beg no more, if more thou'rt pleased to give
I'll thankfully the overplus receive.   1778

    Father of all created things
    Who dwellest above in heaven
    All hallowed by thy holy name
    To thee all praise be given
    The Kingdom of thy blissful grace
    May we still hope to win
    By strict observance of thy laws
    And keeping free from sin.   1831

Grant me Good Heaven,a man of sense refined
Both Great in Merit and of Honest Mind
Be this my portion if I be made a Wife
Or keep me happy in a Single Life.
    *   *   *   *   *   *
        Let Virtue Guide Me.   1810

'ON DEATH'

Death at a Distance we but slightly fear,
He brings his Terrors as he draws more near,
Through Poverty,Pain,Slav'ry we drudge on.
The worst of Beings better please than none
No Price too dear to purchase Life and Breath
The heaviest Burthen's easier borne than Death.   1800

    Happy Soul thy days are ended
    All thy morning days below
    Go by angel guard attended
    to the sight of Jesus go.   1820

    Speak gently to the aged one
    Grieve not the careworn heart
    The sands of life are nearly run
    Let such in peace depart.   1826

'ON TIME'

Swiftly see each moment flies
See, and learn, be timely wise,
Every moment shortens day,
Every pulse beats time away
Thus every heaving breath
Wafts thee on to certain death.
Seize the moments as they fly
Know to live, and learn to die.   1843

'ON A WATCH'

While this gay toy attracts the sight
Thy reason let it warn;
And seize, my dear, that rapid time
That never must return.

If idly lost, no art or care
The blessing can restore:
And heav'n exacts a strict account
For ev'ry mis-spent hour.

Short is our longest day of life
And soon its prospects end
Yet on that day's uncertain date
Eternal years depend.   1796

The second verse of this rhyme appears alone, on samplers up to 1831.

'FLEETING YOUTH'

The finest Rose in Christendom
At length begins to fade
The fairest Virgin in the world
Must in the dust be laid.   During the
                                      nineteenth century

EDUCATION

Tis education forms the youthful mind
Just as the twig is bent the tree's inclined
For what WE learn in youth to that alone
In age we are by second nature prone

So youth set right at first with ease go on
And each new thing is with new pleasure done
But if neglected till they grow in years
And each fond mother her dear darling spares
Error becomes habitual and you'll find
Tis then hard labour to reform the mind.   1829

Industry taught in early days
Not only gives the teacher praise
But gives us pleasure too
When we view the work
that innocence can do.   1830

My time at school well spent
I never shall repent.   1720

NEEDLEWORK

In the glad morn of blooming youth
These various threads I drew,
And now behold this finished piece
Lies glorious to the view.
So when bright youth shall charm no more
And age shall chill my blood,
May I review my life and say,
Behold my works are good.   1831

THE
LADYS CALLING
TEACHETH NO ROMANCE
NO FOND INTRIGUES OF
LOVE NO MODES OF FR
ANCE READING GOOD BOO
KS AND NEEDLE WORK SH
OULD BE THEIR WHOLE
DEVERTION AND FELICITY.   1727

'TO MY EVER HONOURED PARENTS'

On this Fair Canvas does my needle write
With love and duty both this I indite
In pleasing view each pleasing line appears
To show the improvement of my growing years

In gratitude to God my Heart I raise
That I was early taught to sing his Praise
My chief and constant care both morn and night
Will be to give you comfort and delight
And in these lines dear Parents I impart
The tender feeling of a grateful Heart.   1820

The beauteous rose like Youth appears
    Which blooms but for a day
Then drooping quits this Vale of Tears
    Thus fades the Rose away.

Youth buds—the promised flower appears
    But oh! how short the bloom
We live but for a few short years
    Then moulder in the Tomb.

Reflect on this—to die prepare—
    This lesson never spurn
To-morrow we are summoned where
    No travellers return.   1843

Verses from Dr. Isaac Watts' "Divine and Moral Songs for Children"

MORAL SONG VI. 'Good Resolutions' verses 6 and 7

    What though I be low and mean
    I'll engage the rich to love me
    Whilst I'm modest, neat and clean
    And submit when they reprove me.

    If I should be poor and sick
    I shall meet I hope with pity
    Since I love to help the weak
    Tho' they're neither fair not witty.   1820

'DUTY TO GOD AND NEIGHBOUR' verse 2

    Deal with another as you'd have
    Another deal with you:
    What you're unwilling to receive,
    Be sure you never do.   1831

DIVINE SONG XXIII 'Obedience to Parents' verse I

Let children that would fear the Lord
Hear what their teachers say;
With reverence meet their parents' word,
And with delight obey.

Have you not heard what dreadful plagues
Are threatened by the Lord,
To him that breaks his father's law,
Or mocks his mother's word?   1740 to 1850

'OUR SAVIOUR'S GOLDEN RULE'

Be you to others kind and true
As you'd have others be to you,
And never do or say to men
What'er you would not take again.   1825

'THE SUM OF THE COMMANDMENTS'

With all thy soul love God above;
And as thyself thy neighbour love.   1729

'VIRTUE'

Virtue's the chiefest Beauty of the Mind
The Greatest Ornament of Human Kind,
Virtue's our safeguard and our guiding Star
That stirs up reason when our senses err.   1796

True modest virtue it is said,
To be the glory of a maid.   1720

They that walk in the Path of Virtue
are an Ornament to Society.   1833

If wisdom's ways you'd wisely seek
Five things observe with care,
Of whom you speak, to whom you speak
And how, and when, and where.   1839

'MIND SUPERIOR TO BODY'

What is the blooming tincture of the skin
To peace of mind and harmony within?
What is the bright sparkling of the finest eye,
To the soft soothing of a calm reply?
Can comeliness of form, or shape, or air,
With comeliness of words or deeds compare?
No—those at first the unwary heart may gain,
But these—these only, can the heart retain.
And you, ye fair with cautious arm
'Gainst Man's perfidious Arts,
For Youth and Beauty vainly charm
    When Virtue once departs.　　　　1799 to 1832

This verse is entitled 'To Young Ladies' in samplers after about 1820.

'ADVICE'

Learn to contemn all Praise betimes
For Flattery is the Nurse of Crimes
With early Virtue plant thy Breast
The Specious Arts of Vice detest.

Regard the world with cautious eye
Nor raise your expectations high
See that the balanced scale be such
You neither fear nor hope too much.　　　　1800 to 1850

'THE DESIRE'

From my Beginnings may the Almighty Power
Blessings bestow in never ceasing shower
Oh! May I happy be and always blest!
Of every Joy, of every Wish possessed!
May Plenty dissipate all worldly Care
And smiling Peace bless all my revolving years.　　1800 to 1840

HUMILITY

The bird which soars on highest wing
Builds on the ground her lowly nest;
And she that doth most sweetly sing
Sings in the shade when all things rest.
In lark and nightingale we see
What honour hath Humility.　　　　1851

How loved how valued once avails thee not
To whom related, by whom begot.
A heap of dust alone remains of thee
Tis all thou art and all the proud shall be.   1814

DOUBTS ON FRIENDSHIP

Declare thy secret thought to none,
For fear of shame and sorrow.
For he that is thy friend to-day
May be thy foe to-morrow.   1851

In prosperity friends will be plenty
But in adversity not one in twenty.

Reach down reach down Thy Hand of Grace
And teach me to ascend,
Where congregations ne'er break up
And Sabbaths never end.   1818

Jane King will be happy
when christ shall make her free.   1754

Some children combined a number of popular inscriptions which usually are in verse form, so that they appear at first to be prose, one running into the other. Those of Elizabeth Matrom and Anne Wise are examples.

You ask me why I love, go ask the glorious sun, why it throw the world doth run, ask time and fat(e) the reason why it flow ask dammask roses why so full they blow, and all things elce suckets fesh which forceeth me to love. By this you see what car my parents toock of me. Elizabeth Matrom is my name, and with my nedell I rought the same, and if my judgment had beene better, I would have mended every letter. And she that is wise, her time will pris(e) she that will eat her breakfast in bed, and will spend all the morning in dressing of her head, and sat at deaner like a maiden bride, God in His mercy may do much to save her, but what a cas is he that must have her. Elizabeth Matrom. The sun sets, the shadows fleys, the good consume, and the man he deis.   1718

Anne Wise is my name and England
is my nation—Rochester is
my dwelling place—Christ

is my salvation. the Rose is read
The grass is green
The days are past which
I have seen—(When land and money)
—is gon and spent—Learning is
most excellent—This piece of
work my friends may have
When I am gone and lead
in grave—Anne Wise 1714.
Our Father which art in
Heaven Hallowed be thy
Name—Thy Kingdom come thy
Will be done in Earth as
It is in Heaven. Give us this
Day our (daily) Bread & for
Give us (our) trespasses as we
for give them that trespass (against) us and lead us
Not into (temptation) But deliver us from Evil.

A.W.

> This life is nothing heaven is
> All death has not wronged us
> By this fall my days are
> Spent my glass is run and now
> Jesus I com I com.

1714

You took me Robert, when a girl into your home & heart
To bear in all your after life a fond and faithful part.
And tell me have I ever tried that duty to forego
Or find there was not joy for me, when thou wert sunk in woe.
No, I would rather share your tear than any other's glee
For though you're nothing to the world, you're all the world to me.
You make a palace of my shed, this rough hewn bench a throne
There's sunlight for me in your smile and music in your tone.
I look upon you when you sleep, my eyes with tears grown dim
I cry! Oh parent of the poor look down from heaven on him.
Behold him toil from day to day, exhausting strength and soul
Oh look with mercy on him Lord for thou cans't make him whole
And when at last relieving sleep has on my eyelids smiled
How oft are they forbade to close in slumber by our child.
I take the little murmurer that spoils my span of rest

And feel it is a part of thee I lull upon my breast.
There's only one return I crave, I may not need it long
And may it soothe thee when I'm where the wretched feel no wrong.
I ask not for a kinder tone, for thou wert ever kind.
I ask not for less frugal fare, my fare I do not mind.
I ask not for attire more gay, if such as I have got
Suffice to make me fair to thee, for more I murmur not.
But I would ask some share of hours that you on clubs bestow
Of knowledge which you prize so much, might I not something know.
Subtract from meetings amongst men, each eve an hour for me.
Make me companion of your soul as I may safely be.
If you will read I'll sit and work, then think when you're away
Less tedious I shall find the time, dear Robert of your stay.
A meet companion soon I'll be for e'en your studious hours
And teacher of those little ones you call your cottage flowers
And if we be not rich or great, we may be wise and kind
And as my heart can warm your heart, so may my mind, your mind.　　1840

Bibliography

Art of Botanical Illustration, The, Wilfrid Blunt, 1950
Book of Old Embroidery, A, A. L. Kendrick
British Samplers, Mary E. Jones, 1948.
Dictionary of Needlework, Caulfeild & Saward, 1882
English Secular Embroidery, M. A. Jourdain, 1910
Floral Symbolism of the Great Masters, Elizabeth Haig, 1916
Flowerers, The, M. H. Swain, 1955
Grammar of the English Tongue, A, John Brightland, 1711
History of the Horn-Book, The, Andrew S. Tuer, 1897
History of English Embroidery, The, Barbara Morris, 1954
History of Lace, The, Mrs Bury Palliser, 1875
Linen Embroideries, Etta Campbell, 1935
Needlework as Art, Lady Marian Alford, 1886
Oliver Cromwell, John Buchan, 1934
Samplers, Leigh Ashton, 1926
Samplers, Donald King, 1960
Samplers and Stitches, Mrs Archibald Christie, 1920
Samplers and Tapestry Embroideries, Marcus B. Huish, 1900
Spring of Joy, The, Mary Webb
Ten Hours Parson, The, J. C. Gill
Victorian Embroidery, Barbara Morris, 1962
A Gallery of Flowers, Germain Bazin, 1960

JOURNALS AND CATALOGUES
Catalogue of Samplers in the Victoria and Albert Museum, P. G. Trendell, 1922
Connoisseur, Volume 85–86, 'Hannah Smith' by A. F. Kendrick, 1930
Connoisseur, April, 'Earliest dated sampler' by D. King, 1962
Country Life, August 11th, 1960
Embroidery, 1933–1960
Embroidress, The, Volume I
Guide to the Collection of Samplers and Embroideries. National Museum of Wales,
    F. G. Payne, 1939
Magazine of the Daughters of the American Revolution, December 1926
Samplers in the Guildford Museum, R. Oddy, 1951
Some Pictures and Samplers from the Collection of Lady Mary St. John Hope, 1949.

Index

The numerals in **heavy** type denote the figure numbers of the illustrations

Abraham and Sarah, Visitation of, 39, 58: **60**
Ackworth School, 199
Acorn motif, 46, 72, 149, 150: **34, 35, 134, 137, 145, 146, 163, 164**
Acrostic samplers, 95, 186
Adam and Eve, 39, 44, 45, 57, 58, 67, 73, 183, 184: **60, 171, 176**
Adoration motif, 50
Africa, map sampler of, 136
Agur's Prayer, 219: **175**
Aled, Tudur (Welsh poet), 144
Alford, Lady Marian, *Needlework as Art,* 32, 54, 148
Algerian eye stitch, **53, 100**
Alleyne, Anne Rollestone, sampler by, **120**
All-over patterns, 39, 163: **21, 135**
Almanack samplers, 136, 186: **122**
Alphabets, 28, 30, 110ff., 122, 138, 165, 169, 224: **98, 106, 107, 108, 173, 198, 208**
American genealogical samplers, 98
   sampler kits, 232
Angel motif, 44, 67: **60, 103**
Animal motifs, 25, 28, 44, 75, 77, 150, 163, 165, 199, 224: **30, 57, 72–80, 98, 114, 117, 168, 169, 176**
   See also Cat, Dog, Stag, etc.
Anne, Queen, 70, 173: **101**
Annunciation, the, 50
Ansen, Mary Ann, sampler by, **172**
Apple motif, 39, 45
Applied work, 230: **215**
Arcaded borders, 161: **16, 138, 158**
Arnold's School, 136
Arrowhead stitch, 151: **53**
Ash tree motif, 54
Ashton, Sir Leigh, *Samplers,* 22, 29, 139, 149, 163, 199
Ass motif, 77
Axmouth, Devon, 78
'Ayrshire embroidery', 199–201: **125**

B., G. E. F., *see* Barnardiston
B., S. sampler by, 179: **105**

Bacheler, Edward and Ruth, 98
Back stitch, 135–137, 151, 158, 175: **53, 57, 98, 101, 103, 123, 200, 201**
Bacon, Sir Francis (qu.), 163
Band patterns, 29, 39, 69, 75, 116, 117, 146, 154, 158–160, 168, 180: **6, 8, 18, 95, 136, 137**
Barley-ear motif, **217**
Barley, William, *A Booke of Curious and Strange Inventions,* 20
Barnardiston sampler, 204, 205: **202**
Basket motif, 49: **41.** *See also* Fruit Bowl and Basket
Batty, Margaret, sampler by, 184
Bead work 116, 151, 203: **53, 95, 178, 197**
Bear, chained, motif, 150: **53**
Beckett, Sarah, sampler by, 185
Bedford Gaol, sampler from, 93
Bee motif, 81
Belfast Museum and Art Gallery, 202
Bell, Ann, sampler by, 119
Benham, Ann, 138
Berkin, Deborah Iane, 'epistle' sampler, 91
Berlin wool work, 28, 204, 205: **191, 193, 195**
Bestiaries, 19
Betsworth, Ann, 138
   Emma, 138
Biblical inscriptions, 219, 243ff.: **103, 106, 118, 173, 175, 199**
Biblical motifs, 39, 44, 50, 57ff., 181, 183, 209: **60, 170**
Bird motifs, 25, 32, 44, 79, 85, 88, 136, 181, 199, 221, 224: **32, 53, 57, 62, 79–82, 84, 85, 91, 94, 97, 98, 100, 106, 115, 122, 145, 166, 176, 182, 205, 210**
Birds of Paradise, 44, 79: **176**
Bishop, Sarah, sampler by, **101**
Bishop's mitre motif, 229: **211**
Black work, 146, 149, 230; **218, 221**
Blanket stitch, **215**
Blunt, Miss Sybil, 227
Blunt, Wilfred, *The Art of Botanical Illustration,* 26
Boar motif, 77

Boardman, Sarah, sampler by, 126
Bocking, Susanna Pettit, sampler by, 124
Bolton, 124
Bone lace, 159, 160
Border patterns, 28, 146: **16, 17, 25, 128, 129, 142, 150**
Bostocke, Iane, sampler by, 92, 149–152: **53, 131**
'Boten, Lucke', 154
Botticelli, *Virgin and Child*, 51
Bottles, 86: **89**
Boxer motif, 57, 67, 71, 73, 161: **56, 69, 70, 99**
Boyle School, 138
Bradford, 94, 123
Branch, Elizabeth, sampler by, 154: **97**
Branwell family, 107
Brewer, Emma, 138
Brick stitch, **97**
Brierley, Yorks., 94
Brightland, John, *Grammar of the English Tonge*, 110 169
Bristol, 4th Earl of, Bishop of Derry, 174
Bristol Orphanage, samplers from, 28, 35, 111, 113, 138: **198**
Britannia, 136: **121**
British Isles, map samplers of, 135: **121**
Britton, Ann, sampler by, 84, 209, 210: **180, 192**
Broad Clyst School, Devon, 225
Broderer's Guild, 19
Brontë Sisters, samplers by, 107, 219, 234, 243–245: **175**
Brooks, Thomas, *Paradise Opened*, 168
Broom pod motif, 42
Brown, Ann, sampler by, 126
Brown, E., sampler by, 142
Budd, Harriet, 138
Buildings as patterns, 82ff., 181, 183, 206: **118, 173, 176, 180, 192, 195, 221, 222**
Bull, Rev. George Stringer, 94
Bullion stitch, **53, 100, 214**
Bush motif, 32, 180, 183: **53, 64, 104, 106, 118, 123, 176, 182**
Butterfly motif, 32, 180, 183: **57, 62, 64, 65, 98**
Buttonhole stitch, 58, 138, 160, 178, 186: **53, 61, 62, 98, 99, 123, 200, 201, 215**

C., E, sampler by, 141: **215**
C., M, sampler by, 180
Cabinet (embroidered casket), 116, 117
Caernarvon, 126
Calendars, *see* Almanacks
Camel motif, 77: **57**
Campbell, Miss Etta, *Linen Embroideries*, 228
Canting, Hannah, sampler by, 120, 121
Canvas lace work, **191**
Canvas, wool embroidery on, 229: **211, 219**
Carrow Abbey, near Norwich, 144
Carnation motif, 34, 38, 49, 150, 161, 199: **8, 58, 65, 97, 123, 128, 132, 142, 144, 147, 151, 152, 155, 159**
Carr, Ellen, sampler by, 135, 136: **174**
Castles, 84: **195**

Cat motif, 77, 222: **58, 77, 172**
Caterpillar motif, 32: **57, 65**
Catherine of Aragon, Queen, 23, 41, 146
Catlett, Miss Elizabeth, 210
Cattistock, Dorset, 227
Caufeild and Saward, *Dictionary of Needlework* (qu.), 29, 30, 115, 138, 200, 206
Chain stitch, 55, 116, 137, 151, 157: **53, 58, 62, 100, 101, 104, 119, 123, 125, 194**
Champion's School, Shapwick, 124
Charles I, 159
Charlotte, Princess, samplers commemorating the death of, 54, 199, 203, 204, 207: **50, 178**
Chenille work, 85, 195: **174**
Cherrett, Sarah, sampler by, 123
Cherry motif, 40: **104**
Cherubs, **103**
Chevening, 199, 202: **181**
Chichester Family of Arlington, 75
Child labour, 94
Children's deaths, samplers recording, 97
Children's work, 28, Chap. V, Chap. VI: **103, 121, 122, 123, 124, 172, 173, 174, 179, 180, 198**
Chimneys, 85
Christian symbolism, 32ff., 50, 69, 80: **5, 6, 10–26, 53, 54, 58, 65, 138, 153–155**
Christie, Mrs, *Samplers and Stitches*, 226
Christ's Hospital, Hertford, 124
    Scholar, 124: **116**
'Church, the', 84, 209: **180, 192**
Church embroidery, 19, 31
    20th century revival of, 228: **211, 213, 216, 219**
City and Guilds of London Institute, 140
Clements, Elizabeth, sampler by, 122: **115**
Clothes, 67–73, 82: **57, 66–68, 98, 101, 123, 195**
Clox (or clocks), hosiery, 199, 202
Coat of arms motif, 54
Cobb, Eliza, 138
Cock Road Daily School, sampler from, 84: **180, 192**
Cocke, Sarah, sampler by, **103**
Coffee pots, 85: **86**
Cole, Mary, 177
Collars, lace, 159
Columbine motif, 36, 37, 50
Column, or pillar motifs, 88: **100, 103**
Commemorative samplers, 174: **178**
Coptic samplers, 18
Coral stitch, **138, 151**
Cornflower, 36
Cornucopia motif, 51: **127**
Cornwall, map sampler of, 125
Coronet patterns, 115: **110, 112, 118, 216**
    See also Crown motif
Cotgrave's English–French Dictionary, 17
Cottages, 85: **118, 173**
Cottons, colour-printed, 186
Couched stitch, 55, 195, 206: **100**
Couching, 206: **53, 174**
Cousens, E., darning sampler by, 179
Cow motif, 62: **117, 176**

Cowslip, 34, 36, 150
Crane, W., 84
Creasey, Elizabeth, 166
Cridland, Elizabeth, sampler by, 180: **118**
Crochet, 30
Cromwell family, 164, 165
Cromwell, Elizabeth, sampler by, 50, 68, 78, 89, 107, 164: **62**
Crook, Martha, sampler by, 94
Cross stitch, 28, 30, 44, 55, 69, 79, 81, 90, 91, 111, 116, 124, 135, 137, 151, 158, 167, 179, 181, 196, 199, 206, 222, 223, 232: 46, 53, 56, **64**, **65**, **97–101**, **103**, **104**, **107**, **118**, **120**, **123**, **127**, **156**, **172–174**, **177**, **178**, **182**, **187**, **193**, **194**, **199–201**, **202**
Crouzet, Mary Ann, 207
Crown Garland of Golden Roses, 155
Crown patterns, 115, 183: **110**, **111**, **113**, **162**, **198**, **216**
Crucifixion motif, 67: **186**
Crystal Palace, 83: **29**
Cut-and-drawn work, 41, 68, 149, 158, 160: **54**, **96**, **120**
Cut work, 44, 111, 117, 159, 178, 186: **55**, **60**, **63**, **102**, **105**, **203**

D., S. I., sampler by, **63**
Dacca muslins, 200
Daffodil motif, 37
Daisy pattern, 36, 72: **15**, **16**, **58**, **130**
Damask, 216
Danish work, 227
Darning, 115
  on net, 200, 230, 231: **126**
  samplers, 137, 195: **119**, **124**
  stitches, 18, 137, 179: **62**, **97**, **119**, **126**, **165**, **202**, **222**
Davies, John, *Antiquae Linguae Britannicae*, 17
Dawe, Hannah, sampler by, 50: **42**
Day, Ann, sampler, 54, 175: **123**
Day, Janet Mary, 95
Dear, Eliza, 138
Death, samplers commemorating, 95ff., **178**
Derow, Mary, sampler by, 122
Derry, Bishop of, 174
Detached filling, 64
  overcast stitch, **203**, **214**
  stitches, 82, 151: **57**, **62**, **99**
  work, 161
Diaper patterns, 39, 49, 158, 163: **11**, **26**, **38**, **141**, **147**
Dick, Elizabeth, sampler, 174
Diss, Norfolk, 144
Doddridge, Philip, 171
Dog motif, 77, 89: **53**, **57**, **58**, **62**, **77**, **118**, **176**, **194**
Dorset County Museum, 68, 154
Double feather stitch, **199–201**, **215**
  plaited braid, **65**
  running stitch, 44, 111, 175, 228, 230: **5**, **59**, **65**, **74**, **95–99**, **108**, **129**, **218**, **222**
Dovecotes, 85: **118**

Dowling, Margaret, *Some 16th century Pattern Books*, 22
Dragon motif, 77: **62**
Drake family sampler, **177**
Drawn stitches, 82, 230: **202**
Drawn work, 44, 159: **95**, **212**, **214**
Dress-making and repair samplers, 139, 204, 205, 221: **200**, **201**
Dress materials, embroidery on, 201: **188–190**
Duck motif, 79: **80**
Dyers' School, Shapwick, 124

Ecclesiastical embroidery, *see* Church embroidery
Ecklee, Elizabeth, 123
Eden, Garden of, *see* Garden
Edinburgh, 126
  School of Art, 226
Edlin, Martha, sampler by, 116
Edward VI, 146
  VII, Coronation of, 223
Egyptian samplers, 18
Elephant motif, 77
  and castle, 150
Elizabeth I, Queen, 23, 38, 95, 149
  II, Queen, Coronation Robe, 140, 226: **217**
Elizabeth of York, Queen, 144
Elizabethan costume, 149: **57**
Embroiderers' Guild, screen sampler by, 229, 230: **221**, **222**
Embroidery and Alphabet Sampler Book, 28, 139
Embroidery on tambour or hoop, 201
Enclosed garden motif, 69
England, map sampler of, 136: **121**
Epistle samplers, 90
Everitt, Sarah, sampler by, 180
Evershot School, 124
Exhibition of Needlework, South Kensington (1873), 125
Eyelet stitches, 111, 175: **64**, **95**, **96**, **98**, **100**, **104**, **107**, **156**, **201**, **203**, **213**, **214**, **215**

F., M., sampler by, 89, 135, 136: **121**, **200**, **201**
Faggotting stitch, 205
Fair, C. D. (teacher), 142
Falcon motif, 79: **58**
Family figures, 57, 68: **66–68**, **123**, **209**
Fashion, its influence on embroidery, 149
Fear, Sarah, sampler by, 124, 181: **117**
Feather stitch, 138: **199–202**, **215**
Fern motif, 72
  stitch, 157
Fescue, 112, 113
Field family samplers, 107, 165: **62**, **121**
Fieldhouse, Hannah, sampler by, 97, 219: **173**
Fig motif, 40: **22**
Filbert, *see* Hazel nut
Filling stitch, 214: **141**, **203**, **220**
Finny stitch, 157
Fish motif, 80, 231: **62**, **77**, **83**
Fishbone stitch, **202**
Fisher stitch, 157

Fitzwilliam Museum, 41, 71, 115, 154, 179
Flanders Lace, 159, 160
Fletcher, Sarah, sampler by, 39
Fleur de Lys, 35, 149: **11, 12, 216**
Florentine stitch, 206: **100, 120, 193**
Flower motifs and patterns, 24, 26, 33-39, 72, 84, 91, 149, 163, 183, 206: **4-16, 53, 57-59, 62, 70, 97-101, 104, 118, 128, 138-140, 142-144, 149, 151-155, 157, 158, 183, 185, 188-190, 207**
Flower-pot pattern, 50, 88, 175, 181, 183, 199, 221: **42, 119, 123, 159, 160, 172, 176, 180, 182, 184, 195, 206**
Fly stitch, 138
'Forbidden Fruit', the, 39, 40, 43, 45
Fountain with birds pattern, 80: **81, 82**
Four-sided stitch, **62, 107**
France, 20
Freeston, Lincs., 146
French, Ann, sampler by, 172
  Mary, sampler by, 174
French, inscriptions in, 220
French knots, 55, 136, 151, 179: **53, 62, 99, 103, 119, 123, 200, 201**
Fruit bowl or basket motif, 49, 50, 175, 181, 224: **41, 43, 106, 173, 180, 194**
Fruit patterns, 24, 26, 39ff., 72, 149, 150, 163: **3, 6, 21-31, 36, 133, 136, 145, 149, 164, 173, 186**
Fuller, Caroline Lepel, 174, 175
Furber, Robert, *The Flower Garden Displayed*, 26

Garden of Eden, 39, 44, 45, 57, 58, 67, 73, 183, 184: **60, 171, 176**
Gardiner, Ann, sampler by, 126
Gawthorpe Hall, Burnley, 200, 231
Gellett, Susanna, sampler by, 55: **46**
Genealogical samplers, 96ff., **177**
Geometric patterns, 206, 219: **65, 148, 191**
Geometrical satin stitch, **102, 105**
George I, King, 174
  III, King, 202
Gift samplers, 19th century, 92: **199**
Gill, J. C., *The Ten-Hour Parson*, 94
Girl Guide figures, 68
Glasgow, Needlework Development Scheme, 230
Goat motif, 77: **57, 98**
Gobelin stitch, **59, 97**
Goldsmith, Oliver, *She Stoops to Conquer*, 185
Gold thread sampler, 121: **64**
Goodday, Elizabeth, sampler by, 121: **64**
Goodhart, Dr., 42, 154
Goose motif, 79, 168: **80**
Gower, Anne, sampler by, 112
Grant, Jenny, sampler by, 179: **102**
Grape pattern, *see* Vine
Graves, Mary, sampler by, 124: **116**
Grey, Jane, sampler, 210
Gribble, Anne, sampler, 125
Griffin, Eliza, 138
Groombridge and Sons (publ.), *Embroidery and Alphabet Sampler Book*, 28: **86-93**
Guildford Museum, 18

Haig, E., *Floral Symbolism of the Great Masters*, 37, 43
Hair sampler, **199**
Hall, Mary, sampler by, 166
Hare motif, 77, 150, 165: **76**
Harris, William, 93
Harrison, Elizabeth, sampler, 107: **178**
  Mary, sampler, 107
Hart, L., 196
Hawkins, Harriet, 138
Hawkins, William, *Apollo Shroving* (quoted) 112, 156
Hawkshead, 126
Haworth Parsonage, 107, 219
Hayl, Juda (Judith), 120, 121, 166
Hazel-nut motif, 46, 47: **33**
Heart patterns, 18th century, **100, 156, 161, 163**
Hebrew inscriptions, 220
Hedgehog motif, 77: **65**
Hem stitch, **95, 200-202, 212, 215**
Henderson, Robert, Jean and Christian, 98
Henley, Ann, French sampler by, 220
Heraldic emblems, 75, 77, 163, 181: **54, 62, 72, 73**
Herrick, Robert, *Wounded Heart* (quoted), 156
Herringbone stitch, 138, 205: **200**
Hertford, Christ's Hospital, 124
Heythrop School, 139
Higgin's *Handbook of Embroidery*, 30
Hill's Academy, 123
Historical sampler, 207
Hockey, Hannah, 124, 125
Hodges, C., sampler by, 198
Hodgson, Sarah, sampler, 123
Holbein stitch, 141, 146: **56, 62**
Hollie-point lace, 128, 160, 178: **102, 105, 161-164**
Home work, 202, 203
Honeysuckle motif, 34, 38, 52, 72, 150: **5, 6, 13, 138, 153-155**
Hooper, Eleanor Sarah, sampler, 108
Hope, Lady Mary St. John, 83
Hopkins, Hannah, 92
Horn-book, 113
Horse Hill House, near London, 84: **176**
Horse motif, **98**
Household objects, 85: **86-89, 93**
Houses as patterns, 82, 181, 183, 230: **118, 173, 176, 221, 222**
Hughes, Miss, 125
Huish, M. B., *Samplers and Tapestry Embroideries*, 37, 50, 54, 70, 71, 98, 107
Human figure patterns, Chap. III, 181, 225: **55, 57, 58, 60, 61, 63, 66-70, 84, 123, 173, 195, 209**
Hungarian stitch, **100**
Hunt, Ann, sampler by, 185

Ingram, Susan, sampler by, 170
Inscriptions, 90-109, 117ff., 150, 155ff., 207, 224, Chap. XII, 254: **106, 118, 173, 175, 199**
Insect motifs, 25, 32, 77, 80, 91: **57, 59, 64, 65, 90, 98**
Interlacing stitch, **65, 97, 100**
Ireland, map sampler of, 135, 136: **174**

Iris motif, 34, 149
  stitch, 157
Isaac, Sacrifice of, 58, 97
Italian cross-stitch, 53, **58**
Italian cut-work, 157

Jackson, Hannah, sampler by, 97
Jacob's Vision, 58
James I, 159
Jasmine spray motif, **189**
Johnson, Dr Samuel, 177
Jourdain, M., *English Secular Embroidery*, 25, 32, 54,
  73, 87, 125, 144
Judith and Holofernes, 58: **61**
Jugs, 86: **87**

Kay, Frances, 231
Kempsey, 123
Kendrick, A. L., *A Book of Old Embroidery*, 25
Kettles, 86: **88**
Key patterns, 86: **93**
King, Judith, 166
King, Mr Donald, *Samplers* (qu.), 18, 37, 54, 73, 147,
  148
Knitting samplers, 138, 200
Knowles, Elizabeth, ready-reckoner sampler by, 137,
  186: **122**

L., B., sampler by, 93
L., F. C., sampler by, **213**
Lace, 19, 20, 178
  pattern samplers, 149: **54**
  17th century use of, 159, 160
  stitches, 29, 37
Ladder stitch, **53**
Laid work, 151, 157, 206: **216**
Landscapes, 85, 181, 195: **118, 123, 176, 180, 195**
Latin inscriptions, 220
Laurie, R. H., Fleet St. (publisher), 136
Leaf motifs, 46, 55: **33, 34, 36, 37, 137, 146**
Lee, Alice, 92
  sampler by, 97, 150: **48, 51, 53, 133, 135**
Leedes, Joyce, sampler by, 69, 154, 155: **98**
Leek, 37
Leicester, Lettice, Countess of, 156
Le Moyne, Jacques, *La Clef des Champs*, 20
Leopard pattern, 77, 150: **72**
Lettercases, 18th century, 195, 221
Lewis, Sarah, sampler, 123
Liddiard, Ann, 124
Lily motifs, 34, 149: **9-12**
Lily-pot motif, 50: **42**
Limmer, Mary, 92
Linen, 151, 152, 158, 195
  marking, 115: **110-113**
Lingard, A., sampler by, 108
Lion motif, 77: **62, 72**
Little, Mrs Catherine, 228
Lloyd, Mrs, sampler, 57: **55**
Loader, Rachel, sampler 70, 166
Lobster motif, 75
London Museum, 149

Long-armed cross stitch, **98**
Lord's Prayer, 67, 88, 170, 181, 219: **106, 118**
Lotus, 35
Lovell, Miss Valerie, sampler by, 228: **218**
Lucas, Dr, 175
Lucas, Margreet, 119, 166
Lundy Island, 126
Lupton, Miss Agnes, sampler by, 226: **203**
Lurex thread, 232
Lyre motif, **216**

Mackett, Elizabeth, sampler by, 117
Macramé, 30
Mahon, Ellen, 138
Map samplers, 27, 89, 135, 175, 179, 186: **121, 125-
  136, 174**
Marigold motif, 34, 36
Markham family sampler, 98
Marking, 30, 115, 138, 224: **110-113**
Marsden, Mrs C., sampler by, **221**
Martin, Miss Agnes, 202
Mary I, Queen, 41
Mason, Caroline, sampler by, 210
Mayne, Jasper, *The Citye Match* (qu.), 58, 118
Mediaeval embroidery, 19, 32
Meech, Martha, 124
Memorial samplers, 95: **155, 178, 186**
Mermaid, 75: **58, 63, 65, 98**
Metal threads, 151, 159, 232: **53, 54, 57, 65, 97, 141**
Methodism, 171
Middleton, Lord, 148
Milkmaid, 78, 124, 181: **117**
Miller, Mary, 176
Milles, Thomas, 155
  Treasure of Ancient and Moderne Times, 155
Mills, Jane, beadwork sampler of, 203
Milton, John, *Lycidas* (qu.), 33, 156
Minerva, 32
Minshull, Mary, sampler by, 167
Minto, Miss Isobel, 202
Moralizing, 184, 185
Morgan, Margaret, sampler, 209
Morland, *Visit to the Boarding School*, 196
Morris, Barbara, *History of English Embroidery*, 20
  Victorian Embroidery, 28
Mothers, samplers for, 90
Mouse motif, 77: **78**
  stitch, 157
Moxon, Miss Gertrude, sampler by, 227: **212**
Moyse, Mary, 121
Muller, Dr George, 139
Muller Homes, samplers from the, 29, 139: **198**
Mumer, Mary Ives Iane, 92
Muslin, 199, 200: **125**

Nebabri, Susan, 149: **54**
Needle cases, 195
Needle-made lace, 200
Needlepoint, 41, 44, 82, 151: **60, 98**
  fillings, **54, 55, 61, 96, 125**
  lace, 37, 158, 159, 160

Needle-weaving, **202, 204**
Needlework Development Scheme, 230
Needlework, teaching of, Chap. VI: **119, 124, 200,** 201
Negro page boy motif, 70
Nelson, Horatio, Viscount, 115: **112**
Net, darning on, 200, 230, 231: **126**
Net work, 157: **126, 222**
Nevitt, Mary, sampler by, **216**
New stitch, 157
Newton, Rev. John, 210
Nonesuch Palace, 83
Northampton, Henry Howard, Earl of, 88
Northumberland, 126
Numerals, 113, 122, 138, 165, 224: **106, 109, 198**
Nun's work, 178
Nut motifs, 46: **33–35**

Oak leaf motif, 46, 150: **34, 134, 137**
Oak tree motif, 54: **44**
Obelisks, 86: **59, 110**
Olive tree motif, 40: **104**
Open hem stitch, **202, 215**
Ostau, Giovanni, *La Vera perfettione del Designo*, 20, 110
Outlining stitch, 141: **62, 220**
Oversewing, 18, 186: **196**
Owl motif, 32: **98, 210**

Palliser, Mrs B., *History of Lace*, 50
Palsgrave, *Lesclarrisement de la Langue Francoyse*, 17
Pansy motif, 36, 161: **17, 18, 19, 28, 140, 143**
Parker, Annie, sampler by, 93: **199**
  Ellen, sampler by, 94
Parrot, 79: **57**
Patchwork, 205: **196**
Pattern books 19ff., 57ff.: **2, 3, 4,**
Pattern cards, 223
Pavilion pattern, 82, 161: **60, 64**
Payne, Mr Ffransis, *Guilde to the Collection of Samplers and Embroideries*, 84, 115, 144, 210
Pea motif, 36, 42: **27, 28**
Peacock motif, 79, 85: **62, 79, 84, 205**
Pear motif, 39, 72: **57, 99**
Pearls, 151: **53**
Pedestal pattern, 87
Pelican, 79, 150: **53**
Penrhyn Castle, 84, 206: **195**
Perry family memorial sampler, 95, 96
Persephone, 37
Pesel, Miss Louisa, 227, 228
Petal hem stitch, **215**
Pether, Mary, 84
Pets, 85: **77, 91**
Philips family sampler, 70
Philips, Prisca, 120, 121: **114**
Piano, 86: **92**
Picot ring edging, **214, 215**
Pile darning, **97**
Pineapple motif, 52, 121: **98, 100**
Pincushion pattern, 199: **187**

Plaited braid stitch, 151, 159: **57, 58, 65, 100**
Plush stitch, **193**
Plushwork, 206
Pomegranate motif, 40, 52, 149, 150: **25, 26**
Porcupine motif, 77
Porter, Jean, sampler by, 73
Potter and Co., 84
Potter, Elizabeth, sampler by, 155: **96**
Priest, Alice, map sampler by, 136
Prince of Wales Feathers motif, 35: **14**
Pryor, Susannah, sampler by, 196
Purdy, Frances, 177
Puzzle samplers, 95, 186
Pyramid motif, 52, 86, 159: **48, 118**

Quentel, Peter, 20
Quertier, M., sampler by, 199

R., M., sampler by, **58**
Rabbit motif, 77, 165
Raised work, 157, 161
Rammage, Margaret, sampler by, 183
Raymond, Elizabeth, sampler by, 173
Ready-reckoner samplers, 137
Repair samplers, 139, 204, 205, 221: **200–202**
Rhodes, Ann, sampler by, 126, 135
Rhodes, Miss Helen, 230
Rice stitch, **213**
Riche, Barnabe, *Of Phylotus and Emilia* (qu.), 147
Rimington, Jane, 121
Roberts' School, Bolton, 124
Roberts, Miss D. A., 94
Roberts, Sarah, sampler by, **182**
Robertson, Charlotte, sampler by, 172
Robin motif, **32**
Rococo stitch, **57–59, 64, 65, 100**
Rolleston, E., *An embroidered shirt of the 17th century*, 24
Rose bush pattern, 56: **52**
Rose-hip motif, 45: **31, 32**
Rose motif, 34, 38, 49, 50, 150, 160, 167: **52, 58, 64, 65, 96, 97, 101, 131, 139, 141, 150, 206, 207**
Rosemary stitch, 157
Roumanian stitch, **61, 62**
Royal College of Art, 226
Royal Hellenic School of Needlework, 227
Royal School of Needlework, 140, 226: **204, 216, 217**
Royalty, tributes to, 70, 173, 174: **54, 101**
Ruffs, lace, 159
Running stitch, **200, 201, 215**
  See also Double-Running

'S' motif, 19
S-A., S., teaching sampler by, **220**
St. Clement Danes Charity School, 122
St. David's Cathedral, 84
Salesbury, *A Dictionary in Englyshe and Welshe*, 17
Salisbury, 126
Salter, Martha, sampler by, 165

Samplers:
16th Century, 91, 92, Chap. VII: **25, 53, 54, 128–135**
17th Century, 26, 29, 91, 116–120, Chap. VIII: **5–8, 11, 13, 16–19, 21–24, 26–37, 39, 41, 55–65, 69, 74, 75, 95–99, 136–150**
18th Century, 27, 29, 120, 123, Chap. IX: **9, 12, 15, 20, 38, 40, 41, 47, 51, 66, 67, 100–106, 118, 151, 171**
19th Century, 28, 29, 92, 124, 138, 140–142, 184, Chap. X: **14, 41, 43, 46, 50, 52, 86–89, 94, 126, 127, 173–202, 206, 207**
20th Century, 140, Chap. XI: **10, 68, 203–204, 209–222**
Sampler series of coloured cards, 223
Sanderson, Thomas, 97
Satin stitch, 44, 69, 85, 111, 136, 151, 175, 206, 223, 230: **5, 53, 61, 64, 95–97, 99–104, 107, 120, 123, 125, 171, 174, 181, 202, 213, 214**
Scarles, Elizabeth, sampler by, 121
Schonsperger's pattern book, 20
Schools and teaching, Chap. VI, 186: **220**
Schools of Art, 140
Scot, Reginald (qu.), 147
Scotland, Museum of Antiquities 178
Scotland Yard, Black Museum, 94
Scott, Mrs, sampler by, 92: **194**
Scottish Rural Women's Institutes, 229
Scottish samplers, 199–202: **125, 188–190**
Screen samplers, 141, 230
Sequins, 65
Serpent, Biblical, 44: **60**
Heraldic, 77
Seven Deadly Sins, 45
Shakespeare, William, 35, 37, 147
Midsummer Night's Dream, 148
Titus Andronicus, 147
Shamrock, 37: **96, 174**
Shapwick Schools, Somerset, 124
Sharp, Mary, sampler by, 92
Thomas, sampler by, 93
Sheep motif, 77: **123**
Shepherd, shepherdess motif, 70, 71: **123**
Ships, 70, 88, 135: **121**
Shorleyker, Richard, *A Scholehouse for the Needle*, 23, 42: **3, 4, 163**
Sibmacher, Johann, *Schön Neues Modelbuch*, 22, 23, 27, 122, 156: **2**
Sidney, Sir Philip (qu.), 147
Silks, 16th century, 152
18th century, 195
Silver thread, 232: **58, 100**
Silvergilt thread, 232: **58, 100**
Simpson, Mary, 184
Simpson, William, *Second Book of flowers, fruit . . . exactly drawn*, 25
Skelton, John, *Boke of Phyllipe Sparowe*, 144
Garland of Laurell (qu.), 145
Slater family, 97
Smeeth, An, sampler by, 58
Smith, Hannah, sampler by, 117

Snail motif, 77: **65, 97, 98**
Solomon and Sheba, 58
Solomon's Temple, 83
Spanish stitch, 157
'Spanysshe Work', 146: **128. 129**
Spear, Elizabeth, sampler by, 40, 83: **104**
Speckling stitch, **53**
Spectacle cases, 221
Speed, Eleanor, 176, 196
Spies return from Canaan, 181: **170**
Split stitch, 69, 85, 136: **97, 100, 101, 104, 123**
Spot motif, 28, 29, 37, 39, 41, 46, 69, 81, 84, 117, 122, 154, 159, 164, 168: **24, 33, 97, 139, 140, 143, 144, 149, 193, 205**
Squirrel motif, 44, 45, 70, 77, 85, 150: **30, 65, 176**
Stag motif, 77, 121, 181: **53, 58, 59, 62, 97, 98, 100, 104, 114, 118, 168, 169, 176**
Steamship motif, 89
Stem stitch, 55, 135–137, 175: **62, 98, 101, 103, 123**
Stent, Peter (bookseller), 25, 58, 79
Stephens, Sophia, sampler by 44: **176**
Stevens, Miss Dorothy (qu.), 73
Stitches, *See under name*, e.g. Back, Cross, Running, &c.
"Stockingers' Monday", 203
Strawberry motif, 34, 42, 150, 151, 175, 181, 199: **7, 18, 21, 23, 24, 28, 29, 123, 136, 167, 186**
Stump work, 82, 116, 161
Suett, Jemima, 138
Surrey, Countess of, 145
Swain, Mrs Margaret, 201, 202
Swan motif, 79, 122, 165: **62, 115**
Sycamore tree motif, 54: **45**
Symbols, symbolism, 31ff.

T., C. M., sampler by, 229: **211, 219**
T., E., sampler by, **127**
Tabor, Esther, 185
Taffeta, **196**
Tambour (hoop frame), 201
stitch, 125
Tansley, E., sampler by, 141: **214**
Tatting, 30
Taylor, C., sampler, 180: **119**
Taylor, Harriet, sampler by, 88
Taylor, John, *The Needle's Excellency*, 22, 23, 156
Taylor, Sarah, sampler by, 98
Teaching, Chap. VI, 186: **220**
Tea-pots, 86
Ten Commandments, 67, 88, 170, 176: **219**
Tent stitch, 28, 29, 39, 69, 151, 206, 222: **57–59, 64, 65, 97, 100, 102, 123, 193, 213**
Tent work, 157
Thackeray, Wm., *Vanity Fair* (qu.), 222
Thistle motif, 36, 37: **58, 62, 65, 96, 139**
Thomson, Margaret and Alys, 91, 146
Tidy, Austin, sampler by, **179**
Tiffany, 186: **119**
Till, Hannah, 138
Times, The, 207
Timperley, Mrs, sampler by, **222**

Toad motif, 77: **75**
Topiary, 55: **47, 48**
Tradition, 31
Tree of Knowledge, 40, 43, 45, 51, 184: **61, 171, 176**
Tree of Life, 35, 52: **95, 100, 120**
Tree patterns, 40, 41, 51, 181: **44–52, 81, 118, 172
173, 176**
Trinity, symbols of the, 36, 38: **19**
Trollope, Elizabeth, 179
Trophy motif, 72: **70**
Truro, Miss Warren's School at, 125
Truscott, Mrs Oscar, sampler by, **10, 211, 219**
Trusted, Eliza, sampler by, 199
Tuer, A., *History of the Horn Book*, 89, 91, 113
Tulip motif, 36, 38, 49: **20, 127, 157, 158, 160, 183,
188**
Twaites memorial sampler, 96
Twyford, 228
Tye, Elsie, sampler by, 139, 226

Unicorn motif, 77
Urn motif, 199: **50**

Vase motif, 49: **40–42**
Vavassorie, Giovanni Andra, *Esemplario di Lavori*, 20
Victoria and Albert Museum, 18, 23, 70, 82, 87, 88,
117, 136, 139, 148, 149, 154, 227
Vincioli, Frederic di Vinciolo, *Les Secondes Oeuvres,
et subtiles inventions de Lingerie*, 20
*Les Singuliers et Nouveaux Pourtraits pour toutt es
sortes d'ouvrages di Lingerie*, 20
Vine and grape pattern, 48, 70, 150: **36, 37, 39, 133,
135**
Violet motif, 36
Virgin and Child motif, 34, 36, 37, 41, 43, 50, 69, 70

Wakeling, Mary, sampler, 173
Wales, 37
National Museum of, 67, 83, 206
samplers from, 84, 95, 107, 186, 206: **195**
Wallace Collection, 196
Wallis, Mr Cyril, **201**
Walton School, 137: **122**
Wargrave, 175

Warren's School, Truro, 125
Waters, Ann, sampler by, 115, 119
Waters, John, *English and Welsh Dictionary* (qu.), 115
Watlington, St. Leonard's Church, embroidered
kneelers at, 229: **211, 219**
Wattell, Ann, sampler, 166
Watts, Dr Isaak, *Divine Songs*, 170, 171, 173, 208–
210
Webb, Mary, *Anne's Book* (qu.), 231
Webber, Frances Incledon, sampler by, 91
Weeping Willow motif, 54, 199, 203: **50, 178**
Weldon's Practical Publications, 30
Wells, Mary (teacher), 123
Welsh inscriptions, 220
Wesley, John, 171
Westbourne Union School, 138
Wheatley, Frances, *The Schoolmistress*, 196
Whipping stitch, 196
Whitehead, Mary, sampler by, **106**
Whiteside, Margaret, 124
White work, 117, 158, 159, 161, 178, 226
on muslin, 199
William III, 160
Winchester Cathedral Broderers, 227: **213**
Winchester School of Art, sampler from, 141: **218**
'Winchester Work', 227: **213**
Windmills, 85: **118**
Wineglasses, 86: **89**
Winterbourne Telstone and Almer Board School,
123
Wolf, John (publ.), *New and Singular Patternes of . . .
Linnen . . .*, 20
Women's Institutes, 140, 229
Work bags, 221: **182**
Workbox sampler, **218**
Wright, Martha, 167
Wright, Mary, sampler by, 119

'X' motif, 19

York, 126
Young, Mary, sampler by, 58, 97

Zillwood, Eliza, 138